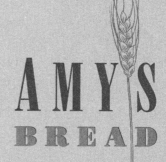

AMY'S
BREAD

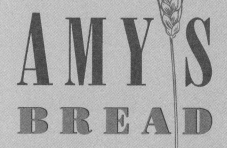

AMY'S
BREAD

Amy
Scherber
and
Toy Kim
Dupree

**photographs by
gentl & hyers**

WILLIAM MORROW AND COMPANY, INC.
NEW YORK

Library of Congress Cataloging-in-Publication Data
Scherber, Amy.
    Amy's Bread / Amy Scherber and Toy Kim Dupree ; photographs by Gentl & Hyers
       p.   cm.
    Includes index.
    ISBN 0-688-12401-1
    1. Bread.   2. Amy's Bread (Bakery)   I. Dupree, Toy Kim.   II. Amy's Bread (Bakery)   III. Title.
TX769.S396   1996
641.8'15–dc20   95-11168
                                                                                                        CIP

Printed in the United States of America

First Edition

1 2 3 4 5 6 7 8 9 10

BOOK DESIGN BY NANCY KENMORE

To
my Grandmother
Florence,
who taught me to put
a little bit of love
into everything
I make.
A. S.

For
my Mother,
who started me on my
culinary adventures
with my first cookbook
when I was
seven years old.
T. D. K.

preface

Making bread is one of the simplest pleasures we know. This nurturing food is a staple of the diet in many cultures. Friends and customers have often told us that bread making is a "noble profession" because it is a way to serve people—to give pleasure, energy, and sustenance to the eater. Bread goes to the very roots of life. Rain, sunshine, and healthy soil to grow the wheat; human hands to harvest, mill, and turn the grain to flour; yeast, which occurs naturally around us in fermenting fruits and starches; and salt from the earth and sea are the basic ingredients. These, along with the warmth of the baker's hands, his or her strength, skill, and passion, and a fiery hearth, are all that are needed to make this elemental food.

Besides this glorious image of "earth to table," we like to make bread because it is always changing, and thus it challenges our skills, intuition, and senses. Does the dough feel right, smell right, and taste right? Is it wet or dry, warm or cool? How is the weather, how is the flour, and how is the oven? The same ingredients, mixed the same way every day, yield slightly different results in the hands of each baker. Some people may find this frustrating, but to be a good baker you must be calm, intuitive, and patient. You must use all of your senses to be aware of the dough, the environment, and your own mood. The challenge and the tasty, tangible reward make bread baking a great pleasure to experience—and to share.

AMY SCHERBER *and* TOY KIM DUPREE

acknowledgments

First we wish to thank the staff at the bakery who work every day to make beautiful bread. Their dedication has helped us to earn our reputation for producing bread of the finest quality. We would like to thank you for picking up slack while we were writing this book—especially Ann Burgunder, Scott Klein, and Amy Quazza who handled our work when we were out.

I would like to thank my parents, Pat and Tony Scherber, and my siblings, Beth and John Scherber and Sally and Dave Hopkinson, who have encouraged me all along the way. I appreciate the time you spent reading rough drafts and tasting lots of bread.

Thank you to Lindsley Cameron and Amy Klobuchar for reading drafts of the manuscript and patiently giving constructive criticism.

We would like to applaud all of our recipe testers who put lots of time, energy, and love into their work. Thank you, Heidi Boyd, Dorothy Jacobs, Tina Higgens, Sue McCracken, Jean Salonek, Pat Scherber, David Schmidt, and Kay Schmidt for your great comments and help.

We are very grateful to have Ann Bramson as our editor. Thank you for your confidence and patience in the early days of this project. Your enthusiasm, creative direction, and support made it all possible. Thank you, Jennifer Kaye, for keeping us informed and for your positive attitude. We also thank Nancy Kenmore and Richard Aquan, our designers, for your vision for the book. A big thank you to Judith Sutton for your tireless editing. You made our clumsy words into a real book. And thank you to Bill Adler who got us into this in the first place.

To our photographers, Andrea Gentl and Marty Hyers, it was a pleasure and an inspiration to work with such imaginative and talented people. Thank you for your sensitive touch. We also thank their assistant Tamara Burke, prop stylists Kemper Hyers and Edward Peterson, and Carolina Gramm for letting us use your beautiful house as a backdrop.

Finally we would like to thank our husbands for their patience and support. Thanks to Kerry Heffernan for your well-educated palate. Your creative inspiration for new breads and delicious food pairings cannot be matched. Thanks to Richard Dupree for your soothing and energizing shiatsu massages. Without them our tired shoulders could not have kneaded our loaves or typed these words.

A.S. *and* T.D.K.

contents

introduction

The Story of the Bakery

◆

Opening Amy's Bread was the fulfillment of a lifelong dream.
I was raised in Minnesota on my mother's home-cooked meals and my grandmother's freshly baked bread and cookies, and the kitchen has always been one of my favorite places. Both of my parents grew up on dairy farms, with big, busy kitchens where delicious, hearty meals were made to feed hungry farmhands.

My professional food career began modestly. Working as a waitress in a pie shop during high school, I served my share of cream pies and oversized burgers to hungry customers. I polished my skills as a dishwasher, food server, and waitress in the college cafeteria. After graduating, I helped launch an innovative local restaurant.

At that point, I made a break for New York City and the business world, where I worked in a marketing agency for three years. Although presentations, client meetings, and promotional plans had their interesting moments, I was confined to a desk in an office cubicle, and I longed to get back in the kitchen.

With the idea of opening a restaurant one day, I went to the New York Restaurant School for culinary training. Afterwards I worked for two years as a cook at Bouley, one of New York's most highly acclaimed restaurants. It was there that I discovered my true passion: bread baking. To learn more about bread, I traveled to France, which has a strong tradition of baking good bread. I worked at boulangeries in three different towns, spending a month at each one. In these bakeries I learned about the production of baguettes and beautiful regional specialties. When I returned to New York, I was brimming with ideas and excitement about opening my own bakery. For the next two years, I worked as a bread baker at Mondrian restaurant, developing recipes and refining my techniques. Then I felt ready to launch my own business.

It was at Mondrian that I met Toy, who was working as an apprentice in the pastry kitchen. She too had changed careers, from computer software development to baking, and she had also studied at the New York Restaurant School. When I broke my hand in a biking accident, Toy came to my rescue, shaping hundreds of loaves and rolls for the restaurant. With her enthusiasm and willingness to take on any challenge, I knew her contribution to the bakery would be invaluable. She has worked at Amy's Bread since we opened in June 1992, and the bakery thrives because of her dedication to quality.

Finding the perfect space for the bakery was my first mission. An old storefront on Ninth Avenue, in the heart of the neighborhood still fondly referred to as Hell's Kitchen, turned out to be that space—and the location and the look of the old shop have become an important part of the bakery's identity. The area has been known for its food markets since the early 1900s. Our building had housed a fish market since it was constructed in 1896 and had been owned by the same landlord for forty years. He was proud of the area's history and had tried to maintain the feel of the neighborhood by keeping the old wood storefront, with its carved trim and bay window, the last of its kind on Ninth Avenue. The dilapidated building, with its high ceilings and decorative moldings, seemed the perfect place for a new Old World bread shop.

With the help and support of my parents, my husband, and a gifted carpenter friend, the tiny six-hundred-and-fifty-square-foot bakery took shape. We did all of the renovations ourselves: We patched, plastered, painted, and in the process exposed a beautiful brick wall that had been hidden behind wood slats and horsehair plaster. We shored up the drooping bay window, gave it a fresh coat of turquoise paint, and replaced the tattered cloth on the old roll-out awning. The store was reborn, looking as it had nearly a century before.

After the renovation, my staff of six dedicated employees, five women and one man, helped finish getting the bakery ready. We scrubbed used equipment and set up the shelves in the retail store. I taught them my recipes and techniques. Then, with little idea of what was to come, we opened our doors.

The first year was the hardest, and we had some difficult times. We learned to handle dough in brutally hot weather, to keep going day after day on only a few hours of sleep, and to get by without money when our wholesale customers didn't pay us. Our space was so small and narrow that we could hardly wheel the racks of dough through it. But the hard early days made us enjoy the good days, when our only problem was too much demand. Sometimes we sold the bread so quickly nothing would be left by noon!

We also learned that a baker's work is never done. The dough keeps rising and must be controlled from beginning to end. The bakery operates twenty-four hours a day, six days a week. Our wholesale customers want bread every day, and on holidays they double their orders. There is no shutting down for a two-week vacation. People need their daily bread.

Entering the bakery, the first thing you notice is a wonderful aroma. The smell of toasty bread and sweets baking transports you to another time and place, the cozy kitchen where you ate cookies fresh from the oven when you were still a child. To your right is the shadow of the words "FRESH BREAD," cast on the wall by the afternoon sunshine as it passes through the large bay window. The red brick wall, pressed-tin ceiling, and black-and-white mosaic tile floor give the bakery a feeling of warmth and intimacy. The wooden counter is decorated with marble and sheaves of wheat painted in the style of beautiful French beaux arts boulangeries. The open white cupboards behind the counter are full of dozens of golden-brown loaves: Semolina with golden raisins and fennel, organic whole wheat with walnuts, fresh rosemary bread. Baskets lined with colorful cloths are brimming with freshly baked bread twists, rolls, and disks of focaccia. A plate of sticky buns beckons, but sliced quick breads studded with fresh fruit

Big Crusty Loaves

Big crusty rounds of country sourdough bread are coming out of the oven. Their color is almost that of dark walnut furniture, or rich sautéed mushrooms. The crusts are hard and cracked and ridges have formed where the loaves burst open from the intense oven heat. Each loaf smells like wheat and caramel and wonderful hot toast. They crackle and snap when they are removed from the oven, singing as their crusts shrink slightly in the cool, dry air. They are heavy but light: The hefty loaves feel hollow and airy inside, and their hard crusts protect a soft, moist crumb. The reward of seeing these fresh-baked loaves is the reason we are bakers. We hope that you will experience this pleasure too. It is these rustic loaves that fuel our memories and our imaginations and make us feel proud of the tradition we carry on.

and plump, glossy chocolate buns vie for your attention. Then your eyes light on a rustic boule, a deep brown round of bread with a craggy top that is bursting open. The crust is slightly glossy and cracked, and the loaf looks rich and robust. You select the country sourdough boule and resist the sticky bun. You'll try it next time–you know you'll be back.

HOW WE CREATE YOUR DAILY BREAD

The day begins at 5:00 A.M. with the mixing of the dough. Our large mixer is filled with flour, water, sourdough starter, salt, and a pinch of yeast. Before long, a mass of creamy, glossy dough, smelling of robust wheat, is slapping and snapping as it is pulled and stretched by the fork kneader. The dough is lifted from the bowl to rest and rise slowly at a cool temperature, then divided into portions to be shaped later in the day.

By noon, there are several rolling racks of rising dough waiting to be cut and formed by our team of shapers. The radio is turned up to the beat of Latin pop, coffee is brewed, and six people surround the smooth wood worktable. With this much hand power, it doesn't take long to fill the racks with hundreds of loaves of every shape and size, from boules and ficelles to logs and bâtards. Skilled hands gently mold the dough, piece by piece, being careful to seal the breads tightly while leaving some of the open air pockets intact–a feat a machine could never achieve. The bread is left to rise again and then is placed in a 50°F retarding walk-in refrigerator, where it will ferment and rise slowly until it is ready to be baked in the middle of the night. The air in the retarder is moist, cool, and intoxicating with the smells of sourdough, wheat, and fennel.

The pace slows slightly, but then the night crew arrives. Up goes the volume of the radio, this time rock, or reggae, and on go the ovens. The room becomes warm and steamy as the first batch of dough is loaded into the stone hearth oven. It's a thrill to watch through the oven window as the intense heat transforms the short loaves into plump domes. When the crust has reached a deep rich dark brown, the loaves are pulled from the oven with a long wood paddle, called a peel, and placed on a rack to cool. Soon we share our favorite moment of the day: We hear the song of the crackling, snapping crust as the hot bread hits the cool air of the room. The loaves look gorgeous with their glossy dark crusts decorated with stripes of flour and flared cuts, and they smell delicious.

After the bread has cooled, it is packed into brown paper bags for wholesale deliveries to some of the finest stores and restaurants in the city. Drivers stop throughout the night to pick up the sacks of fresh bread. At 8:00 A.M. we open our store to retail customers, to the tune of classical music. By then most of the bread is baked, cooled, and stacked on the shelves, ready to be tasted and enjoyed. Meanwhile, we have already begun the whole process again!

The Philosophy of the Bakery
◆

Our philosophy of life is to enjoy the way we spend our days. Many of us have changed professions because we love making bread and have made our passion our career. We are proud of what we do, and our pride shows in the beautiful bread we make each day.

With this book, we hope to show you the honest pleasure that comes from putting your heart into what you make. We believe so strongly in this important ingredient we will mention it again and again. Think of the foods most dear to you–most often they were made by someone who put love, and even passion, into the preparation. Your grandmother's pie, your father's bacon and eggs, your best friend's chocolate chip cookies–all were lovingly made. These food memories carry with them a powerful emotion. With practice, some of our recipes can become your specialties as you begin to put more of yourself into the preparation. Your perseverance will pay off in beautiful baked goods that will give greater pleasure to those who eat them.

At the bakery, every bread is formed by hand, and we believe that using hands rather than machines really makes a difference. In most of our recipes we recommend that you knead the dough by hand. You will learn more about the dough than you would if you let a machine knead it, and you'll have more fun getting your hands into the action. Our hand-formed loaves and rolls have a better crumb with more irregular holes than machine-shaped breads. The few misshaped loaves we make each day add the human touch to the process.

PRACTICE AND PATIENCE ARE THE KEYS TO SUCCESS

As each day passes, we refine our definition of the quintessential bread. It gets heartier, earthier, and more fragrant at each new level we reach. Mastering fermentation is the baker's biggest challenge, and a good baker continues to learn and make changes. Like ours, your bread will get better and better with each new level of understanding. Our constant search for a better bread keeps us challenged and gives us something to look forward to. We hope you will also keep experimenting. Each time you make bread, you will become more skilled and more confident. Keep notes on what you try and what you learn. You will find your bread becoming more sophisticated, with a lighter crumb or a crunchier crust, with every new batch you make.

Artisan Baking

◆

From New York to California, artisan baking is on the rise. People everywhere are tasting hearth-baked loves made with long fermentation times, thick crusts, and chewy crumbs. We're pleased that the time has come for delicious artisan breads to replace the soft, squishy, plastic-bagged bread so long associated with America.

Artisan bakers are a new generation of bread makers with a passion for baking sophisticated specialty breads of the highest quality. They have returned to making bread in small batches, using their hands to shape the dough and reviving practices that had become a lost art. Artisan bakers use the best flour, often from organically grown wheat that is milled in small mills, and many leaven their bread with sourdough starters, using natural fermentation. Like us, these other artisan bakers are driven by the desire to make better the staff of life and to reeducate the public about how good real bread tastes, and how important the daily ritual of buying bread locally can be.

Artisan bakeries are part of the community. Small, abundantly stocked stores, they are filled with fresh baked goods that draw people to them every day. Most breads baked by artisan bakers are made with wholesome ingredients, little fat or sugar, and no preservatives. They make an important contribution to a healthful diet. Since the USDA's Food Guide Pyramid recommends six to eleven servings of bread and grains per day, fresh-baked bread is the natural accompaniment to every meal.

Artisan baking is also becoming a popular movement in home kitchens. Through wonderful recent bread books like Dan Leader's *Bread Alone* and Joe Ortiz's *The Village Baker*, professional recipes based on classical French techniques have been made accessible to home bread bakers. Our purpose in writing this book is to carry on this tradition of sharing, as well as to satisfy the many recipe requests we have had from our loyal customers. We're not attempting to write the "definitive" bread book, whatever that may be. Rather, we're passing along our favorite recipes and the techniques we use to make loaves that live up to our high expectations. We hope you will get as much pleasure and satisfaction from them as we do.

The Bread Bakers Guild of America

Growing as fast as the artisan baker movement is the Bread Bakers Guild of America, a young organization with the goal of uniting artisan bakers across the country and furthering their education through a bimonthly newsletter and a directory of members. The Bread Bakers Guild was established with the hope of building awareness of the needs and goals of small, individually run artisan bakeries and of raising the standards of education for these bakers. The Guild offers seminars and educational trips. It plans to establish an apprenticeship program for American bakers. It is responsible, too, for organizing a team of American bakers who compete at the international bread baking competition, the Coupe du Monde, held in France every two years. The Bread Bakers Guild has provided us with a link to other small bakeries that have questions and problems like our own. We also enjoy sharing our pride and our passion with other bakers who feel the same way we do. For more information on the guild, see page 190.

The Power Workout: Working in a Bread Bakery

Every job in a bread bakery requires skill and strength. Imagine making two thousand pounds of dough a day. The person who mixes all the dough starts the process by taking fifty-pound bags of flour, adding at least 65 percent more weight in the form of water, and mixing in other ingredients to form beautiful, supple dough. Besides possessing the skills required to measure accurately and the intuition to know if the amount of moisture and the degree of kneading are correct, the mixer has to hunch over a huge bowl, cutting, lifting, pulling, scraping, and moving large amounts of living dough from one place to another. Pulling, stretching, and lifting two thousand pounds of dough is great for upper body development and forearm strength!

After the dough has risen, the pans and tubs of dough are lifted and dumped out onto a table by a lone benchperson, to be cut and weighed into individual pieces to fulfill customers' orders. This is excellent for shoulder and biceps development: Cut, weigh, move; cut, weigh, move. With more than two thousand repetitions a day, portioning dough makes a fantastic toning exercise.

After the dough is portioned, it is shaped into loaves. If you are shaping, you must have very strong hands. After pressing, rounding, stretching, and rolling for eight to nine hours a day, the hands and forearms develop tremendous dexterity, tone, and definition. Look at all those hand, wrist, and forearm muscles you never noticed before! (Remember, through all of this you are supported by two legs that must stand, pivot, flex, and walk for those eight or nine hours. This work cannot be done from a sitting position.)

Now comes the total body workout: working at the deck oven. Here you must lift each and every loaf of the day's bread, along with the pans, boards, baskets, and cloths that the loaves are rising on, onto the loader, then move the loaves off the boards and baskets and into and out of the oven. You place the breads on a metal loader that is elevated up into the oven and then retracted. After that you must shimmy side to side to return the loader to its starting position. Talk about hips, calves, biceps, lower back, ankles, and forearms: They're all screaming! When the bread is baked, you lift the loaf pans—groups of four pans welded together filled with hot breads, weighing ten to twelve pounds each—flip them, move the loaves to the cooling rack, and put the heavy pans away. Repeat thirty times. (Did I mention that you are doing this total body workout at a room temperature of 80° to 100°F? It's a great way to sweat it out.)

Finally, the people bagging bread for deliveries move every loaf from the cooling racks to brown satchel bags, then carry the bags, thirty pounds at a time, on extended arms to the front of the bakery. Each trip is thirty to fifty feet each way—this job is for track stars only. Packers have been known to log six miles a day.

Given the nature of the work, you might guess that most people working in the bakery are trim and strong, with nicely toned muscles. They are sustained by plenty of cool water and snacks of bread throughout the day. No wonder we always laugh when people say, "Doesn't working in a bakery make you fat?"

1

Essentials for Making Good Bread

Ingredients: Building Blocks for Delicious Loaves

◆

One of the most wonderful things about bread baking is that something so beautiful and satisfying to eat can be made with just four simple ingredients: flour, water, salt, and yeast. By combining different types of flour and adjusting the amounts of water and yeast, you can make a wide variety of delicious loaves. If you expand the ingredients list to include cracked grains, nuts, seeds, fruits, vegetables, sweets, dairy products, eggs, and fats, the possibilities are endless. At Amy's Bread the only ingredient taboos we have are fast-acting yeast products and additives or preservatives that artificially extend shelf life. Our preference is for organic products, although not everything we use falls into this category. Our general rule is to use natural products of the highest quality.

FLOUR

Flour is a subject of intense interest for artisan bakers. So many kinds are available, each with its own special characteristics that affect the volume, flavor, texture, and aroma of a finished loaf of bread. But the fact is you don't really need to know a tremendous amount about different flours to make delicious loaves in your home oven. At first, simply follow the specifications for flour types in each recipe and use whichever brand is available to you at the supermarket or the nearest natural food store. Once you've mastered the techniques and feel confident working with those flours, go for it! Experiment with the wide variety of interesting flours available from mail-order sources (see page 189) and gourmet specialty stores. Avoid self-rising flours and instant flours, which are unsuitable for bread baking, but don't be afraid to mix and match. Do taste tests using organic and nonorganic flours. We think organic flours win hands down, but don't take our word for it! Eventually you'll develop your own unique list of favorites.

Wheat Flour

Wheat flour is the main ingredient in most of our recipes because the flour is the highest in gluten-forming plant proteins. It is these proteins that combine with water to form the flexible web in kneaded dough that traps carbon dioxide gas to make bread rise. Generally the more protein there is, the stronger the web of gluten. The amount of protein in a specific wheat flour is determined by the variety of wheat from which it is milled and the part of the wheat kernel from which it is extracted. Hard wheats are highest in protein, and red spring wheat and durum wheat are the hardest wheats grown.

Unbleached all-purpose flour is made from a combination of hard spring wheat and softer winter wheat so it can be used for a variety of different baking jobs. It is milled from the starchy endosperm of the wheat grain. Strictly speaking, the flour is not "unbleached," as it has in fact been whitened by a natural aging process, but "bleached flours" are lightened with chlorine compounds and other chemicals. We prefer the light cream color of unbleached flour over the unnatural whiteness of chemically bleached all-purpose flour. The best unbleached all-purpose flour is organic. It can be purchased from natural food stores; the most conscientious stores keep their flours in special temperature-controlled rooms. There are also several good mail-order sources (see page 189). Hecker's/Cresota unbleached flour, which can be found in most supermarkets, will also give you good results. The protein content of most all-purpose flour is about 11 percent.

High-gluten, or bread, flour is the highest-protein "white" flour, milled from the endosperm of hard red spring wheat. The best of this type is unbleached organic bread flour, which can sometimes be found in natural food stores. Specialty gourmet food stores and mail-order catalogues (see page 189) are other good sources. More often, you'll find bleached and bromated versions that include malted barley flour as a booster, such as the Pillsbury and Gold Medal brands in your local supermarket. Most of the time we use this strong flour in combination with unbleached all-purpose or other whole-grain flours. The protein content of high-gluten flour varies with the brand, but it is usually at least 13 percent.

Don't confuse high-gluten flour with an ingredient called *vital wheat gluten*. Vital wheat gluten is what's left when the starch has been removed from wheat flour through a water-washing process. It is essentially a natural gluten booster for yeast breads

> ### Protein Is Tough Stuff!
>
> *Too much protein in flour can be almost as much a problem as too little. If there is too much gluten formation, you'll get tight, rubbery dough, resulting in a very dense loaf with a tough crumb and crust. At Amy's Bread we like to combine our highest-protein flours with unbleached all-purpose flour to temper the strength of the gluten.*

that are made with weaker nonwheat flours and/or significant amounts of nuts, seeds, and raisins. None of the recipes in this book call for this product, because they all use gluten-rich wheat flours as their main ingredient. Vital wheat gluten is approximately 40 percent protein.

Clear flour, sometimes called common flour, is less refined and even higher in protein than bread flour. It is milled from the extreme outer layer (the "first clearing") of the wheat endosperm and has a slightly darker color than other wheat endosperm flours. It is most often used in combination with rye flour to produce the dense chewy texture associated with traditional Jewish rye bread. We thank George Greenstein for bringing this flour to our attention, in his delightful book *Secrets of a Jewish Baker*. Clear flour is 16 percent protein.

Patent durum flour is a fine, silky grind milled from a super-hard cold-weather wheat variety of the same name. Never bleached, this flour retains its lovely pale yellow color. Its high protein content makes it a wonderful flour for bread, but it's best combined with a softer flour. At the bakery we use it in combination with unbleached all-purpose flour to make our Italian-style semolina breads. When durum wheat is ground less fine, as coarse as cornmeal, it is called semolina flour, used primarily for pasta. Don't use semolina flour to make semolina bread—you'll get dense yellow rocks! The protein content of durum flour is about 12 percent.

Pastry flour and **cake flour** are both fine-milled from soft winter wheat. Whole wheat pastry flour is milled using the whole kernel; unbleached pastry flour and cake flour are milled from the endosperm. Cake flour is almost always bleached and enriched. At the bakery we use unbleached pastry flour in combination with all-purpose flour to lower the gluten content when making certain quick breads and other sweets. The protein content of pastry flour is around 9 percent. Cake flour is about 8 percent protein.

Whole wheat bread flour is milled using the whole kernel of hard red spring wheat. It contains not only the complete endosperm, but also the hull and germ, which are rich in fiber and nutrients. At the bakery we use organic stone-ground whole wheat flours, both coarse grind and fine grind. We love the coarse texture and wheaty fragrance and flavor they impart to breads. Being milled from hard wheat, they are generally high in protein, around 13 percent, though we've noticed that the protein levels of the whole wheat flours tend to be less consistent than those of other wheat flours.

Store grains and flours in thoroughly airtight containers in a cool location. Whole-grain flours and berries are especially susceptible to heat and humidity because the oil in the germ goes rancid quickly. If you're not going to be using them on a regular basis, the refrigerator or freezer is the best place for them. Remember to let cold flour come to room temperature before you use it.

Wheat bran is the outer hull of the wheat, separated from the rest of the kernel during milling. We use it occasionally for additional texture in some of our whole-grain breads. **Wheat germ** is the nutrition-rich heart, or embryo, of the wheat kernel. It contains a high percentage of oil and must be kept refrigerated to keep it from turning rancid. It can be used raw or lightly toasted to add a slightly crunchy texture and a rich, nutty flavor to breads.

Rye Flour

The **rye flour** and **pumpernickel flour** we use at the bakery are both milled from whole rye berries, containing the bran, germ, and endosperm. Our finely ground organic rye flour is the rye equivalent of fine whole wheat flour. Pumpernickel, sometimes called rye meal, is the rye equivalent of coarse whole wheat flour. Although rye flour does contain some gluten, the percentage is so low that rye flour is almost always combined with some type of wheat flour when making bread. This fragrant, fruity-smelling grain is especially prone to fermentation and, as a result, it makes a good base for a sourdough culture (see page 43). We love to use it in our "white" bread recipes to add depth and complexity to their flavor and texture. There is also a white rye flour, milled from the endosperm of the rye berry, but none of our recipes use this product.

CORN

Cornmeal adds extra flavor and crunch to some of our breads. We like to use it in our semolina breads to enhance the yellow color and slightly sandy texture of the durum flour. we also use it to dust peels, baking pans, and stones to prevent dough from sticking before baking. We prefer the coarse-textured bright yellow stone-ground variety to the finer pale cornmeal that is found in supermarkets. It is available at natural food stores, through mail-order sources (see page 189), and sometimes in the ethnic food sections of supermarkets. You can substitute Italian polenta for cornmeal in any of our recipes.

Corn germ is the dehydrated embryo of the corn kernel. It is full of nutrients and has twice as much fiber as wheat germ. We like it for its crunchy texture and the fresh-corn flavor it adds to bread. It's a fairly new product that can be found in natural food stores. The Fearn Natural Foods brand (made by Modern Products, Inc., Milwaukee, Wisconsin 53209) is the only one we've seen so far.

Cornstarch is used to make a glaze that can be applied to many breads before and after baking to give them a professional-looking glossy finish. (Instructions are included in the recipes when such a glaze is recommended.) It is similar to the glossy finish we get in the bakery simply from baking in our steam-injected ovens.

OATS

Rolled oats are used in several of our recipes. Full of proteins, minerals, and fat, they add flavor and moisture to breads, keeping them fresh longer. We prefer the heavy old-fashioned variety to the lighter quick-cooking kind, so if you only have the quick-cooking oats available, be sure to use the weight rather than the cup measure called for in the recipe to achieve consistent results.

LIQUIDS

Moisture is necessary in bread making to activate the yeast and promote the formation of gluten strands from the protein in the flour. **Water** is the liquid we use most often because it helps create a loaf with the chewy crumb and crunchy crust that we prefer. At the bakery and at home we use plain tap water, except when we're making sour-dough cultures. Fortunately, in New York City, we're blessed with excellent-tasting water right out of the faucet. If your tap water doesn't taste so great, you may want to use bottled spring water or boil your tap water (and cool it) before you use it. If you're in doubt, try a recipe once with tap water and once with bottled or boiled water, and let your taste buds make the decision for you. When a recipe specifies "very warm water" or "warm water," we suggest adding a little boiling water to cold tap water, or warming the water in the microwave until you get the desired temperature, to avoid water soft-eners and other undesirables that may come through your hot water pipes.

Milk in a bread dough softens the crust and gives it a rich brown color. It also contributes to a finer-textured, more tender crumb and helps the bread stay fresh longer. We use milk in some of our yeasted sweet breads and many of our quick breads and breakfast items. Skim milk or low-fat milk can be substituted when whole milk is called for if you prefer. **Buttermilk** is used in our scone recipe (page 153) to add flavor and tenderness.

SALT

The kosher salt marketed in some regions of the country looks like small rock-salt crystals instead of flakes. If your kosher salt is this type, you will probably want to use a slightly smaller measure of salt than specified in our recipes; e.g., if a recipe calls for two tablespoons of kosher salt, use about one tablespoon plus two-and-a-half teaspoons of these larger crystals. (Or weigh the salt instead—the two types of kosher salt should be equivalent.)

Salt helps to control the activity of yeast, tightens the gluten, and enhances the flavor of the other ingredients in bread dough. At Amy's Bread we prefer to use **kosher salt** because we like its mild flavor and the fact that it contains no additives. It has a coarser texture than regular salt, but the crystals are actually fine flakes. We think the flakes dissolve more easily in dough and can be sprinkled more evenly on pizza, foccacia, rolls, bread sticks, and the like. If you want to substitute kosher salt for regular salt in other bread recipes, be sure to double the *measured* amount (not the weight) of salt specified in the recipe; e.g., if the recipe calls for a tablespoon of regular salt, substi-tute two tablespoons of kosher salt. The reverse is true if you want to substitute regu-lar salt for the kosher salt in our recipes—use half the measured amount specified. Kosher salt and regular salt are actually equal if you *weigh* them; e.g., half an ounce of kosher salt can be substituted for half an ounce of regular salt. In any case, you may want to adjust the amount of salt in a recipe to suit your personal taste.

SWEETENERS

Granulated sugars (white and brown), **honey, molasses,** and **maple syrup** are the sweeteners we use to enhance the flavor of certain doughs. Sweeteners can accelerate yeast activity if used in small amounts, but will inhibit yeast activity if used in large amounts. They can also tenderize the crumb and cause the crust to brown faster during baking.

FAT

Butter, olive oil, canola oil, and **walnut oil** are the fats that you will see in our recipes. We use them when we want to add richness to the flavor of the bread and softness and moisture to the crumb. Breads that contain fat stay fresh longer. In addition, you will notice that doughs that contain fats are usually softer, smoother, and more malleable than those that are fat-free.

EGGS

Using **eggs** in a bread gives it a tender, almost cake-like texture. The yolks add color, richness, and moisture and the whites increase the volume of the loaf. We use them in our sweet yeast breads and quick breads.

SPECIALTY INGREDIENTS

In artisan bread baking, specialty ingredients are anything other than the four most basic ingredients, flour, water, salt, and yeast. When we consider all the things that can add an incredible variety of flavors, textures, and colors to a simple loaf of bread, we sometimes feel like kids in a candy store. The possibilities are endless! You'll see many of our favorite ingredient combinations in the recipes in this book; we hope these will serve to inspire you to try new combinations of your own.

Grains and **seeds** add crunch as well as flavor. We like to use whole wheat berries and rye berries, as well as the cracked versions of these grains. The cracked grains can be used as they are, but the whole berries should be cooked until they become nice and plump, then drained and cooled before you use them. If you store cooked berries in the refrigerator in an airtight container, they will keep for at least a week. You will also find millet, flaxseed, poppy seeds, sunflower seeds, and sesame seeds in our recipes. We prefer the rich, earthy flavor of natural unhulled sesame seeds (available in natural food stores) to the tasteless white, hulled variety found in most supermarkets.

Nuts are another of our favorite crunchies. Chopped or whole almonds, hazelnuts, pecans, and walnuts add their own unique flavors and textures to a loaf of bread. We always toast our nuts before we use them. Generally, we add nuts at the end of mixing the dough, after most of the gluten development has already taken place. If you add the nuts early in the mix, the sharp-edged pieces have a tendency to break the developing strands of gluten.

Olives are one of the most traditional and widely used ingredients for specialty breads. We stay away from the canned varieties and choose instead the more flavorful cured imports, such as Greek Kalamata, Amfissa, and Atalanti olives. Use your own favorites, and try a combination of complementary types. Rinse any brine from the olives and drain them before incorporating them into the dough at the end of the kneading time. If you add olives to a recipe, you may want to decrease the amount of salt to allow for the saltiness of the olives.

Dried fruits add sweetness to bread without using sugar. Cut into coarse chunks, they add color and texture as well. Use them as they are, or soak them briefly (fifteen to thirty minutes) in just enough warm water to cover them. Then drain off the water, and save it to use as part of the liquid in your dough. Our recipes use dark raisins, golden raisins, currants, apricots, prunes, and figs.

Vegetables add flavor, color, and extra nutrition to bread. Use them raw or lightly cooked and coarsely chopped, finely diced, or pureed. Even dried peas or beans can be cooked or ground into coarse flour and added to a bread dough. We've used onions, garlic, scallions, potatoes, red bell peppers, jalapeño peppers, pumpkin, and dried lentils in the recipes in this book.

Fresh herbs are one of the most pleasing additions to bread dough. We particularly like basil, rosemary, sage, and thyme. When you experiment, practice moderation. The herbs should enhance the flavor of the bread, not overpower it. Dried herbs can be used too, but often they're a pale substitute for their fresh counterparts.

Small amounts of **spices** go a long way in a loaf of bread. We use them in both sweet and savory combinations with other ingredients. You'll see cinnamon, caraway, mustard seeds, and dill seeds in the recipes in this book.

Cheese has always been a favorite partner for bread. We incorporate imported Parmesan into one of our doughs and use several other varieties in our pizzas.

Tools: A Few Implements to Make Your Job Easier

◆

Bread baking at home requires only a few simple tools. (We use the same equipment listed here at the bakery; the only difference is that we also use a large mixer/kneader.) It won't take a large investment in equipment to get you started. In fact, for most jobs, your hands are the best tools of all.

Baking Stone or Quarry Tiles We recommend using a baking stone, sometimes called a pizza stone, to simulate a stone hearth in your oven. The best stones have a large surface area for baking; we prefer a square stone to a round one because we can fit more loaves on it. See page 29 for information on using a stone. Unglazed quarry tiles, usually six inches square, can also be used for baking; they can be purchased at tile stores. The only problem with tiles is that they can slide around, letting the dough fall between them or leaving grooves or creases on the bottom of the loaves. They also tend to crack more easily than the thicker pizza stones.

Baskets, Bannetons, and Cloths Willow baskets, cloth-lined baskets called *bannetons,* and heavy baker's canvas are all tools used for letting dough rise. They provide a structured place for the rising dough and result in a finished loaf with an attractive appearance. See page 28 for information about how to use rising baskets and how to make your own.

Cooling Rack It is important to place your bread on a cooling rack after baking so the air can circulate around the crust, keeping the outside firm and the inside moist.

Dough Cutter A dough cutter, also called a bench cutter or dough scraper, is a rectangular metal blade set into a rounded handle made from wood, metal, or plastic. The dough cutter is an essential tool for cutting and dividing dough and for scraping it up off the work surface during kneading.

Electric Mixer We prefer to knead bread by hand, and a mixer is not required for any of our recipes. However, it can simplify and shorten the kneading process. Use a heavy-duty stationary electric mixer, such as a KitchenAid, with a dough hook and a paddle. A mixer is helpful when making sticky, wet doughs that can be difficult to knead by hand. For complete instructions on using an electric mixer, see page 17.

Food Processor Many bread books recommend the food processor for kneading. We prefer to knead by hand. The processor may save time, but it's more satisfying to make bread with your own hand power.

Kitchen Scale We strongly recommend that you purchase a scale with a capacity of two pounds. A kitchen scale that measures in quarter-ounce increments is precise enough for any of the recipes in this book. If you don't have a scale, you can measure the ingredients using measuring cups, but the measurements won't be as accurate.

La Cloche La Cloche is a two-piece ceramic bread baker with a round base and a domed top that fits onto the base. It acts as a self-contained baking hearth. The base of the cloche is sprinkled with cornmeal, and the dough is placed on it to rise. Some bakers recommend that you soak the top in water for thirty minutes, then drain it just before baking. When the bread has risen, the soaked lid is placed over the loaf and the whole thing is put into the hot oven. The dome creates a moist baking chamber, resulting in a loaf with a wonderful crunchy brown crust with a slightly glossy appearance. The dome lid can also be left unsoaked and placed over the base for baking; it will still provide a moist environment for baking, because the loaf gives off its own moisture. The only drawback of La Cloche is that the loaf spreads slightly and doesn't spring up as high during baking because it takes longer for the oven heat to penetrate the dome. However, although the bread comes out flatter, we like the results we get from La Cloche, especially the crunchy quality of the crust.

Measuring Cups, Dry and Liquid Use dry measuring cups to measure dry ingredients such as flour and grains. To measure flour, dip the cup into the flour gently and scoop it up; don't pack it into the cup. Level the top off with a knife.

Liquid measuring cups should only be used for measuring the water and other liquids. They do not give an accurate reading for dry ingredients.

Measuring Spoons These are essential for accurately measuring salt, yeast, and other such ingredients. Dip the spoon into the ingredient, then level off the top with a knife to get a precise measure. Do not try to use other spoons as measuring spoons.

Mixing Bowls Use stainless steel, plastic, or ceramic mixing bowls to mix your dough. We prefer ceramic over metal because it holds a constant room temperature and doesn't react with acidic sourdough starters. You will need two or three medium to large bowls for our recipes.

Oven See page 33 for information on understanding your oven.

Pans Loaf pans are used in several of our recipes. These are good for making the standard sandwich-bread—shaped loaves. We recommend 9 by 5-inch pans for most of our recipes, but the 8^1/$_2$ by 4^1/$_2$-inch pans can be used; they will result in taller, more compact loaves.

Cookie sheets, usually 12 by 17 inches, are needed for several recipes. For bread sticks and twists, a flat sheet is fine, but you'll need a pan with a rim for focaccia and rolls. A 9-inch square baking pan is used for making sticky buns. If you are purchasing pans, invest in the new heavy-weight nonstick baking pans. They conduct heat evenly, allowing the top and bottom of loaves or bread sticks to color at the same rate, and produce a wonderful golden-brown crust. They require minimal oiling before use, resulting in lower-fat baking. We also like to use baguette molds to keep our baguettes straight and even.

Parchment Paper Parchment paper is a valuable tool for the baker. Used to line a pan for sweet breakfast breads or bread sticks, it keeps them from sticking to the pan without a lot of extra oil or butter for greasing. It can also be used in place of cornmeal to keep loaves from sticking to a peel or pan before they are baked on a baking stone. We find that parchment works better than cornmeal when sliding loaves made from wet, sticky dough onto the baking stone. Parchment can be purchased at specialty cookware stores and in some supermarkets.

Pastry Brush A 1½ to 2-inch-wide pastry brush is used in several recipes to brush olive oil or a glaze onto dough. You can use a narrow basting brush, but it will not coat as efficiently or as gently.

Peel A peel is a wooden paddle used to slide bread or pizza onto a baking stone in the oven. Available in cookware stores, wooden peels are also a good place to let dough rise before baking. If you don't have a peel, use the back side of a sheet pan lined with parchment paper.

Plant Sprayer or Mister This is one of the simplest but most important tools for a baker. The water mister helps to produce steam in the oven, giving breads a better crust. It also comes in handy for "gluing" seeds and other garnishes onto shaped loaves.

Plastic Containers We prefer to use deep clear plastic containers for letting our starters and sponges rise. It is fun to be able to see the structure of the bubbles through the sides of the container, but, more important, you can mark the level of the starter at the beginning of the fermentation process so you can see just how far and how fast it rises.

Plastic Scraper A plastic scraper is a stiff thin plastic rectangle with one curved side. It can be used to scrape the sides of a bowl during kneading or to scrape dough bits off your worktable. It is also handy when working with quick breads and pastry.

Razor Blade A razor blade mounted on a three-inch handle, known as a *lame,* is ideal for scoring bread. It can be ordered from baker's supply catalogues. (See page 189 for mail-order sources.) You can also use a sharp single-edge razor blade.

Refrigerator We use our refrigerator for cooling, or retarding, our doughs. It is ideal if the inside temperature is around 40°F, or even slightly warmer. A very cold refrigerator will stop the rising process completely and chill the dough so much that it will take longer for it to come to room temperature for the second rise.

Thermometers An instant-read thermometer is one of the most important tools you can buy. Instant-read thermometers are long-stem thermometers that read from 0° to 220° F. They are used to measure the temperature of both the water you mix into the dough and the final mixed dough.

It is also helpful to have a portable room thermometer to find the ideal place for your dough to rise. It is important to know the temperature of the room where the dough is mixed and, more important, where it rises.

It's a good idea to buy an oven thermometer too, since most home ovens fluctuate in temperature and their thermostat settings are not extremely accurate.

Timer A timer is an important tool when mixing, shaping, and baking bread. Purchase a digital timer that can be set for several hours so you can use it when you're making our slow-rising doughs. It's helpful to have a timer with multiple settings, for timing several procedures at once or when making more than one batch of bread at a time.

Worktable Any Formica or wood countertop will work well for kneading. You will need a space about three feet by two feet. It is best to work at a table or counter that is just above waist height so you can knead comfortably without straining your back and shoulders.

> **Bread Machine**
>
> *We prefer to make bread by hand, so we have never tried to use a bread machine. If you have one, you may also have instructions for converting recipes for the machine. But we believe in a long, slow, cool fermentation process and like the shapes of free-form loaves baked on a stone.*

Techniques: Our Secrets and Tips

◆

This chapter contains plenty of basic information on techniques that will help you make great bread. We've also included more technical information in Chapter 12. Our skill, knowledge, and intuition have come from practice and experience. Time will teach you about the best dough texture, dough temperature, the first rise, and the ideal flavor of the ripened sourdough starter. You will learn about flour strength and gluten development, about molding and dough handling, about long, slow fermentation at a cool temperature. As you incorporate these techniques into your bread making, you will find that the more you control the variables affecting the dough, the better your bread will be. When you get everything right and make the big, beautiful, crusty loaf of your dreams, you will feel wonderfully satisfied.

MEASURING INGREDIENTS

One technique that will greatly improve your results is to weigh all the ingredients on a kitchen scale instead of measuring their volume using measuring cups. Both the weather and the humidity can affect the volume measurement of flour, and different types and brands of flour may have different volumes. Besides, each person measures flour differently. The same is true for liquid measurements. We have found that liquid measuring cups often have inaccurate volume markings, so we weigh our liquids as well. So although we have given both weights and measures in our recipes, we strongly recommend that you use a scale for greater accuracy.

A few of our recipes contain both honey and oil. When measuring these ingredients using a measuring cup, we find it works well to pour the oil into the cup first, then pour the specified amount of honey on top of the oil. When you pour the ingredients into your mixing bowl, the honey will be released easily from the cup without sticking, thereby giving a more accurate measure and an easier clean-up.

CONTROLLING THE TEMPERATURE OF THE DOUGH

Another important technique is to control the temperature of the bread dough. Purchase an instant-read thermometer and use it to check the temperature of both the warm water you are mixing into the yeast and the cool water used in the dough. After mixing, take the temperature of the dough: We like our final mixed dough to have a temperature of 75° F. We also like to let the dough rise at a cool room temperature, between 75° and 77° F. We refer to this technique as a "slow, cool rise." The best way to keep the dough temperature in the desired range is to use the guidelines on page 179.

Besides giving the bread a better flavor, a cool rise gives the loaf a moister interior and a chewy texture. If you use the cool-rise method, you will taste the wheat, the crust, and any other ingredients in the bread, but you won't taste a strong yeast flavor. We find that the slow, cool rise gives our bread a beautiful appearance as well. When the yeast ferments slowly, it gives off small bubbles that form beneath the crust. If the bread is given plenty of steam in the oven, the crust becomes glossy, bubbly, and golden brown.

MAKING DOUGH WITH THE RIGHT AMOUNT OF MOISTURE

One of the most common mistakes in bread baking is to make the dough too dry. Some people hold back part of the flour at first, then try to knead it all in to create a firm, resilient dough. Or they throw lots of flour on the table and on the dough as they're kneading it, making dough that feels like stiff clay. The bread comes out with a dense, tough texture and very small holes in the crumb.

We think it's better if you hold back a little of the water instead of the flour when you're mixing dough. Once you start kneading, you'll be able to feel the texture of the dough. If the dough seems firm, you can add more water by the tablespoon until it is supple and moist. Just flatten the dough on the table and dimple the surface with your fingertips. Sprinkle on one to two tablespoons of water, fold the dough in thirds, and knead gently until the water is absorbed. The dough will become slippery at first, then smooth and supple. A moist dough feels supple, soft, and stretchy when it is kneaded.

The benefits of a slightly wetter dough are a wonderfully moist, chewy bread with a glossier crumb, a longer shelf life, and an appealing texture with more open holes. The secret to the doughs we make in the bakery is *wetter is better*. Of course dough can be made too wet, resulting in a bread that spreads and flattens and has a sticky, gummy crumb. After you have tried the same recipe two or three times, you will learn how wet you should mix the dough to get the exact results you want. (To determine the moisture content of a dough you can calculate the hydration rate, or the ratio of water to flour in that dough; see page 179 for more information on this calculation.)

AUTOLYSE

Autolyse is a French word that refers to a rest period given to dough during the kneading process. This rest lets the gluten in the dough relax so that the flour can absorb more water than it otherwise would, resulting in dough that is smooth and supple. Using the autolyse method means the dough is kneaded for less time in all. Using an autolyse at the bakery has helped us make dough that is moist, stretchy, and easier to shape. The finished loaves have greater volume, look beautiful, and taste better.

With the French method, the only ingredients that are mixed together before the autolyse are flour and water, but we have tried adding other ingredients with good results. First some or all of the dough ingredients are mixed together to form a shaggy mass. The dough is kneaded for a few minutes to begin the gluten development, then it rests, covered, for twenty minutes. After the autolyse, the dough is kneaded for a few more minutes or so, depending on the type of dough, until it is stretchy and smooth. Bread doughs containing a high proportion of white flour derive the greatest benefit from an autolyse. We give specific instructions for timing the autolyse with each recipe.

KNEADING THE DOUGH

Although we make very moist doughs in the bakery, we have made the doughs in these recipes slightly drier so they will be easy to knead by hand. In recipes where the dough is difficult to handle, we recommend using an electric mixer (see complete instructions below). Otherwise, we prefer hand kneading because we enjoy getting our hands and our whole body into the therapeutic rhythm of pushing, turning, and folding the dough. It's also interesting to feel the properties of the developing gluten as the dough changes from a lifeless mass to a stretchy, springy, rising dough. Once you get used to the feel of moister doughs and you practice working with a dough cutter to scrape up the dough from the table, you'll find it easy to improve any bread recipe yielding firm dough by adding a little more water.

To knead dough by hand, first mix the wet and dry ingredients together in a bowl with your fingers until the dough comes together and forms a crumbly, shaggy mass. Then move to a very lightly floured surface to continue kneading. You don't need to beat the dough or work so vigorously that you work up a sweat. The experienced baker uses a quick, confident hand that does not warm the dough too much yet provides enough strength to develop the gluten. Gentle kneading will develop the gluten in the dough.

Knead the dough by pushing down and forward on it with the palms of your hands, then lift and turn the dough a quarter turn. Fold the dough in half over itself and repeat the process, using a push-turn-fold motion. *Use as little flour on the work surface as possible.* If the dough sticks to the table during kneading, use a dough cutter to lift the dough off the table and scrape up the sticky dough residue, then dust *lightly* with more flour.

Kneading Dough

The rhythm of pushing,
turning, and folding the dough
is very relaxing

A shaggy mass takes form in the bowl

The dough mass is moved to the table where kneading begins

The dough is turned and folded

Then the dough is pushed away

These steps are repeated until you get a smoothly kneaded dough

Using an electric mixer to knead the dough

To knead dough using a heavy-duty stationary mixer such as a five-quart KitchenAid, it works best to mix the wet and dry ingredients with a paddle first, until they gather into a moist, solid mass, then switch to a dough hook. On most machines the dough hook doesn't reach the bottom of the bowl and thus is not as effective for gathering the ingredients together as the paddle. (A longer hook has recently been introduced for newer models of the KitchenAid mixer, making the use of the paddle unnecessary.)

If you use an electric mixer for the recipes in this book, follow our timing instructions for hand kneading, but reduce the kneading time after the rest period, or autolyse, by about two or three minutes. Using the kneading time given, mix the dough on low, or #2, for all but two minutes before the autolyse, then move to medium speed (#6) for the last two minutes. Let the dough rest in the mixer bowl during the autolyse. After the autolyse, mix for one to two minutes on low speed (#2) and two minutes on medium speed (#6). (Dough speeds are for a KitchenAid stationary mixer with ten speeds.) Watch for the dough to pull away from, or "clean," the sides of the mixer bowl, and use our description of the desired dough texture for each recipe to tell if the dough has been kneaded for the right amount of time.

KNEADING COARSE INGREDIENTS INTO THE DOUGH

To knead coarse ingredients such as raisins or nuts into a dough, let the dough relax for five to ten minutes after kneading so it is less resistant. Pat the dough into a rectangle and sprinkle or spread the ingredients evenly over the surface. Fold the dough in thirds, forming a narrow rectangle, then roll the dough up into a rough log. Gently knead the dough to distribute the ingredients. The dough will separate and look stringy before it comes together into a smooth mass. The kneading process should take only two to four minutes. Do not overwork the dough; if the coarse ingredients keep popping out, stop kneading and wait until after the first rise, when the dough can be given a gentle turn to finish incorporating the ingredients.

Kneading Coarse Ingredients into the Dough

Pressing the ingredient into a flattened piece of dough

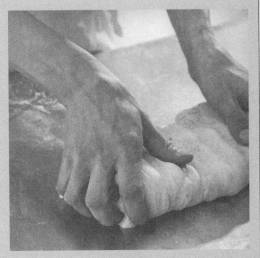

Rolling up the dough

Kneading the ingredient into the dough—
the dough becomes shredded

The finished dough is smooth

KNOWING WHEN THE DOUGH IS FULLY KNEADED

The dough is fully kneaded when it is stretchy and smooth and does not stick to your hand when you slap it. To test a dough made from mostly white flour, pull off a bit of dough and stretch it to form a thin membrane. If you can stretch it so it's almost transparent, as thin as a balloon, it's ready. The stretch test does not work as well with coarse-grained whole wheat or rye doughs; to test these doughs, use your thumb and forefinger to pull up a piece of the dough about an inch above the dough surface. If the dough holds the pinch and stands in a little ridge without springing back, it is fully kneaded.

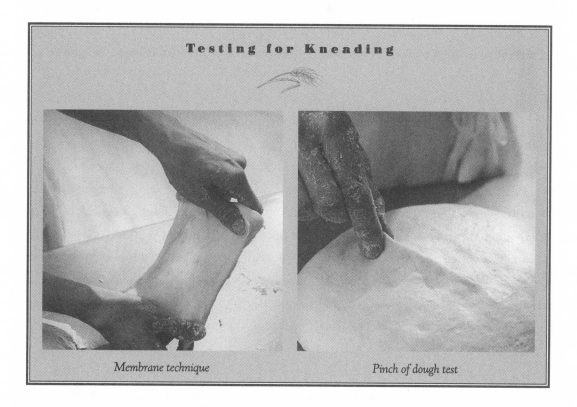

Testing for Kneading

Membrane technique   *Pinch of dough test*

COVERING THE DOUGH

After the dough has been kneaded, it is usually placed in a bowl to rise. Lightly oil the bowl to prevent the dough from sticking; we use vegetable oil. Turn the ball of dough in the bowl to coat it with oil. Then cover the dough with plastic wrap to keep it from drying out. We spray the plastic wrap with nonstick cooking spray so it won't stick to the dough. The same piece of oiled plastic wrap can be used to cover the loaves after they have been shaped.

LETTING THE DOUGH RISE

It's a good idea to use a portable room thermometer to help you find the best place to let your dough rise. The ideal room temperature for rising is between 75° and 77° F. At temperatures over 80° F, the bread will ferment too quickly and will taste very yeasty or bitter, or like beer. Putting dough into a warmed oven or on a radiator to rise is too drastic.

Each rise of the dough plays an important role in the development of the bread. The first rise is the most critical, for it is then that the greatest flavor development takes place. During the first rise the yeasts begin to multiply, feeding on the sugar and starch in the flour. The tangy characteristics of a sourdough bread are developed at this time. The organic acids that form help to give the dough strength and aid in the development of a thin, crisp crust as well. For flavorful bread with a wonderful texture, be sure to let the dough expand fully and double, or almost double, depending on the dough, during the first rise.

The second rise takes less time than the first, because the yeasts have multiplied so more yeasts are at work in the rising dough. The second and any subsequent rises contribute more to the light texture of the bread and the openness of the crumb.

After the first rise, you must deflate the dough and prepare it for shaping or additional rises. Do this gently; "punching down" is not necessary. Simply take the bowl of risen dough, turn it over, and dump it gently onto a lightly floured worktable. The action of dumping it out of the bowl will deflate the dough enough. If you are going to shape the dough into loaves, divide it into the number of pieces given in the recipe and proceed from there. Or, for an additional rise, gently fold the dough in half, then in half again, and form it into a loose ball. Put it back into the bowl to rise again.

RETARDING THE DOUGH (SLOWING THE FERMENTATION)

You can slow down the fermentation of the dough by retarding (refrigerating) it after the first rise has begun. Retarding intensifies the benefits of the cool rise, further enhancing the texture and flavor of your bread. Breads that have been retarded will stay fresh longer too. After you mix the dough, let it rise for about an hour at room temperature, or until it has begun to increase in volume but has not doubled. Then chill the dough overnight, or for at least eight hours and up to twenty-four. The second half of the rise takes place in the refrigerator. After the dough has been retarded, let it come to room temperature and soften before the shaping and second rise.

Retarding dough also gives you more flexibility. You can mix it one day and finish shaping and baking it the next. Some doughs work better not chilled overnight. We indicate in each recipe whether or not the dough is enhanced by the retarding method.

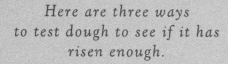

Tests for Rising

Here are three ways
to test dough to see if it has
risen enough.

Small ball of unrisen dough in bowl

Dough has visibly doubled in volume

Testing volume by poking finger into dough

Indentation does not spring back

Slight indentation in risen loaf does not spring back

HOW TO KNOW IF THE DOUGH IS FULLY RISEN

To tell if dough is fully risen, or "proofed," you can use three tests. The most obvious is a visual test. You can see that the dough has increased substantially in volume; most doughs will almost double in size. You can also poke the dough to see if it has risen enough. For the first rise, you should be able to push your finger deep into the mass of dough and leave an indentation that does not spring back. For loaves that have been shaped and are on their second rise, touch them lightly with your index finger. When they are ready for baking, the dough should feel soft and the slight indentation should not spring back. Another test for a free-form loaf on its second rise is to gently place your fingers under the loaf and lift it up to see if the dough feels light and airy. You will be able to tell when the network of bubbles has expanded inside the loaf because the dough will not feel as dense.

We give most of our breads two rises before baking. With certain doughs, a third rise makes a better bread. If the yeast has enough potency to rise the bread again, a third and sometimes even a forth rise will give the bread a lighter crumb and more delicate crust.

If your dough has risen too much and overproofed on the second rise, so the shaped loaves are beginning to spread and deflate, gently pat the loaves to flatten them, then reshape them and let them rise again. It is almost always better to reshape them than to bake overproofed and deflating loaves. We actually prefer to leave most of our loaves very slightly underproofed in the final rise. They will inflate more in the oven and have a more attractive appearance.

SHAPING THE LOAVES

Here we describe how to make five basic bread shapes; see page 171 for directions for other shapes. When shaping your loaves, the most important thing to remember is to be gentle with the dough. Your goal is to form an even loaf with a taut skin, while leaving some larger air holes inside.

Log. Very lightly flour the work surface. Start by *forming an envelope*: Place the dough on the table. Press and flatten it gently with your fingertips to form a rectangle with a short side facing you, leaving a lot of air bubbles in the dough. Fold the top edge down over the middle of the rectangle, then fold the bottom edge up. Give the dough a quarter turn and repeat the process, folding the top edge down and the bottom edge up again and overlapping the edges slightly in the middle so the dough looks like an envelope. Pat the seam to seal it. Now you have a smaller, tighter rectangle.

Form a cylinder: Starting from the top edge of the rectangle, fold the top third of the dough over itself with one hand. With the heel of your other hand, gently press the

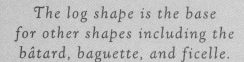

The log shape is the base
for other shapes including the
bâtard, baguette, and ficelle.

The dough has been flattened. Now we begin a
business letter fold

Shaping an envelope

First fold to shape a log

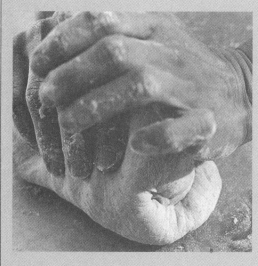

Sealing with the heal of the hand after the first fold

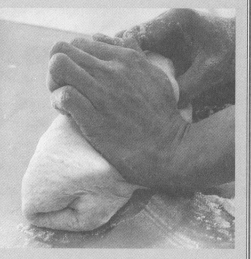

Sealing the final seam of the log

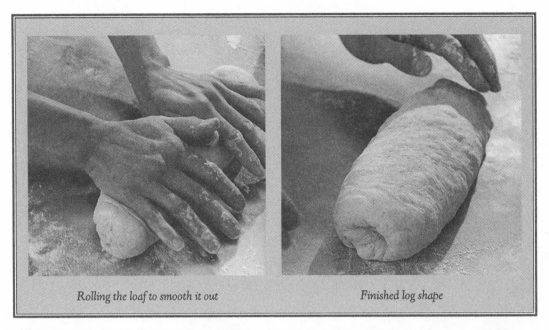

Rolling the loaf to smooth it out   *Finished log shape*

seam to seal it. Fold the dough one third of the way down again and work from one end to the other to seal the seam. Try to keep the skin of the dough smooth and tight but not so tight that the skin tears. Repeat this process one or two more times, until the loaf is a nice round log. Seal the final seam completely with the heel of your hand. Ideally your seam should be straight and tight with no openings or flaps of dough hanging out; with practice, this will become natural. If any dough is protruding from the ends of the log, poke it back in with your finger.

The plain log shape can be placed in a loaf pan or left on a cloth for a free-form second rise. From the log shape, you can make other cylindrical shapes.

Bâtard. Begin to form the basic log shape, making an envelope. Flatten the envelope and fold the top two corners in toward the center of the rectangle to form a triangle. Using your fingers, fold the point of the triangle down into the center of the loaf, forming a half-moon shape. Then fold the dough over itself one third of the way down and, working from one edge to the other, seal the seam with the heel of your hand. Give the loaf two to three more folds, each time folding the ends in further so they become more tapered. Seal the final seam tightly with the heel of your hand. Now roll the loaf back and forth on the table under your palms, working from the middle out to the ends of the loaf and pushing down on the ends to taper them. This technique will smooth out, elongate, and taper the loaf. The bâtard should be between eight and ten inches long, depending on the weight of the dough. Place the loaf on a floured cloth or board to rise.

Bâtard Shape

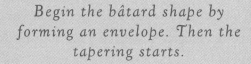

Begin the bâtard shape by forming an envelope. Then the tapering starts.

Folding in the corners of the rectangle

Forming a crescent shape

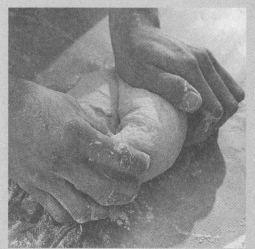

Folding and sealing

Sealing the final seam on the bâtard

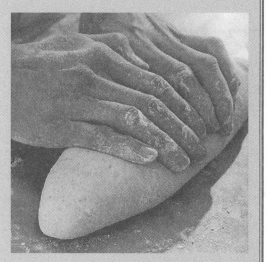

Rolling the finished loaf

Baguette. To make either a baguette or a thinner rope called a ficelle, first shape a loose log and let it relax for a minute or two. Then, keeping the seam up, flatten the log slightly. Working from one end to the other, fold the dough one third of the way down over itself and seal the seam with the heel of your hand. Repeat the process two or three times, making the log longer and thinner. Seal the final seam. Place both palms over the middle of the loaf and roll it back and forth to elongate it, working out toward the ends. (If the loaf springs back, let it rest for two minutes, then roll it out again.) Return your hands to the center of the loaf and repeat the process, pushing down and rolling until the loaf is the length you want. Do not stretch the dough so much that the skin tears. The baguette can be placed in a mold or on a floured cloth or board to rise.

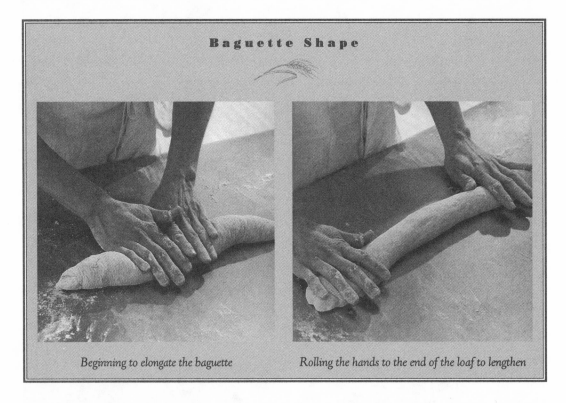

Baguette Shape

Beginning to elongate the baguette   Rolling the hands to the end of the loaf to lengthen

Boule. To shape the dough into a round ball-shaped loaf, or boule, place it on a very lightly floured surface and gently pat it to flatten it slightly. Then, working around the circle of dough, fold the outside edges of the dough into a point in the middle, section by section. Dust the flour off a small part of the worktable and turn the ball over onto the clean spot. Rotate the ball against the table to tighten and seal it completely: With your right hand, pull the loaf toward you and with your left hand push it away, working in a clockwise motion. You are using the stickiness of the dough to create tension against the table. Continue to shape, or round, the ball until the skin of the loaf is pulled tight, being careful not to let the skin tear. When the loaf is shaped, turn it over and rub a little bit of flour on the seam to prevent sticking, then put it seam side down on the rising place of your choice.

Folding the dough into the center   Rounding the boule against the table

Roll. To shape a roll, place a piece of dough on an unfloured table and cover it with your palm. Your fingers should form a cage over the roll. Rotate your curved fingers against the table in a clockwise motion and tighten the skin over the roll by pushing it against the table. The piece of dough will move under your palm in the opposite direction. Continue until the roll is firm and has a tight skin; work quickly and try not to warm up the dough too much with your hand. Place the rolls on a pan or floured cloth to rise.

Roll Shape

Forming a roll by making a cage over the dough with your fingers

CHOOSING A RISING PLACE FOR THE SHAPED LOAVES

When you're going to bake the bread on a baking stone (see page 29), you have a choice about where to let the loaves rise. Since they must be slid onto the hot stone, it's easiest to let the shaped loaves rise on a peel or on an upside-down baking sheet lined with parchment paper. You can also let them rise somewhere else, such as the work surface, and then move them to the peel just before baking. Moving the loaves after they have risen can work well, but there's a danger of deflating the loaves. Wherever the loaves rise, be sure to cover them with plastic wrap so a dry skin doesn't form while they proof.

If you are letting your bread rise on a peel, coat it generously with cornmeal before putting the loaves on it. We use coarse cornmeal because it is better than fine at keeping the loaves from sticking (and is easier to clean off the baking stone and out of the corners of the oven). If you don't have a peel, you can use the back side of a baking sheet lined with parchment paper. Sprinkle the paper with a little cornmeal and put the loaves on the paper. When you're ready to bake, slide the loaves and the paper onto the stone. After the crust becomes firm, the paper can be removed, allowing the loaves to touch the stone for better crust development.

Bread can also rise on baker's canvas, or a *couche*. At home you can use a heavy cotton dish towel with a smooth "nonlooped" surface or a small cotton tablecloth. Simply sprinkle a generous amount of flour over the cloth and rub it into the surface to prevent the dough from sticking. If you bake bread often, you can fold up your floured cloth to use again without washing it. Over time it will become well seasoned, and doughs will be released easily from it. Place the floured cloth on a counter or a pan, then place the shaped loaves on the cloth to rise.

Another option is to let the bread rise in a special rising basket, or *banneton*. These baskets must be well floured each time you use them. We use bannetons at the bakery to give loaves a uniform shape and to create a decorative flour pattern on the crust. Dough tends to rise more slowly in these baskets because it is insulated from the warmth of the room. They can be ordered from a baking supplier (see page 189 for mail-order sources), or you can make your own by placing a well-floured dish towel in a medium colander or in any woven basket. We have tried all sorts of different-sized deep and shallow bowls lined with a cloth. They give interesting new dimensions to boule-shaped loaves.

Standard loaf pans and baking sheets are another choice for letting bread rise. After the first rise the loaves are shaped, then placed directly in or on the pans where they will bake. If you want to make baguettes or ficelles that are longer and straighter than those baked free-form, a baguette mold is very handy. Most molds hold two to five baguettes. Because baguettes placed in a mold are not disturbed after they are proofed, they come out fatter and more uniform after baking. The only drawback is that the crust is not quite as crisp when baked in a mold.

If you are using a peel, cloth, pan, baking sheet, or bread mold, place the loaves seam side down to rise. Conversely, if using a cloth-lined basket or bowl, place the loaves seam side up to rise; just before baking, they will be dumped out onto the peel seam side down, revealing the tops of the loaves.

USING A BAKING STONE

Any serious home baker should invest in a baking stone. A stone helps loaves bake more evenly and gives them a much better crust. If you are using a baking stone, you should preheat the stone in the oven for at least thirty minutes to ensure that the stone is heated through. In a gas oven, place the stone on a rack in the lower third of the oven. In an electric oven, place the stone on a rack in the center of the oven. The stone should be in the center of the rack, leaving at least one or two inches all around to let air and steam circulate.

We have experimented with using two stones in a home oven to simulate the intense top and bottom heat we get in our commercial oven. Placing one stone on a rack a few inches above the baking loaf, allowing space for rising, and the other stone nearer to the bottom of the oven has enabled us to bake loaves that spring higher and have a more complex, toasty, crunchy crust. If you try this technique, be sure to preheat the two stones well, and use more steam in the oven, quickly sprinkling a little water on the top stone when you begin to bake.

SCORING THE CRUST

Scoring the crust serves both a functional and decorative purpose. When the yeast's activity is accelerated by the heat of the oven, the carbon dioxide gas it releases needs a place to escape, and the cuts provide that outlet. If left unscored, most loaves will crack open where you don't want them to. Decorative cuts on the crust are also considered the baker's signature. You can use our ideas or create your own cuts to give your loaves a beautiful appearance and make them unique.

Scoring bread properly requires a sharp blade and a quick, steady hand. At the bakery we use a *lame,* a double-edge razor blade mounted on a three-inch handle. To make a cut that opens to form a flared ridge on a loaf such as a baguette, hold the blade at a 30-degree angle, nearly parallel to the loaf. This allows you to cut just below the surface, or skin, of the loaf. A blade held at a 90-degree angle, or perpendicular to the loaf, will create a smooth opening with no ridge. This is nice when cutting a star, a cross, or a tic-tac-toe pattern on a round loaf. Whatever cut you choose, it is important to keep it shallow but long. Don't drag the blade too slowly, or the skin will gather or tear. And don't use a heavy hand when you score the bread, because too much pressure on the loaf will cause it to deflate. Certain heavy-grained doughs do not require much scoring because they are not high in gluten and will not burst open in the oven.

Scissors work well for scoring very wet doughs, where a blade would drag, or on decorative loaves such as crowns or epi. Additional ideas for scoring and making decorative patterns can be found on page 177.

Scoring the Crusts

Here are two techniques for scoring bread using a lame. Note the angle and direction of the cuts.

Angle to hold the blade for a flared ridge on the loaf

Correct pattern of the cut from one tip of the loaf to the other for best appearance

Angle to hold the blade for a flat, smooth opening

OVEN SPRING

When raw yeast dough is placed in a hot oven, the drastic change in temperature causes the yeasts to act rapidly. They give off carbon dioxide in a last flurry of life before reaching 140° F, the temperature at which they expire. The carbon dioxide gas is trapped in the web of gluten in the dough, leaving open air bubbles in the bread. This action of bursting is known as *oven spring*. To get the fullest rise from your loaves, be sure the oven has had time to preheat and the dough is not overproofed when you are ready to bake it. (Overproofed loaves should be gently deflated and reshaped, then allowed to rise again.) Breads with a lighter texture, such as baguettes, are best baked slightly underproofed. The loaves will rise higher in the oven, giving them a more open-holed crumb. The cuts will also burst open further, making the loaf more attractive.

ALL ABOUT THE CRUST

For many people the texture and the flavor of the crust are the most memorable parts of a loaf of bread. Getting a perfect crust takes practice, and, no matter what, factors beyond your control, such as humidity and the kind of oven you use, can change the results. To get the best texture in the crust, make sure to start with a moist dough and see that it is properly proofed on the first and second rise. Use a baking stone that has been preheated for at least thirty minutes at 425° F or hotter, and use plenty of steam in the oven. Bake the loaves until they have a deep brown color; a pale crust will soften and have less flavor. More information about the crust can be found on page 181.

To get a crunchier crust, bake the bread at a temperature over 425° F. For loaves without any sweet ingredients, such as raisins or honey, the oven can be preheated to 450° F or 500° F and turned down to 400° F or 425° F after the first ten minutes of baking. Sweet breads require a cooler oven, between 375° and 400° F. Experiment with your oven to see what temperature gives the bread a good rise and a crisp crust without burning the bottom of the loaf.

After the bread is baked, the best way to keep the crust dry and crisp is to let air circulate around the loaf, both during and after cooling. Don't wrap the bread in plastic wrap or chill it, or the crust will soften. If the bread has softened, you can restore a crunchy crust by reheating the bread for five to eight minutes in a preheated 400° F oven.

SLIDING LOAVES ONTO THE BAKING STONE

When you are ready to slide risen loaves onto a preheated baking stone, shake the peel gently to release them or loosen the loaves with your fingers. To slide the loaves onto the stone, simply hold the peel over the stone and use a smooth, quick jerking motion to release the loaves. Draw the peel out smoothly so the loaves land where you want them to be.

If your batch of dough makes more loaves than will fit on your baking stone, you can hold one or two risen loaves in the refrigerator while you bake the other loaves. After the first batch has baked, let the stone heat again for about five minutes. Then take the waiting loaves from the refrigerator and bake them.

STEAM IN THE OVEN

Creating steam in the oven while the loaves bake will make the crust browner and glossier; it also helps produce a thin, crunchy crust. The best ways to create steam in a home oven are to pour hot water into a preheated pan in the oven and to spray the loaves and the oven walls with a plant sprayer at the beginning of the baking process.

If you're using a water pan, place it on an oven rack directly under the baking stone. Put the pan in the oven at the same time you put the stone in to preheat. We recommend using a wide shallow pan that will let the water evaporate more quickly. Use an old, dispensable pan, because it will become warped and discolored from sitting empty in a hot oven. After you slide the risen loaves onto the baking stone, quickly but carefully pour one cup of very hot water into the water pan and shut the oven door. Be careful not to burn your hand on the hot steam that will immediately rise from the pan. (In our home ovens, one cup of hot water will have evaporated completely after ten to twelve minutes of baking; the amount you will need depends on your oven and the size of your water pan. After the first ten to twelve minutes of baking, the oven should be allowed to dry out so the crust can develop the crunch you want.) After one minute, open the oven door and quickly mist the walls of the oven and the loaves six to eight times with a plant sprayer. (If you've made a decorative flour pattern on the loaves, don't spray them directly.) Repeat the misting process again a minute later.

If you don't use a water pan, mist the loaves and the oven walls eight to ten times when you put the bread into the oven. Repeat the misting process two minutes later and again after two more minutes, shutting the oven door rapidly each time.

If the crust develops white streaks as it bakes and is not browning because you don't have enough steam in the oven, you can brush the loaf with a little oil during the last ten to fifteen minutes of baking. Although the crust won't be as crisp as you might like, the oil will make it browner and more attractive.

UNDERSTANDING YOUR OVEN AND ROTATING THE LOAVES

Use an oven thermometer to check the accuracy of your oven. Many home ovens have some hot spots or other unevenness. Check the bread as it bakes to see that it is coloring evenly. We usually rotate the loaves from one side of the oven to the other and turn them around halfway through the baking time to get more even coloration. If you are baking on two different oven racks, it is essential that you switch the position of the loaves at least once. Quickly shut the oven door after you rotate the bread.

(Note: To test our recipes, we baked our breads in old New York City gas ovens. You may find that with newer ovens with tightly sealed doors or with electric ovens, the oven temperatures we give are too hot. If your oven temperature proves to be accurate when tested with an oven thermometer, and if your loaves seem to be browning too fast, lower the temperature by 10° F in all our recipes.)

TESTING FOR DONENESS

Telling whether or not bread is fully baked is easy. The first test is color. A properly baked loaf will range from golden to deep brown. Pick up the loaf and tap it on the bottom. It should sound hollow and produce a nice "thunk" when tapped. If it feels heavy and does not quite sound hollow, bake it for five minutes longer and check it again. Another test for doneness is to check the internal temperature of the loaf. Push an instant-read thermometer into the center of the bread: It should register between 200° and 210° F. After baking, the bread should be allowed to cool on a rack before cutting. It will continue to firm up and finish cooking on the inside as it cools.

GLAZING LOAVES

If you like a glossy crust on your loaves and steaming has not produced the gloss you desire, you can glaze the loaves as soon as they come out of the oven. This will give them a firm crust and a shinier appearance. For some breads, a glaze can be applied before baking to produce a tender, shiny crust. Glazing before baking is most suitable for breakfast breads and other doughs that contain sugar, fat and/or eggs. We have included a glaze recipe with each bread that is enhanced by glazing.

SLICING BREAD

We enjoy tearing right into a freshly baked loaf, but you might prefer to slice it with a serrated bread knife. Serrated knives stay sharp for a long time and the teeth cut through a thick, hard crust without compressing the loaf. A bread knife is a small but worthwhile investment for any bread lover. When you cut a loaf yourself, you can make thick, rustic slices, unlike those produced by a slicing machine.

STORING BREAD

To store fresh bread, it's best to leave it at room temperature for the first two days. Leave the bread unwrapped, and place the loaf cut side down on a bread board, in a cupboard, or in a bread box. Leaving the bread unwrapped keeps the inside of the loaf soft and the outside crusty. After a couple of days, you can put the bread in a plastic bag to keep it moist.

To refresh bread, or return it to its just-baked state, cut off the amount you want and mist the crust with water. Put the bread directly on an oven rack in a preheated 400° F oven. (An oven that is too cool will draw the moisture out of the bread, leaving it tough and dry.) Let it crisp for five to eight minutes, until it feels very hot and just slightly crisp and crusty. Remove it from the oven, let it rest for a few minutes, then slice and serve warm.

You can also freeze freshly baked bread as soon as it has cooled completely. Wrap the loaf tightly in foil, place it in a heavy-duty freezer bag or wrap it in two layers of plastic wrap and freeze. Allow the bread to thaw in the wrapping at room temperature, then unwrap and refresh the loaf in the oven. We do not recommend refrigerating bread. It may keep a long time in the refrigerator, but it dries out. We absolutely never microwave bread. It becomes spongy at first, then rock-hard.

2

The Magic
of Making
Bread Rise

Mix up a little flour, water, and salt, add some leavening, such as yeast or sour-dough, and the magic begins! *Webster's New World Dictionary* says the word *leaven* comes from the Latin *levare,* "to make light, lift up, raise." In France the leavening is called *levure* or *levain,* in Italy *lievito* or *biga.* No matter where you are or what you call it, the leavener is the miracle ingredient that gives life to a lump of dough.

One warm summer morning when the bakery had only been open for about a month, we found out just how much life leavened dough can have. Susan, the mixer, made a large batch of our Country Sourdough Bread and portioned it into several shal-low plastic dough boxes. She stacked them inside the small walk-in refrigerator so the dough could have its first cool rise. About an hour later, while we were working up front in the retail store, we heard Susan opening the door to the walk-in. Suddenly there was a shriek of surprise, and the *I Love Lucy* theme song came floating out of the refriger-ator. The scene that greeted us as we peered around the open door really did look like something that only Lucy and Ethel could have cooked up. Great globs of creamy-colored dough were oozing out of the plastic boxes like rivers of lava. The boxes themselves were tipping and tilting in a crazy slow-motion rumba to the rhythm of the fast-rising dough. It was quite a mess!

The dough felt almost hot when we touched it. Susan recalled that the dough temperature had been a few degrees higher than usual at the end of the mix

> Sugar in small amounts increases yeast activity. However, large quantities of sugar in dough will have just the opposite effect. That's why most recipes for sweet breads require larger amounts of yeast.
>
> Salt also retards yeast activity. If you for-get to add salt to your bread dough, it will rise much faster and exhaust the yeast sup-ply sooner than it would otherwise. At the bakery we always taste our doughs after they're mixed to be sure the salt has been included.

because of the warm weather. The extra warmth accelerated the activity of the yeast in the dough, and the madly reproducing yeast generated even more heat as the dough began to rise. The shallow plastic boxes acted like insulators, keeping the dough's heat in and the cool air of the refrigerator out. We learned a lot about leavening power that day.

At the bakery we use four different kinds of leaveners, or "starters": commercial baker's yeast, biga (a sponge starter), old dough (from the previous day's mix), and sour-dough. All of them use yeast in one form or another. Yeast is a minute one-celled fungus that is present in everything around us. There are at least a hundred and sixty different species in the air, on our skin and on the skins of fruits and vegetables, and in the flour we use for baking. Not all of these fungi are benevolent. Some can cause food to rot, others promote a variety of unpleasant diseases. Baking yeast, however, belongs to a favorable genus called *Saccharomyces* (sugar fungi). These yeasts thrive and multiply in any warm, moist environment where they can feed on carbohydrates (sugars and starches). As they eat, the yeasts metabolize the carbohydrates through a process called anaerobic fermentation. Alcohol and carbon dioxide are the by-products. In bread dough, the carbon dioxide is trapped by a complex web of gluten strands in the moist dough, causing it to expand, or "rise," and creating a sponge-like network of holes throughout the dough. In the intense heat of baking, the yeast dies and the alcohol evaporates, but the network of holes remains to give leavened bread its wonderful characteristic texture.

At Amy's Bread we use the minimum amount of yeast necessary to leaven our bread. We want the dough to rise slowly at a temperature of about 77° F so the flavors of the wheat, and any other grains, will be more prominent than the flavor of the yeast. Yeast generates heat as it metabolizes the sugars and starches in the dough. A large amount of yeast can result in too much activity, making it difficult to control the temperature of the dough and the proofing time. To help control rising time, we use less yeast in our doughs during the hot summer months (when yeast activity is intensified) than we do in the cooler months. Most of the recipes in this book contain considerably less yeast than standard bread recipes.

Using Baker's Yeast

◆

There are four types of commercial baking yeast: active dry yeast, compressed cake yeast (sometimes called fresh yeast), quick-rise yeast, and instant yeast.

Active dry yeast is what we use in the recipes in this book, because it is the easiest to find. Most grocers carry the strips of three $1/4$-ounce foil packets. Each packet contains about $2^1/4$ teaspoons of dried yeast granules. Look for boxed displays of Fleischmann's or Red Star brand yeast in the dairy case; sometimes it is with the flours and baking supplies. Be sure to check the expiration date ("pull-date") that's stamped on the back of the package, and don't buy it if it's past the pull-date. You can store the unopened packets at room temperature, but they retain their potency better in the freezer. Once a package has been opened, store any leftovers in an airtight container. You can simply fold up the foil-wrapped package and place it in a plastic bag in your freezer. An opened packet of yeast that is not used immediately will be damaged by exposure to warmth, air, and moisture.

You can also buy active dry yeast in 4-ounce jars or in bulk from your local natural food store. Be sure to get *active dry yeast,* not brewer's yeast or torula yeast, which are intended for nutritional purposes only and will not cause bread to rise. Although it's more economical to buy yeast in bulk, unless it has been stored by your supplier in airtight containers in a cool place, you may be in for some disappointing results when you use it to make bread. (See page 189 for a list of mail-order suppliers.) Keep the yeast in an airtight container in your freezer.

You don't have to bring active dry yeast to room temperature or "preproof" it before you use it. In the recipes in this book, we give the yeast a "head start" by dissolving it in a little warm water and letting it sit for about three minutes. If you're dubious about the potency of your yeast, preproof it by adding a pinch of sugar to the yeast and warm water and let it sit a while longer. If the yeast is nice and bubbly after ten minutes, you can use it.

Compressed cake yeast is cultivated from a different genetic strain of the same species as dry yeast and has very different characteristics. The moisture content of cake yeast is 70 percent, compared to the 8 percent of dry yeast. We use compressed cake yeast at the bakery because it activates more easily at the cooler dough temperatures we prefer and has a milder flavor than dry yeast. If you want to use it in place of active dry yeast in our recipes, you must double the *measured* amount of yeast specified; e.g., if the recipe calls for half a teaspoon of active dry yeast, use a full teaspoon of cake yeast to replace it. Some grocers stock small 0.6-ounce cubes or larger 2-ounce cakes of moist yeast in the dairy case. You may also be able to purchase a chunk of it from a local bakery. In either case, the yeast should have an even light tan color with no mold or discoloration. It should feel slightly moist and crumble easily, breaking with a clean edge. Don't be surprised by its pungent yeasty odor.

> **Here are some weights and measurements you may find helpful:**
>
> *1 packet active dry yeast = ¼ ounce/
> 2¼ teaspoons/7 grams*
>
> *1 ounce cake yeast = 1 ounce/2 tablespoons plus
> ¼ teaspoon (firmly packed)/28 grams*
>
> *1 packet active dry yeast = ½ ounce (15 grams)
> cake yeast*

Cake yeast must be kept refrigerated, wrapped in plastic and/or put in an airtight container. It survives freezing well and maintains its potency longer if frozen than if refrigerated. It stays potent for only a week or two if refrigerated; if frozen, it's good for up to two months. Don't buy more than you'll be able to use within that period of time and, of course, don't buy a package that has passed its pull-date. If you're in doubt, preproof the yeast by dissolving it with a pinch of sugar in a quarter-cup of very warm water (105° to 115° F). If it's nice and bubbly in ten minutes, you can use it.

Quick-rise yeast is a different strain of the same low-moisture granulated yeast as active dry yeast. You can cut your rising time in half with this product because it proofs at a higher temperature, which accelerates the activity of the yeast, but the flavor and texture of the bread will generally suffer. We don't recommend it because we prefer the quality produced by a slow, cool rise. If it's the only kind of yeast you can find, follow the directions on the package but use slightly less than the amount of yeast specified to slow down the rising time somewhat. Quick-rise yeast is packaged the same way as active dry yeast and should be stored in the same manner.

Instant yeast is yet another dried yeast product. The most commonly available brands are imported from Europe. It is a very low moisture granulated yeast, but it is combined with a sugar and an emulsifier so it will activate immediately upon contact with warm liquid. We don't recommend it because the dough has to be very warm to activate instant yeast (at least 85°F), and some manufacturers suggest eliminating the first proofing period of the dough. Obviously, it doesn't lend itself to our "slow, cool" philosophy of bread making. If you want to try instant yeast just for the experience, you can find small bulk packages at gourmet cooking stores or through mail-order sources (see page 189 for a list of suppliers). Follow the directions on the package.

The Simplicity of the Sponge Starter

◆

Many of our recipes use a sponge starter made from flour, water, and a small amount of yeast. The sponge, which has the consistency of a stiff batter, is allowed to rise once at room temperature and then can be used immediately or stored, covered with plastic wrap, for a day or two in the refrigerator. If you don't use a refrigerated sponge within three days, throw it away and make a new one. In France the sponge is called *poolish,* in Italy it is called *biga.* We like sponge breads because they have a moist, chewy texture with more flavor, a nicer crust, and a longer shelf life than straight yeast breads. These are many of the same qualities that make sourdough breads so appealing, but you can achieve them without the extended process of making a sourdough starter.

Sponge Starter

Makes 28 ounces

• •

1½ cups (12 ounces) very warm water (105° to 115°F)

¼ teaspoon active dry yeast

3½ cups (16 ounces) unbleached all-purpose flour

• •

Equipment: One 2-quart clear plastic container

Mix all the ingredients together in a medium bowl and stir vigorously with a wooden spoon for 2 to 3 minutes, until a smooth, somewhat elastic batter has formed. The batter will be very stiff; it gets softer and more elastic after it has proofed. You may find it easier to mix the sponge using an electric mixer, with a paddle or a dough hook, on medium speed for 1 to 2 minutes. Scrape the sponge into a 2-quart clear plastic container and cover with plastic wrap. At this point you have two options:

If you plan to make your dough later that same day, let the sponge rest at room temperature until it has risen to the point where it just begins to collapse. This may take from 6 to 8 hours, depending on the temperature of the sponge, the temperature of the room, and the strength of the yeast. The sponge will triple in volume and small dents and folds will begin to appear in the top as it reaches its peak and then begins to deflate. The sponge is now in perfect condition to be used in a dough. It's best if you have already weighed or measured out all of your other recipe ingredients before the sponge reaches this point so you can use it before it collapses too much.

If you're not planning to make your dough until the next day or the day after, put the covered sponge in the refrigerator and let it rise there for at least 14 hours before taking it out to use in a recipe. Be sure to compensate for the cold temperature of the starter by using warm water (85° to 90°F) in the dough instead of the cool water specified in the recipe. Or let the starter sit out, covered, until it reaches room temperature (this may take several hours)–but don't let it collapse too much before you use it.

Sponge Starter

Scrape your mixed sponge starter into a clear, high-sided plastic container. Mark the time and the level of the sponge on the container or on a piece of tape, then watch it rise.

Just mixed sponge starter showing the level on the side of the container

Rising sponge, halfway up the side of the container

Sponge that is ready to use

Saving a Lump of Dough: The Old Dough Starter

◆

At the bakery, we usually mix fifty or sixty extra pounds of our Country Sourdough Bread to use as "old dough" (we call it a "chef") for several different kinds of bread in our next day's mix. Using an old dough starter is similar to using a sponge, but instead of making a flour and water batter, you simply incorporate a piece of mature dough into a new batch of dough. Because your piece of old dough is already mature, it contains lively yeast and the flavor of wheat from the flour has had some time to develop. The old dough method produces a full-flavored loaf with a lighter, open-textured crumb than a straight yeast dough and an extended shelf life.

You don't have to bake bread every day to have mature dough available for one of our old dough recipes (such as Grainy Whole Wheat and Seeds, page 68). Instead, you can make a little batch of dough using our Old Dough Starter recipe. Once the starter dough has doubled in volume (usually about five hours), you can mix the base dough in the recipe calling for an old dough starter, knead it briefly, and allow it to rest. Then the old dough starter is kneaded into the new dough until a smooth, homogeneous mass is formed. You can save a piece of this final dough to use as the "old dough" for next day's bread or freeze it and use it the next time you need old dough for a recipe.

Old Dough Starter

Makes 14½ ounces

¼ teaspoon active dry yeast

¼ cup (2 ounces) very warm water (105° to 115°F)

2 cups (9 ounces) unbleached all-purpose flour

1 teaspoon kosher salt

½ cup less 1 tablespoon (3½ ounces) cool water (75°F)

1. Place the yeast and very warm water in a medium bowl. Stir with a fork to dissolve the yeast and allow to stand for about 3 minutes.

2. Mix the flour and salt together and add to the yeast mixture along with the cool water. Stir until a shaggy mass has formed.

3. Move the dough to a lightly floured work surface and knead until the dough is smooth and supple, about 7 minutes.

4. Put the dough in a lightly oiled bowl, turn it to coat with oil, and cover it with plastic wrap. Let it rise at room temperature (75° to 77°F) until it has doubled in volume, about 5 hours.

This starter can be made ahead and frozen. Deflate the dough after it has risen and wrap it securely in aluminum foil, leaving a little room for the dough to expand. Wrap it again in plastic wrap or place in a heavy-duty freezer bag, and freeze. It will maintain its potency as a starter for about 6 months. Move it to the refrigerator to thaw the day before you want to use it, then take it out at least 2 hours before you begin making the recipe to allow it to warm and soften slightly. If the old dough is cold and stiff, it will be difficult to incorporate into the new dough mass and it will lower the overall temperature of the dough, making the proofing times longer.

Sourdough Starter: A Project for Ambitious Bakers

◆

For artisan bakers, using a sourdough starter is the ultimate way to create a perfect loaf of bread with the most complex flavor, the best-textured crumb, the crunchiest crust, and the longest shelf life. By using a sourdough starter, you are going back to the source, using pure, wholesome ingredients to capture yeast in its wild state and then encouraging it to thrive and multiply by creating the most favorable environment for it. With regular feeding, you can eventually tame it enough to be used for leavening bread. Like all of the best things in life, this process requires patience and careful attention to detail, but the end result is definitely worth the effort.

When most Americans think of sourdough, they picture the crusty, assertively sour loaves that are produced in the bread mecca of America, San Francisco. But bread made from a sourdough starter doesn't have to be intensely sour. The level of acidity that produces the sour taste depends to a large extent on the consistency and maturity of the starter that is used. If you're one of those people who dislikes sourdough bread, don't stop reading here. We're going to show you how to make a starter that will produce a loaf as mild or as sour as you like.

These instructions are for making a quick and easy starter that begins as a rye culture and is then divided in half. One portion remains a rye culture that is "refreshed" with pumpernickel flour to become a "rye mother"; the other portion is transformed into a white culture, refreshed with unbleached white flour, to become a "white sourdough mother." You store the mothers in the refrigerator and feed them on a regular basis. Then, when you want to make bread you use part of one of the mothers to make a starter for the dough. Each time you remove part of the mother, it must be fed again so you'll always have enough when you need it.

Use organic flour and spring water to start, to ensure that the yeast and bacteria you are trying to cultivate haven't been damaged by pesticides and fungicides and that they won't be inhibited by the chemicals and/or fluoride in your tap water. Once you get your culture going, you can go back to nonorganic flour and tap water to maintain it if you prefer.

Rye flour loves to ferment. Once you've completed Stage 1, use containers that are large enough to let the batter quadruple in volume. Do not use containers with airtight lids, as the lids need to pop up easily to release pressure from the gases produced during the fermentation process. The first time we tested this recipe, one of our containers that was covered with a tight plastic lid literally exploded–that's why we call it "dynamite" sourdough starter. (We're still finding little globs of dried rye sour in unexpected places.) If necessary, cover your container with a double layer of cheesecloth, secured with a rubber band, or punch lots of little holes in the lid.

(This section is just to get you started. If you want more detailed information and some alternative methods for making sourdough starters, see page 168.)

Dynamite Sourdough Starter

Stage 1

· ·

½ cup (2 ounces generous) organic rye flour, at room temperature

½ cup (4 ounces) spring water

· ·

Equipment: One 1-pint clear plastic container with lid;
instant-read thermometer

1. Put the flour and spring water in a 1-pint clear plastic container and stir together vigorously until well combined. (The batter should be about the consistency of very thick pancake batter; if necessary, add more water or flour to achieve the desired consistency.) Taste the batter now so you can appreciate how the taste changes as your sourdough culture develops. Check the temperature of the batter with an instant-read thermometer. Ideal temperature is 75° to 77° F; a little cooler is okay, but a little warmer is not. If the temperature of the batter is over 80° F, you'll incubate the wrong kind of bacteria and your culture will have an unpleasant bitter taste. If the temperature *is* over 80° F, put the batter in the refrigerator for about 20 minutes, or until the temperature has dropped into the desired range.

2. Cover the container with a lid. (At this early stage an airtight lid is okay, but don't use cheesecloth, because mold seems to grow more readily with a cheesecloth cover than it does with a plastic one. Once the batter really begins fermenting, cheesecloth is fine.) Use a marker or a piece of tape to mark the level of the batter on the outside of the container so you can tell when it has doubled in volume. Set it aside at room temperature (75° to 77° F) to ferment for 36 to 48 hours. You should start to see tiny bubbles forming in the batter after about 24 hours. By the time it has doubled, there will be a noticeable network of small bubbles throughout the batter (you can see them through the sides of the clear plastic container), and it will be bubbling and foaming on top.

If mold forms on the top of the batter, discard it all and begin again. If the batter has not doubled within 48 hours, feed it with $^1/_4$ cup (2 ounces) spring water and $^1/_2$ cup (generous 2 ounces) rye flour (or more of either ingredient if necessary to achieve the consistency of thick pancake batter). Stir it vigorously, cover it, and let it sit for 24 hours, or until you see some definite activity. Proceed with Stage 2.

Stage 2

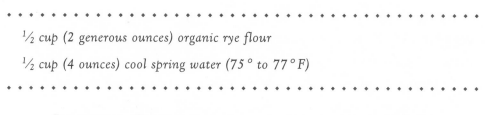

$^1/_2$ cup (2 generous ounces) organic rye flour

$^1/_2$ cup (4 ounces) cool spring water (75° to 77°F)

Equipment: One 1-quart clear plastic container with lid

1. If there is a dry crust on top of the batter, carefully scrape it off and discard it. Stir the culture down with a wooden spoon. Notice how soupy it has become (water is one of the by-products of fermentation). The batter should have a noticeably sour smell and a mildly tangy taste at this point. Add the additional flour and water to refresh it and stir vigorously until well combined. (The yeasts in the culture like the energetic stirring. It redistributes their food supply and provides them with fresh oxygen to help them multiply.)

2. Transfer the refreshed culture to a 1-quart clear plastic container. The temperature should be under 80°F. If it is not, refrigerate until it is 75° to 77°F. Mark the outside of the container with a marker or tape to show the level of the culture, and cover it (not tightly) with a lid. The culture should be showing a fair amount of activity at this point. You should see lots of foaming and bubbling through the sides of the container, as well as on top if you lift the cover. Let it ferment for 12 hours to develop its acidity (sour taste). If it threatens to overflow the container, stir it down, transfer it to a larger container, and let it continue fermenting for the remainder of the 12-hour period. Don't be concerned if the culture deflates and loses volume. This means the yeast has exhausted its food supply, but it will still continue to increase in acidity. Don't worry if your culture isn't dramatically active yet. As long as there is some noticeable activity going on and the mixture smells and tastes sour, you're on the right track.

continued

Stage 3

· ·

¾ cup (6 ounces) cool spring water (75° to 77°F)

⅔ cup (3 ounces) pumpernickel rye flour

⅔ cup (3 ounces) unbleached all-purpose flour

· ·

Equipment: Two 1-quart clear plastic containers with lids or cheesecloth and rubber bands

1. The culture should now have a pronounced sour, fruity taste and smell; it should not taste musty or bitter (if it does, discard it and start again, paying close attention to the temperature of the culture at all times). Using a wooden spoon (the acid in the sour-dough reacts with metal utensils), divide the culture between two 1-quart clear plastic containers, putting approximately 6 ounces in each one. The next step is to thicken the culture by increasing the proportion of flour to water, this time using equal weights of each ingredient. You're also going to "customize" the cultures by feeding one with pumpernickel rye flour (which has a coarser grind than regular rye flour) and the other with unbleached all-purpose flour. (We prefer to maintain our rye sour with pumper-nickel flour because we like the texture and flavor it gives to our breads.) After repeated feedings with unbleached flour, the second culture will eventually be "all white," unless you choose to throw in an ounce of pumpernickel rye flour now and again for extra flavor.

The proportion of water to flour in a sourdough culture affects the fermentation rate. Wet cultures ferment more quickly and generally have a higher level of acidity than drier cultures. So if you want a mild-flavored sourdough bread, use a dry levain-style starter, as we do in our recipe for Country Sourdough Boule (page 141). For a more San Francisco–style sourdough, use a wet starter, as we do in our recipe for Tangy Twenty-Four-Hour Sourdough (page 129).

2. Add ¼ cup plus 2 tablespoons (3 ounces) each of the spring water and the pumpernickel flour to one of the cultures. Add the remaining ¼ cup plus 2 tablespoons (3 ounces) spring water and the unbleached flour to the other culture. Stir each one vigorously. Check the temperature, as in the preceding stages. Cover each container with a loose-fitting lid or a double layer of cheesecloth (secured with a rubber band), and mark the level of the cultures with a marker or tape. Let them ferment for another 12 hours.

You now have two healthy sourdough cultures, approximately 12 ounces in each container. At this point you need to refresh them again, setting up a maintenance level of 12 ounces for the rye culture and 8 ounces for the white sourdough culture. (You could maintain larger amounts but it's not necessary for the recipes in this book and they would only take up extra space in your refrigerator.) These will be the "mothers" that you use to build the sourdough starters needed in individual recipes. Each time you take part of the mother out to build a starter, you must refresh it with equal weights of flour and water to bring it back up to its maintenance level. We describe how to do this below. (In recipes that include small amounts of a sour starter just for its flavor, you can use some of the mother instead of building a separate sourdough starter.)

Maintaining the Rye Mother

Makes 12 ounces

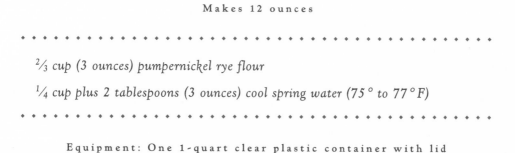

²⁄₃ cup (3 ounces) pumpernickel rye flour

¹⁄₄ cup plus 2 tablespoons (3 ounces) cool spring water (75° to 77°F)

Equipment: One 1-quart clear plastic container with lid

1. Place 6 ounces (²⁄₃ cup) of the rye culture in a clean 1-quart clear plastic container. Discard the rest of it. (Unless you plan to make large batches of dough using the rye sourdough starter, you only need to maintain a mother with a total weight of 12 ounces— 6 ounces of mother plus 6 ounces of fresh flour and water; any more is just surplus and takes up unnecessary space in the refrigerator.) Add the flour and water and stir vigorously to combine. Cover the container and mark the level of the mother with a marker or tape. Let it sit at room temperature until it has doubled in volume. A strong mother will double in 8 hours. If yours doesn't do that, let it continue to sit out until it has a nice tangy taste and smell; discard all but 6 ounces and repeat this step again. (Flour that has been sitting on the shelf too long, or flour that has not been stored properly, does not contain as much potentially active yeast as fresher flour, so it takes a little longer for starters made with older flour to build up strength.) Repeat this procedure as many times as necessary until the mother doubles within 8 hours. It may take several days. Don't get discouraged, it's worth the effort.

continued

2. Store the refreshed rye mother in the refrigerator. Repeat the refreshing procedure, using 6 ounces ($^2/_3$ cup) of the mother and 3 ounces each of flour ($^2/_3$ cup) and water ($^1/_4$ cup plus 2 tablespoons), at least once a week–twice a week is best–so the mother will be active when you need to use it. Be sure to refresh the mother the same way, with equal weights of flour and water, whenever you remove some of it to build a rye sour starter to use in a recipe.

Building a Rye Sour Starter

Makes 10 ounces

. . . .

Generous $^1/_2$ cup (5 ounces) Rye Mother (cold from the refrigerator)

$^2/_3$ cup (3 ounces) pumpernickel flour

$^1/_4$ cup plus 1 tablespoon ($2^1/_2$ ounces) warm water (85° to 90°F)

. . . .

Equipment: One 1-quart clear plastic container

1. Place all the ingredients in a 1-quart clear plastic container and stir vigorously to combine. The mixture will be stiffer than the rye mother. Cover the container with a lid or plastic wrap and mark the level of the starter with a marker or tape. Let it sit at room temperature until it has doubled in volume. (If the starter hasn't doubled within 8 hours, discard all but 5 ounces [generous $^1/_2$ cup] of it, and feed it again in the same manner. Sometimes it takes more than one feeding if you haven't been refreshing the rye mother often enough.)

2. When the starter has doubled, it is ready to use in a recipe. Measure the amount needed and discard any that remains. If you're not ready to use the starter right away, you can store it for up to 24 hours in the refrigerator.

> Rye Sour is used in Toy's Teddy Bread (page 75), Dense Rye Bread (page 85), Moist Potato-Rye Wands with Dill (page 115), Tangy Twenty-Four-Hour Sourdough (page 129), and Chewy Pumpernickel (page 137).

Maintaining the White Sourdough Mother

Makes 8 ounces

• •

½ cup less 1 tablespoon (2 ounces) unbleached all-purpose flour

¼ cup (2 ounces) cool spring water (75° to 77°F)

• •

Equipment: One 1-quart clear plastic container with lid

1. Place 4 ounces (²/₃ cup) of the white sourdough culture in a clean 1-quart clear plastic container. Discard the rest of it. (Unless you plan to make large batches of dough using the white sourdough starter, you only need to maintain a mother with a total weight of 8 ounces–4 ounces of mother plus 4 ounces of fresh flour and water; any more is just surplus and takes up unnecessary space in the refrigerator.) Add the flour and water and stir vigorously to combine. Cover the container and mark the level of the mother with a marker or tape. Let it sit at room temperature until it has doubled in volume. A strong mother will double in 8 hours. If yours doesn't do that, let it continue to sit out until it has a nice tangy taste and smell; discard all but 4 ounces and repeat this step again. (Flour that has been sitting on the shelf too long, or flour that has not been stored properly, does not contain as much potentially active yeast as fresher flour, so it takes a little longer for starters made with older flour to build up strength.) Repeat this procedure as many times as necessary to get the mother to double within 8 hours. It may take several days. Don't get discouraged; it's worth the effort.

2. Store the refreshed white sourdough mother in the refrigerator. Repeat the refreshing procedure using 4 ounces (²/₃ cup) of the mother and 2 ounces each of flour (½ cup less 1 tablespoon) and water (¼ cup) at least once a week–twice a week is best–so the mother will be active when you need to use it. Be sure to refresh the mother the same way, with equal weights of flour and water, whenever you remove some of it to build a starter to use in a recipe.

> *The White Sourdough Mother is also used to build a white sour sponge for our Tangy Twenty-Four-Hour Sourdough (page 129). Instructions for building the sponge are included in that recipe.*

The White Sourdough Mother is used to build a *levain* starter, which is used in the Country Sourdough Boule recipe on page 141.

Building a Levain Starter

Makes 9 ounces

• •

¼ cup (2 ounces) White Sourdough Mother (cold from the refrigerator)

¼ cup (2 ounces) warm water (85° to 90°F)

1 cup plus 2 tablespoons (5 ounces) unbleached all-purpose flour

⅛ teaspoon kosher salt

• •

Equipment: One 3-cup clear plastic container with lid

1. Combine all the ingredients in a small bowl and use your hand to stir and knead them together until a shaggy mass of dough has formed. It will be very dry and stiff.

2. Remove the mass from the bowl and knead it on a lightly floured worktable until you have a smooth, cohesive ball of dough. This is your *levain*.

3. Place the *levain* in a 3-cup clear plastic container, and mark the level of the dough with a marker or tape. Cover with a lid or plastic wrap and let sit at room temperature until it has doubled in volume. (If the starter hasn't doubled within 8 hours, discard all but 2 ounces of it and feed it again in the same manner. If it is very stiff and dry, you may have to add another tablespoon of water. Sometimes it takes more than one feeding if you haven't been refreshing the mother often enough.)

4. When the starter has doubled, you have a *levain* that is ready to use in a recipe. Measure the amount needed and discard any that remains. If you're not going to use it right away, you can store it for up to 24 hours in the refrigerator.

> If you prefer a very mild flavored sourdough loaf, you can minimize the acidity in your starter by doing two things:
>
> 1. Refresh the White Sourdough Mother about 8 hours before you plan to make the levain starter, using twice as much flour and water as you would normally use. That is, feed 4 ounces of the mother (⅔ cup) with 4 ounces (¾ cup plus 2 tablespoons) of flour and 4 ounces (½ cup) of water. Let it double at room temperature.
>
> 2. Build the levain starter as soon as the mother has doubled so the mother doesn't have time to become more sour and acidic. (Use cool water [75° to 77°F] instead of the warm water called for in the recipe.) Let the levain double at room temperature and then use it as soon as possible. If you can't use the levain starter immediately, refrigerate it until you are ready to make your dough. But the longer you delay, the more sour it will become.

3

Easy Recipes to Get You Started

Here are five basic breads that taste delicious and are easy to make. After you have tried and perfected them, you'll be ready to tackle the recipes in the following chapters. Relax, experiment, and enjoy the process.

Big Beautiful White Pan Loaves

A straight dough bread

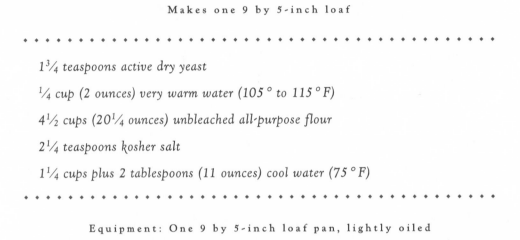

A plump, golden loaf of bread is a pleasure for all to behold. My mother, grandmother, and great-grandmother all lovingly baked this basic loaf to feed their families and to nourish their souls. The procedure and ingredients are the simplest there are. Our technique, which gives the dough a rest period, or autolyse, during kneading makes the dough bouncier and easier to work with. And the baked loaf has a better flavor and texture because it is not overworked by aggressive kneading.

Makes one 9 by 5-inch loaf

• •

1¾ teaspoons active dry yeast

¼ cup (2 ounces) very warm water (105° to 115°F)

4½ cups (20¼ ounces) unbleached all-purpose flour

2¼ teaspoons kosher salt

1¼ cups plus 2 tablespoons (11 ounces) cool water (75°F)

• •

Equipment: One 9 by 5-inch loaf pan, lightly oiled

1. Combine the yeast and warm water in a small bowl and stir with a fork to dissolve the yeast. Let stand for 3 minutes.

2. Mix the flour and salt together in a large mixing bowl. Add the yeast mixture and the cool water. Using your fingers, mix the dough into a sticky mass.

3. When all of the flour is incorporated, move the dough to a lightly floured work surface and knead for 4 minutes. The dough should be sticky and will not look smooth. If the dough feels stiff or dry, knead in additional cool water a tablespoon at a time.

4. Put the dough in a lightly floured bowl, cover, and let rest for 20 minutes. (This rest period is the autolyse.)

5. Return the dough to the lightly floured surface and knead it for 7 to 8 minutes. The dough will go from being sticky to smooth and will become supple but not too firm.

6. Place the dough in a clean bowl lightly dusted with flour. Cover the bowl with a towel and allow the dough to rise at room temperature (75° to 77°F) for 2 to 2¹⁄₂ hours, until it doubles in volume. (An indentation made by poking your finger deep into the dough should not spring back.)

7. Place the dough on a very lightly floured surface. Gently deflate the dough and pat it into a rectangle with a short side facing you. Fold the top edge down and the bottom edge up, overlapping them slightly, then turn the dough a quarter turn and fold the top down and the bottom up again to form an envelope. Shape the dough into a log shape following the instructions on page 22.

8. Place the loaf seam side down in a lightly oiled 9 by 5-inch loaf pan. Gently press down on the loaf to spread it to fill the corners of the pan, and cover it with oiled plastic wrap.

9. Let the loaf rise for 1 to 1¹⁄₄ hours, or until it has doubled and risen about 1 inch above the sides of the pan.

10. Meanwhile, position a rack in the center of the oven and preheat the oven to 425°F.

11. Gently place the loaf pan on the center oven rack. Using a plant sprayer, quickly mist the loaf 6 to 8 times, then shut the oven door. After 3 minutes, mist the loaf again.

12. Bake for 10 minutes, then reduce the oven temperature to 400°F and bake for 30 minutes longer, or until the top is a deep golden brown. Remove the loaf from the pan–it should come out with ease. The bread should sound slightly hollow when tapped on the bottom, and the sides of the loaf should be brown. Place the loaf on a wire rack to cool. Serve slightly warm, with butter and lots of homemade jam!

> ### Making "Old Dough"
>
> *You can make a double batch of this basic white dough and freeze half to use later in recipes calling for an old dough starter. Divide the batch of dough in half and shape and bake one half as described in the recipe. Divide the other half into 2 equal pieces and place each piece in a plastic bag. Tie the bags closed, leaving some space for rising. Wrap the bags in aluminum foil and place in the freezer. Each piece is enough to make one batch of old dough bread. The frozen dough should be used within 6 months.*

The Farm

Memories of bread smells wafting from the oven and filling the big kitchen transport me to the family farm where my mother, her father, and his father were raised. Built in 1892, the house has been warm and welcoming to family, friends, and neighbors for more than a century. Today my cousin and his wife and their three children carry on the family tradition.

When I was growing up, we would drive to the farm on Sunday afternoons to visit my grandparents and to take in the sights and smells of the country. As soon as we entered the house, our senses were awakened. From our Grandmother's kitchen came the fragrant aromas of roasting chicken or beef and caramelized onions and carrots. Pots simmered on the stove and  steam clouded the windows. The table was set for lots of people and anticipation was in the air. Above all of the wonderful smells was the lingering aroma of those big, beautiful white pan loaves perched on their racks to cool. They were golden brown and plump and still slightly warm. To me they were the highlight of the meal, with a soft, tender texture that would almost melt in your mouth. We always had strawberry or raspberry jam with dinner. That was to show off my grandmother's preserves, made with fresh berries from her extraordinary garden. I remember holding a soft slice of fresh bread, its edges gently drooping over the sides of my small hand, and spooning on that wonderful homemade jam! Who needed roast beef?

The Smell of the Grain

Every summer I spent a week at my grandparents' farm, much of the time playing and exploring in the big barn. My uncle raised dairy cows and he had a huge hayloft in the cow barn where hay, straw, and oats were stored. We played on the thick rope swing that hung from the rafters, pushing off from great piles of hay bales and flying through the air from one side of barn to the other. We stacked the bales in special configurations to make our own private forts, where we hid from each other. In hot weather the hay was pungent, nearly fermenting, and the sweet tangy smell 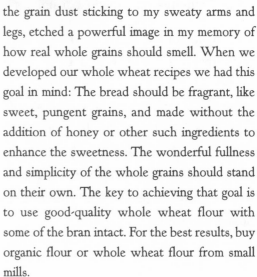 was intoxicating. Although we weren't supposed to play in the feed storeroom, sliding on the big pile of slippery oats was great fun and would kick up even more earthy, tangy, grainy smells.

Those hot days, with the grain dust sticking to my sweaty arms and legs, etched a powerful image in my memory of how real whole grains should smell. When we developed our whole wheat recipes we had this goal in mind: The bread should be fragrant, like sweet, pungent grains, and made without the addition of honey or other such ingredients to enhance the sweetness. The wonderful fullness and simplicity of the whole grains should stand on their own. The key to achieving that goal is to use good-quality whole wheat flour with some of the bran intact. For the best results, buy organic flour or whole wheat flour from small mills.

A.S.

Golden Whole Wheat Bread
An old dough bread

This is a fragrant and versatile bread that uses an old dough starter to give it a moister texture. Make an effort to find top-quality whole wheat flour for these loaves. We like to use organic flour or a coarsely ground whole wheat from a small flour company, such as Hodgson Mill or King Arthur. The aroma and flavor of "real" whole grains shine through.

Makes two 14-ounce round loaves

- -

¼ teaspoon active dry yeast

¼ cup (2 ounces) very warm water (105° to 115°F)

2¼ cups (11¼ ounces) organic whole wheat flour

¼ cup (¾ ounce) wheat bran

2 teaspoons kosher salt

¾ cup (6 ounces) cool water (75°F)

1 recipe (14½ ounces) Old Dough Starter (page 42)

Additional wheat bran for coating

- -

1. Combine the yeast and warm water in a small bowl and stir with a fork to dissolve the yeast.

2. Combine the flour, bran, and salt in a medium bowl. With your fingers, mix in the yeast mixture and the cool water until the dough is a granular mass. Fold the dough over onto itself and knead briefly in the bowl. If the dough seems too stiff, add 1 to 2 tablespoons of water.

3. Move the dough to a lightly floured work surface and continue to knead until it becomes firm and springy, about 5 minutes. Sprinkle the work surface with additional flour only if necessary; you should need very little flour to knead this dough.

4. Let the dough rest on the work surface for 20 minutes, covered with a cloth or plastic wrap. (This rest period is the autolyse.)

continued

5. Lightly flour the area under the dough and gently stretch the dough into a rectangle about $^3/_4$ inch thick. Place the old dough on top of the whole wheat dough and stretch it to cover the wheat dough. Fold the whole mass up like a business letter, folding the top third of the dough down and the bottom third up over it. Fold the two sides in and begin gently kneading to bring the two doughs together.

6. Knead for 7 to 8 minutes, until the two doughs are well combined. Don't overmix. The dough should feel smooth, springy, and still slightly firm.

7. Shape the dough into a loose ball, place it in a lightly oiled bowl, and turn to coat with oil. Cover the bowl tightly with oiled plastic wrap and let the dough rise at room temperature (75° to 77° F) for about 2 hours, until it has nearly doubled in volume.

8. Sprinkle a peel or the back of a baking sheet generously with cornmeal or line it with parchment paper. On a lightly floured surface, divide the dough into 2 equal pieces. Shape each piece into a boule (see page 26). Using a plant sprayer, mist the loaves with water, then roll each loaf in wheat bran to coat the entire surface. Place the loaves seam side down on the peel or pan, leaving 3 to 4 inches between them for rising. Cover with oiled plastic wrap and allow the loaves to rise for about $1^1/_2$ hours, or until they have nearly doubled in size. Watch the loaves carefully; if they begin to spread and grow together, bake them a little early, even if they are slightly underrisen.

9. Thirty minutes before baking, preheat the oven to 450° F. Place a baking stone in the oven to preheat and place an empty water pan directly below the stone.

10. Snip a shallow circle or crown pattern into the top of each loaf with scissors (see page 177), then gently slide the bread onto the stone. Pour 1 cup of very hot water into the water pan and immediately shut the oven door. After 1 minute, quickly mist the loaves with water 6 to 8 times, then shut the oven door. Mist again 1 minute later.

11. Bake for 15 minutes, then reduce the oven temperature to 375° F and bake for 15 to 20 minutes longer, until the loaves are deep golden brown and sound hollow when tapped on the bottom. Place the loaves on a rack to cool. Serve warm or cool–and inhale the wheaty fragrance.

Cinnamon Raisin Bread

An old dough bread

This easy recipe for cinnamon raisin bread makes a wonderful breakfast loaf that can be sliced and toasted to accompany a Sunday feast of eggs, bacon, and fresh fruit. Save the extra slices, if there are any, and use them for French toast the next day.

Makes two 9 by 5-inch loaves

. . . .

1¼ teaspoons active dry yeast

¼ cup (2 ounces) very warm water (105° to 115°F)

4¼ cups plus 2 tablespoons (20¼ ounces) unbleached all-purpose flour

1 tablespoon plus 1 teaspoon kosher salt

1⅓ cups (11 ounces) cool water (75°F)

1 tablespoon ground cinnamon

1 recipe (14½ ounces) Old Dough Starter (page 42)

3 cups (15 ounces) dark raisins

¼ cup plus 1 tablespoon granulated sugar (optional)

. . . .

Equipment: Two 9 by 5-inch loaf pans, oiled or buttered

1. Combine the yeast and warm water in a small bowl and stir with a fork to dissolve the yeast. Allow to stand for about 3 minutes.

2. In a medium bowl, combine 4¼ cups (20 ounces) of the flour and the salt. With your fingers, mix in the yeast mixture and the cool water until the dough forms a shaggy mass. Fold the dough over onto itself and knead briefly in the bowl.

3. Move the dough to a lightly floured work surface and knead until it is smooth and supple, about 7 minutes. If it feels too dry, add 1 to 2 tablespoons of water.

4. Let the dough rest on the work surface for 20 minutes, covered with a cloth or plastic wrap. (This rest period is the autolyse.)

5. Lightly dust the work surface with flour. Stretch the dough into a rectangle about ¾ inch thick. Sprinkle the cinnamon over the dough. Place the old dough on top of the white dough and stretch it to cover the dough completely. Fold the whole mass up like a business letter, bringing the top third of the dough down over the middle and the bottom third up over it. Fold the two ends in and begin gently kneading to bring the two doughs together.

6. Knead for 5 to 7 minutes, or until the two doughs are well combined and the dough is silky and elastic. Shape the dough into a ball, place it in a lightly oiled bowl, and turn to coat with oil. Cover the bowl tightly with oiled plastic wrap and let the dough rise at room temperature (75° to 77° F) for $1^1/_2$ to 3 hours, or until it has doubled in volume.

7. While the dough is rising, place the raisins in a bowl or a plastic container and add warm water to come just below the top of the raisins. (If you use too much water, you will rinse away the natural sweetness of the raisins.)

8. When the dough has doubled in volume, gently dump it onto a lightly floured work surface, without folding it over itself. Gently stretch the dough to form a rectangle about 14 inches by 12 inches. If you want a sweet bread, sprinkle the sugar evenly over the dough. Drain the raisins and toss them with the remaining 2 tablespoons flour ($^1/_4$ ounce). Spread the raisins evenly over the dough and gently press them into it.

9. Starting at a long side, roll the dough into a log. Roll the dough tightly, keeping the skin of the dough slightly taut and tucking in any raisins that fall out, but don't stretch the dough so tight that the skin tears. Seal the seam of the log gently but tightly using the heel of your hand against the surface of the table, or pinch it shut with your fingers. Cut the log in half to make 2 loaves, and tuck in the ends of each log.

10. Place each loaf in an oiled or buttered 9 by 5-inch loaf pan and cover with oiled plastic wrap. Let the dough rise at room temperature for $1^1/_2$ to $2^1/_2$ hours, or until the loaves have risen almost 1 inch above the sides of the pans.

11. Meanwhile, position a rack in the center of the oven and preheat the oven to 450° F.

12. Place the loaf pans on the center oven rack. Using a plant sprayer, mist the loaves 8 to 10 times, then quickly shut the oven door. Spray the bread again after 2 minutes.

13. Bake for 15 minutes, then reduce the oven temperature to 375° F and bake for 20 to 30 minutes longer, until the crust is deep brown and the loaves sound hollow when tapped on the bottom. The crust may color quickly because of the cinnamon and raisins in the dough; watch carefully and cover the tops of the loaves loosely with foil if they are browning too fast. Let cool in the pans for 5 minutes, then remove the bread from the pans and place the loaves on a rack to cool. Let cool completely before slicing, or the bread will fall apart. This bread keeps well for at least 2 days.

The Baguette

A straight dough bread

Although most people think the baguette is a French creation, the shape actually was developed by an Austrian baker and was only brought to France in the middle of the nineteenth century. Our baguette has a chewy, open-holed texture and a thin, crunchy crust. If you can get the loaf to dry out properly in your oven, you should see little cracks appearing in the crust as the bread cools, giving way to little squares of thin crust. This is the look of an authentic baguette. The difference in our baguette is that we give it several rises, which result in a wonderful texture.

Makes three 14-inch-long loaves

$1\frac{1}{4}$ teaspoons active dry yeast

$\frac{1}{4}$ cup (2 ounces) very warm water (105° to 115°F)

3 cups ($13\frac{1}{2}$ ounces) unbleached all-purpose flour

1 cup ($4\frac{1}{2}$ ounces) cake flour (see Note)

$2\frac{1}{4}$ teaspoons kosher salt

$1\frac{1}{4}$ cups plus 1 tablespoon ($10\frac{1}{2}$ ounces) cool water (75°F)

Equipment: Baguette pan (optional)

1. Combine the yeast and warm water in a small bowl and stir with a fork to dissolve the yeast. Let stand for 3 minutes.

2. Combine the flours and salt in a large bowl. Pour the cool water and the yeast mixture over the flour, and mix with your fingers to form a shaggy mass.

3. Move the dough to a lightly floured work surface and knead for 4 minutes. It should be supple and resilient but not too smooth at this point. Let the dough rest on the work surface for 20 minutes, covered with plastic wrap or a light towel. (This rest period is the autolyse.)

4. Knead the dough for 5 to 7 minutes. Don't overknead it: The dough should be smooth, stretchy, and resilient.

continued

5. Place the dough in a lightly oiled bowl, turn to coat with oil, and cover with oiled plastic wrap. Let rise at room temperature (75° to 77° F) for $1^1/_2$ to 2 hours, or until nearly doubled in volume.

6. Gently deflate the dough and fold it over itself in the bowl. Reshape it into a ball and cover with oiled plastic wrap. Let it rise for $1^1/_4$ hours, or until it has nearly doubled again.

7. Gently deflate the dough again. Reshape it into a ball, cover, and let rise for about 1 hour.

8. Place the dough on a very lightly floured surface and divide it into 3 equal pieces (about 10 ounces each). Gently stretch one piece into a rectangle, leaving some large bubbles in the dough. Fold the top third down and the bottom third up as if you were folding a business letter. Now form the loaf into a log, following the instructions on page 22; you want to gently draw the skin tight over the surface of the baguette while leaving some air bubbles in the dough. Seal the seam, being careful not to tear the skin of the dough or deflate its airy structure. Set aside on the work surface to relax before elongating it, and repeat the shaping process with remaining pieces of dough.

9. Now elongate each baguette, starting with the first one you shaped, by rolling it back and forth on the work surface. Begin with both hands over the center of the loaf and work them out to the ends until the loaf reaches the desired length. (Don't get carried away, or the baguettes won't fit in your oven!) Place the finished loaves on a peel or upside-down baking sheet lined with parchment paper and generously sprinkled with cornmeal or on a baguette pan. Cover the loaves with well-oiled plastic wrap or a floured cloth and let rise for 30 to 40 minutes, until the loaves are slightly plump but not doubled in volume. The final rise is short because you want the baguettes to be slightly underproofed; this will give them a better oven spring, resulting in loaves with a light, airy crumb and more flared cuts.

10. Thirty minutes before baking, preheat the oven to 500° F. Place a baking stone in the oven to preheat, and place an empty water pan directly under the stone.

11. Ten minutes before baking, uncover the loaves to allow the surface to dry slightly.

12. Use a *lame* or very sharp razor blade to make 3 to 5 slashes, depending on the length of your loaves, down the length of each baguette. The cuts should run from one end of the loaf to the other, rather than across it, and the blade should be held at a 30° angle to the loaf to create the cuts that will pop open in the oven (see photograph on page 30). Be careful not to press down too hard, or you may deflate the loaves. Using a plant sprayer, mist the loaves.

13. Gently slide the loaves onto the preheated stone, or place the baguette mold on the stone. Pour 1 cup of very hot water into the water pan and quickly close the oven door. After 2 more minutes, spray the loaves again and the oven walls.

14. Bake for 10 minutes, then lower the oven temperature to 425° F and bake for 12 to 16 minutes longer or until the loaves are golden brown and crisp. Move them to a rack to cool.

15. Enjoy your baguettes still slightly warm with some soft, ripe French cheese and a glass of wine.

Note: If cake flour is not available, you can substitute the same amount of unbleached all-purpose flour, but cake flour will give the baguette a lighter texture.

Henri Lovera and the Most Beautiful Loaves

At one bakery where I trained in France, I worked with a baker named Henri Lovera. Half-French and half-Italian, he was a dedicated bread baker who worked in the early morning hours, devoting eight hours a day, six days a week, to making perfect baguettes. For him the most satisfying accomplishment each day was to glance over the hundreds of finished loaves to see that each one had the proper dimensions, a gorgeous brown crust, and even cuts. He knew that inside each toasty, golden loaf was a light, delicious crumb. He was proud of the fact that he did not use additives in his dough to make the baguettes puff up, a common practice in many boulan-geries. Although his baguettes might look a little smaller than those of his neighbors, they weighed the same—the size of a baguette is governed by French law!

At the end of the day, Henri would sweep the bakery, change his clothes, and then survey the loaves again to choose the ones he would take home to his family. I was accustomed to working in restaurants where the employees chose the less-attractive products to taste, leaving the most beautiful creations for the paying customer. Not Henri! Every day he picked the two most perfect, impeccably beautiful loaves to serve at his table. He believed that after all his hard work, his family should be treated to only the best. Besides, who else would have an eye exacting enough to appreciate that perfection?

A.S.

Amy's Crusty Italian Loaf

A sponge starter bread

Here's another technique for creating an airy, crunchy bread with a toasty crust. The most basic ingredients are combined with a sponge starter to make a soft, moist dough. Just before baking, each loaf is stretched to elongate the gluten strands and the open holes in the bread, making for a lighter loaf. This bread is delicious with a hearty pasta dish or a crisp salad of bitter greens. We also recommend scooping out some of the interior crumb and stuffing the shell of the loaf with sliced meats, cheeses, greens, tomatoes, and a drizzle of olive oil and vinegar for an incredible party sandwich.

Makes 3 long loaves

$^3/_4$ teaspoon active dry yeast

$^1/_4$ cup (2 ounces) very warm water (105° to 115°F)

1 cup (8 ounces) cool water (75°F)

1$^1/_2$ cups (12 ounces) Sponge Starter (page 40)

3$^1/_2$ cups (16 ounces) unbleached all-purpose flour

1 tablespoon plus 1 teaspoon kosher salt

1. Combine the warm water and yeast in a large bowl and stir with a fork to dissolve the yeast. Let stand for 3 minutes.

2. Add the cool water and sponge to the yeast mixture and mix with your fingers for about 2 minutes, breaking up the sponge. The mixture should look milky and slightly foamy.

3. Add the flour and salt and mix with your fingers to incorporate the flour, scraping the sides of the bowl and folding the ingredients together until the dough gathers into a mass. It should be wet and sticky, with long strands of dough hanging from your fingers. If necessary, add 1 tablespoon of water.

4. Move the dough to a lightly floured surface and knead for about 5 minutes, until it becomes supple and fairly smooth. This is a sticky, wet dough; don't be tempted to add a lot of flour to the work surface. Just dust lightly and use a dough scraper as necessary to loosen the dough from the table during kneading. Allow the dough to rest for 15 minutes, covered with oiled plastic wrap. (This rest period is the autolyse.)

5. Knead for dough for 3 to 5 minutes, until it is stretchy and smooth yet still slightly sticky. Shape the dough into a loose ball, place it in a lightly oiled bowl, and turn the dough in the bowl to coat with oil. Cover the bowl tightly with oiled plastic wrap and let the dough rise at room temperature (75° to 77° F) for about 1 hour, or until the dough looks slightly puffy but has not doubled.

6. Place the dough in the refrigerator for at least 8 hours, or preferably, overnight to let it relax, develop flavor, and become more manageable.

7. Take the dough from the refrigerator and let it sit at room temperature for 1 to 2 hours, until it warms up and starts to rise.

8. Flour a work surface well and gently dump the dough onto it. Divide the dough into 3 equal pieces (about 13 ounces each). Gently flatten one piece, pressing out some of the air bubbles, and stretch it into a rectangle. Form the dough into a log and then into a short baguette about 12 inches long, following the instructions on page 26. The loaf will be loose and slightly irregular in shape. Cover an area at one side of the work surface with a thick layer of flour and place the loaf seam side down on the flour. Repeat with remaining pieces of dough, leaving plenty of space between the loaves–they will spread as they rise. Cover the loaves with well-oiled plastic wrap and let them rise for about 1 hour.

9. Thirty minutes before baking, preheat the oven to 475° F. Place a baking stone in the oven to preheat and position an oven rack just below the stone.

10. Sprinkle a peel very generously with cornmeal. Line an upside-down baking sheet with parchment paper and sprinkle very generously with cornmeal. Lift one loaf and flip it over onto the peel so the floured side is on top. Gently tug on the ends to stretch the loaf to the full length of the peel (about 14 inches). Repeat with the remaining loaves, placing another one on the peel and the last one on the pan. Dimple each loaf with your finger in about six places, but don't deflate them too much.

11. Be sure the loaves are loosened from the peel, then carefully slide them onto the baking stone. Place the pan of bread on the rack below the stone. Using a plant sprayer, quickly mist the loaves 8 to 10 times, then quickly shut oven door. Mist the loaves again after 1 minute. Then mist again 1 minute later.

12. Bake for about 10 minutes, then reduce the temperature to 450° F and bake for 15 minutes longer, or until the loaves sound slightly hollow when tapped on the bottom and the crust is a medium to dark brown. (If the crust is not brown enough, the loaves will soften as they cool.) Transfer the bread to a rack to cool for at least 30 minutes before serving.

Crunchy Creations

Artisan bakers are judged by their peers on the quality of the basic breads they produce. But our creativity soars when we start adding other ingredients to plain dough. Both of us especially love breads that *crunch!* when you eat them. With such an endless variety of healthy whole and cracked grains, nuts, and seeds at our disposal, we have no problem indulging ourselves. The recipes in this chapter are some of our crunchiest favorites. They're all good examples of healthy breads that have interesting textures and wonderful flavors without a lot of sugar, butter, or milk.

Coarse-Grained Whole Wheat with Toasted Walnuts

An overnight sponge starter bread

Amy developed this recipe when she was working at Mondrian in New York City. The chef wanted a bread that was crunchy and earthy, with a deep walnut taste, to comple-ment a new prosciutto and fig dish. The bread was served lightly toasted to enhance its nuttiness. When the fig dish was dropped from the menu, the bread remained–to be served with nothing less than foie gras! If you don't have any foie gras around, it tastes perfectly good by itself, or with richly flavored cheeses, such as aged, soft Camembert or St. André.

This dough is refrigerated overnight to intensify its walnut flavor and to allow the walnut skins to impart a slightly purple color to the dough.

Makes two 1-pound round loaves

- $^3/_4$ teaspoon active dry yeast
- $^1/_4$ cup (2 ounces) very warm water (105° to 115°F)
- $1^2/_3$ cups (8 ounces) organic whole wheat flour
- 1 cup ($4^1/_2$ ounces) unbleached all-purpose flour
- 2 tablespoons plus 2 teaspoons (1 ounce) coarse cornmeal
- 1 tablespoon kosher salt
- 1 cup (8 ounces) Sponge Starter (page 40)
- 1 cup (8 ounces) cool water (75°F) and/or reserved wheat berry cooking liquid
- 1 tablespoon ($^1/_2$ ounce) honey
- 1 tablespoon ($^1/_2$ ounce) walnut oil (or vegetable oil)
- $1^1/_2$ cups (6 ounces) walnut pieces, toasted (see box, page 68)
- $^1/_2$ cup (3 ounces) cooked wheat berries (see box, page 67)

1. Place the yeast and warm water in a medium bowl and stir with a fork to dissolve the yeast. Allow to stand for about 3 minutes.

2. Whisk the whole wheat flour, unbleached flour, cornmeal, and salt together in a medium bowl. Set aside.

3. Add the sponge starter, cool water, honey, and oil to the yeast mixture. Mix the ingredients with your fingers for 1 to 2 minutes, just to break up the sponge. The mixture should look milky and be slightly foamy. Add the flour mixture and stir with your fingers to incorporate the flour, scraping the sides of the bowl and folding the dough over itself until it gathers into a shaggy mass.

4. Move the dough to a lightly floured surface and knead for 5 to 7 minutes, until it becomes supple and elastic. If the dough seems too stiff and hard to knead, add additional cool water 1 tablespoon at a time until you get a malleable dough. Shape the dough into a loose ball and let it rest, covered with plastic wrap, on the work surface for 20 minutes. (This rest period is the autolyse.)

5. Combine the walnuts and wheat berries in a small bowl. Set aside.

6. Flatten the dough and stretch it gently with your fingers to form a rectangle about an inch thick. Spread the walnuts and wheat berries evenly over the dough. Fold the whole mass into an envelope (see page 23) and knead it gently until the nuts and berries are well distributed, about 2 to 3 minutes. If the dough resists, let it rest for 5 minutes and then continue kneading it. Some of the nuts and wheat berries may pop out of the dough, but they can easily be incorporated after the first rise, when the dough has softened.

7. Shape the dough into a loose ball and place it in a lightly oiled bowl, along with any loose nuts and berries. Turn the dough to coat with oil and cover the bowl tightly with oiled plastic wrap. Let the dough rise at room temperature (75° to 77° F) for 1 hour, or until it looks slightly puffy but has not doubled.

8. Refrigerate the dough overnight to intensify the walnut flavor.

9. Remove the dough from the refrigerator and allow it to rise at room temperature for 2 hours.

10. Gently remove the dough from the bowl and place it on a lightly floured work surface, pressing in any loose nuts and wheat berries. Divide it into 2 equal pieces and

> ### Cooking Wheat Berries
>
> *To save time, you can cook the wheat berries a day ahead. Place the berries in a saucepan with water to cover them by at least 1 inch, cover, and bring to a boil. Reduce the heat to low and cook until they're plump, 30 to 40 minutes. Let the berries cool, then drain, saving the cooking liquid to use as part of the water called for in the recipe. Refrigerate in an airtight container if you don't plan to use them immediately. (Whole rye berries can be cooked the same way, but you should increase the cooking time by 10 minutes.)*
>
> *Wheat berries (and rye berries) triple in volume when they are cooked. To determine how many dry berries you need to cook, simply divide the measured amount in the recipe by 3 (e.g., if the recipe calls for ¼ cup of cooked berries, you need to cook about ¼ cup of dry ones). Or cook a bit more and sprinkle on your morning cereal, or toss with a salad.*

shape each piece into a boule (see page 26). Dust a peel or the back of a baking sheet generously with coarse cornmeal. Place the loaves on the peel or sheet, seam side down, leaving several inches between them so they won't grow into each other as they rise. Cover with oiled plastic wrap and allow to rise for 2 to 3 hours, or until they have doubled in size (a finger pressed lightly into the dough will leave an indentation).

11. Thirty minutes before baking, preheat the oven to 450°F. Place a baking stone in the oven to preheat and place an empty water pan directly below the stone.

12. When the loaves have doubled, cut a shallow X on top of each one with a very sharp knife. Shake the peel or pan slightly to be sure the loaves aren't sticking and slide them onto the baking stone. Quickly pour 1 cup of very hot water into the water pan and immediately shut the oven door. After 1 minute, using a plant sprayer, mist the loaves quickly 6 to 8 times, then shut the oven door. Repeat the misting procedure 1 minute later.

13. Bake for 20 minutes, then reduce the oven temperature to 400°F and bake for 15 to 20 minutes longer, until the loaves sound hollow when tapped on the bottom. Transfer the loaves to a rack and allow to cool before serving. This bread freezes well, wrapped tightly in aluminum foil and a heavy-duty plastic freezer bag.

Grainy Whole Wheat and Seeds with Apricots, Prunes, and Raisins
An overnight old dough bread

When Amy was developing recipes for a magazine article, she wanted to create a healthy breakfast bread that would be low in fat and sugar but still satisfy that "morning sweet tooth." These plump, seeded wedges filled with moist chunks of apricots, prunes, and raisins were the answer. Try one warm from the oven with your favorite jam–it's an addictive combination. One serving of this satisfying breakfast treat provides a whopping eleven grams of dietary fiber, and only 13 percent of the calories are from fat. On the other hand, if fat's not a problem for you, try a piece split, toasted, and spread with a little cream cheese . . . pure heaven! This is an overnight dough, so prepare it in the late afternoon or early evening the day before you want to serve it.

• •

1 teaspoon active dry yeast

¼ cup (2 ounces) very warm water (105° to 115°F)

2 cups (9½ ounces) organic whole wheat flour

2 teaspoons kosher salt

¾ cup (6 ounces) cool water (75°F)

1 tablespoon flaxseed (sold at natural food stores)

1 tablespoon millet seed (sold at natural food stores)

½ cup (2½ ounces) dark raisins

Generous ½ cup (3 ounces) dried apricots, coarsely chopped

Generous ½ cup (3 ounces) pitted prunes, coarsely chopped

1 recipe (14½ ounces) Old Dough Starter (page 42)

Generous ½ cup (3 ounces) sesame seeds

⅔ cup (4 ounces) cooked wheat berries (see box, page 67)

1 tablespoon canola oil or melted butter for glazing during baking

• •

Equipment: One 12 by 17-inch baking sheet, lined with
parchment paper

1. Place the yeast and warm water in a small bowl. Stir with a fork to dissolve the yeast and allow to stand for about 3 minutes.

2. Combine the whole wheat flour and salt in a large bowl. Mix in the dissolved yeast mixture and the cool water, stirring with your fingers until the dough forms a sticky mass. Fold the dough onto itself and knead briefly until all of the flour is incorporated.

3. Move the dough to a floured work surface. At first the dough will feel very wet, but it will become drier as you knead it; flour your hands and the work surface frequently to keep the dough from sticking and tearing. If necessary, add more whole wheat flour 1 tablespoon at a time until you get a soft malleable dough that feels moist but not mushy. Continue kneading the dough until it is smooth and supple, about 4 to 5 minutes. Shape it into a loose ball, cover it with plastic wrap, and let rest on the work surface for 20 minutes. (This rest period is the autolyse.)

continued

4. Meanwhile, combine the flaxseed and millet seed in a cup and add warm water just to cover. Set aside. Combine the raisins, apricots, and prunes in a medium bowl and just barely cover them with hot water. (Too much water will wash away the flavor of the fruit when you drain it.) Set aside.

5. Flatten the dough on the lightly floured work surface and stretch it gently to form a rectangle about $1/2$ inch thick. Stretch the old dough into a rough rectangle of about the same size and place it on top of the whole wheat dough. Fold the whole mass into an envelope (see page 23) and begin kneading gently to merge the two doughs. Continue kneading for 3 to 4 minutes, or until the doughs are almost completely combined. Flatten the dough into a rough rectangle, cover it with plastic wrap, and let it rest for 10 minutes to relax the gluten strands.

6. Drain the millet and flax, if necessary, and combine them with the sesame seeds and wheat berries in a small bowl. Drain the dried fruit.

7. Gently stretch the dough into a more defined $1/2$-inch-thick rectangle. Spread the seeds and wheat berries evenly over the dough and gently press them into it. Spread the dried fruit on top, sprinkle lightly with flour to absorb some of the moisture, and gently press the fruit into the dough. Carefully fold the dough into an envelope and knead it until the fruit and seeds are well distributed, 3 to 5 minutes. Flour your hands and the work surface frequently (but moderately) to keep the dough from sticking. If the dough resists, let it rest for 5 minutes to relax the gluten strands, and then continue kneading. The dough will become sticky and begin to shred and separate slightly as the large clumps of wet fruit begin to surface. As you continue to knead, the dough will come together again and form a compact, cohesive mass. Some of the seeds and fruit may pop out of the dough, but they can easily be incorporated after the first rise, when the dough has softened.

8. Shape the dough into a loose ball and place it in a lightly oiled bowl, along with any loose seeds and fruit. Turn the dough to coat with oil and cover the bowl tightly with oiled plastic wrap. Let the dough rise at room temperature (75° to 77° F) for 1 hour, or until it looks puffy but has not doubled.

9. Refrigerate the dough overnight to allow it to relax and develop the flavors of the wheat, fruit, and seeds.

10. Remove the dough from the refrigerator and let it rise at room temperature for 2 hours.

11. Gently remove the dough from the bowl and place it on a lightly floured work surface, pressing in any loose seeds and fruit. Flour your hands lightly to keep the dough from sticking, and divide it into 2 equal pieces. Shape each piece into a boule (see page 26).

12. Line a 12 by 17-inch baking sheet with parchment paper and place the boules on it, seam side down, leaving several inches between them so they won't grow into each other as they rise (positioning them on a diagonal seems to work best). Slightly flatten the boules into disks about 2 inches high, then deeply score each disk into 6 wedges with a floured dough cutter; don't worry if you cut almost all the way through the dough. If necessary, gently push the wedges together to form a ring (the tips of the wedges should be touching in the center of each ring). Cover the rings with oiled plastic wrap and let rise at room temperature for about 2 hours, or until they have doubled in volume (a finger pressed lightly into the dough will leave an indentation).

> ### "Old Dough"
>
> *You don't always have to make "old dough" from scratch. Whenever you're making plain white bread or French bread, weigh out a 14½-ounce piece of dough after the first rise and freeze it. As long as it's wrapped in aluminum foil, leaving a little room for the dough to expand, and then wrapped again in plastic wrap or a heavy-duty freezer bag, it will maintain its potency as a starter for about 6 months. Thaw it in the refrigerator overnight before you want to use it, then take it out at least 2 hours before you begin making the recipe to allow it to warm and soften slightly. If the old dough is too cold and stiff, it will be difficult to incorporate into the new dough mass.*

13. About 15 minutes before baking, position an oven rack in the lower third of the oven and place an empty water pan directly below it. Preheat the oven to 450°F.

14. Place the pan of bread on the rack above the water pan. Quickly pour 1 cup of very hot water into the water pan and immediately shut the door. After 1 minute, using a plant sprayer, mist the loaves 6 to 8 times and shut the oven door. Repeat the misting procedure 1 minute later.

15. Bake for 10 minutes, then reduce the oven temperature to 400°F and bake for 20 to 25 minutes longer, until the loaves are dark golden brown and sound hollow when tapped on the bottom. (If the bottoms of the loaves start to brown too quickly, move the pan to a rack in the top third of the oven.) Remove the loaves from the pan and put them on a wire rack to cool. This bread can be served warm or completely cooled. Don't break the rings into individual wedges until just before serving, to ensure that each piece stays moist.

Coarse Cracked Corn with Four Peppers

A sponge starter bread

Take crunchy toasted corn and spicy hot pepper, add a hint of fresh garlic, and you have an irresistible and surprisingly versatile flavor combination. This moist, savory loaf is delicious plain alongside a crisp green salad in the summer. Or toast thick slices and serve with a big bowl of chili in the winter. Combine it with a mild cheese, such as Monterey Jack, to make a memorable grilled cheese sandwich for lunch, or spread a toasted slice with a generous layer of jalapeño jelly for breakfast. You can even use the dough to make a most unusual pizza crust. The combination of yellow durum flour and red and green peppers makes a festive-looking loaf that is perfect for gift giving.

For an interesting variation, replace the cool water in the recipe with tomato juice (decrease the salt by a quarter-teaspoon if the juice is salted). You'll create a whole new list of bread-eating possibilities!

Makes three 1-pound round loaves

· ·

1 teaspoon active dry yeast

$\frac{1}{4}$ cup (2 ounces) very warm water (105° to 115°F)

$3\frac{3}{4}$ cups (or more as needed) (19$\frac{1}{2}$ ounces) patent durum flour

$\frac{2}{3}$ cup (4 ounces) cracked corn, toasted (see box)

1 tablespoon plus 1$\frac{1}{4}$ teaspoons kosher salt

1$\frac{1}{2}$ teaspoons coarsely ground black pepper

$\frac{1}{2}$ teaspoon ground cayenne pepper

$\frac{2}{3}$ cup (3 ounces) jalapeño pepper, cut into $\frac{1}{8}$-inch dice

$\frac{2}{3}$ cup (3 ounces) red bell pepper, cut into $\frac{1}{4}$-inch dice

2 teaspoons garlic, minced

1$\frac{1}{4}$ cups (10 ounces) Sponge Starter (page 40)

1$\frac{1}{2}$ cups (12 ounces) cool water (75°F)

Coarse cornmeal for coating (about 2 cups)

· ·

1. Place the yeast and warm water in a large bowl. Stir with a fork to dissolve the yeast and allow to stand for about 3 minutes.

2. Whisk the durum flour, cracked corn, salt, black pepper, and cayenne pepper together in a medium bowl. Set aside. Mix the jalapeño pepper, red bell pepper, and garlic in a small bowl. Set aside.

3. Add the sponge starter and cool water to the yeast mixture. Mix with your fingers for 1 to 2 minutes, just to break up the sponge. The mixture should look milky and be slightly foamy. Add the flour mixture and incorporate well with your fingers, scraping the bowl and folding the dough over itself until it gathers into a shaggy mass.

4. Move the dough to a lightly floured surface and knead it for 5 to 7 minutes, until it becomes supple and elastic. This dough should not be too wet, or it will be difficult to handle when the vegetables are added. If it feels wet and mushy, add another $^1/_4$ cup of durum flour as you knead. If the dough seems too stiff and hard to knead, add cool water a tablespoon at a time until you have a soft but not mushy, malleable dough. Shape the dough into a loose ball, cover it with plastic wrap, and let it rest on the lightly floured work surface for 20 minutes. (This rest period is the autolyse.)

5. Flatten the dough and stretch it gently to form a rectangle about an inch thick. Spread the peppers and garlic evenly over the dough and sprinkle lightly with durum flour to absorb some of the moisture. Fold the whole mass into an envelope (see page 23) and gently knead until the peppers and garlic are well distributed, about 2 to 3 minutes. The garlic may give the dough a somewhat sticky texture, so handle the dough gently and keep your hands and the work surface lightly floured. If the dough resists, let it rest for 5 minutes and then continue kneading. Some of the peppers may pop out of the dough, but they can easily be incorporated after the first rise, when the dough has softened.

6. Shape the dough into a loose ball and place it in a lightly oiled bowl, along with any loose peppers. Turn to coat the dough with oil and cover the bowl tightly with oiled plastic wrap. Let the dough rise at room temperature (75° to 77° F) until it has doubled in volume, about 2 hours.

continued

Cracked Corn

Cracked corn comes in many shapes and sizes. For this recipe we prefer coarsely ground pieces that are about a quarter of the size of a grain of rice, larger than coarse cornmeal or corn grits. If you can't find it in a natural food store, substitute one of the following:

Hominy, finely chopped	*1 cup*	*5¼ ounces*
Corn germ (see page 5)	*1 cup*	*4 ounces*
Polenta (coarse, not quick-cooking)	*²⁄₃ cup*	*4 ounces*

You may have to add a little more durum flour or cool water to the dough to accommodate the way the substitute ingredient absorbs moisture.

Toast the cracked corn (or the hominy, corn germ, or polenta) on a cookie sheet in a preheated 350°F oven for 8 to 20 minutes (depending on the ingredient you use), or until very lightly browned and fragrant. Let cool completely, then store in an airtight container at room temperature.

7. Spread about 2 cups of coarse cornmeal on a flat dish or baking sheet. Loosen the dough from the bowl with lightly floured hands, and pour it onto a floured work surface. (The dough will be very sticky because the peppers will have released some of their juices.) Press in any loose peppers, and divide the dough into 3 equal pieces. Gently shape each piece into a tight boule (see page 26) and roll each one in the coarse cornmeal to coat completely. Dust a peel or the back of a baking sheet generously with additional cornmeal and place

Take great care when handling hot peppers. Wear rubber gloves (or cover your hands with plastic bags), then wash your hands very thoroughly afterwards with detergent and hot water to remove any volatile hot pepper oils from your skin. Sometimes those insidious oils even sneak through rubber gloves. Remember not to touch your eyes, nose, or lips until your hands have been well washed.

the shaped loaves seam side down on the peel or sheet, leaving several inches between the loaves so they won't grow into each other as they rise. Cover with oiled plastic wrap and allow to rise for $1^1/_2$ to 2 hours, or until they have almost doubled in size.

8. Thirty minutes before baking, preheat the oven to 425° F. Place a baking stone in the oven to preheat and place an empty water pan directly below the stone.

9. When the loaves have doubled, cut a shallow X on top of each one with a *lame,* a razor blade, or a very sharp knife. Shake the peel or pan slightly to be sure the loaves aren't sticking and slide them onto the baking stone. Quickly pour 1 cup of very hot water into the water pan and immediately shut the oven door. After 1 minute, using a plant sprayer, mist the loaves 6 to 8 times and shut the oven door. Repeat the misting procedure 1 minute later.

10. Bake for 20 minutes, then reduce the oven temperature to 375° F and bake for 25 to 30 minutes longer, until the loaves are browned and sound hollow when tapped on the bottom. Transfer the loaves to a rack and allow to cool before serving. This is a moist bread that will last for days stored at room temperature. It also freezes well, wrapped tightly in aluminum foil and a heavy-duty plastic freezer bag.

Toy's Teddy Bread

A sourdough bread

Although this bread can be formed into any shape, Toy originally developed the recipe so she could make teddy bears out of bread. At the bakery we like to call the bears "huggable edibles." They've been used as table centerpieces for birthday parties and baby showers and sent as get-well gifts to hospitals. A couple of them have even been permanently encased in fiberglass resin to become part of private teddy bear collections! However, this dense, chewy bread was made to be eaten. It has a wonderful rich grainy flavor that is perfect for picnic baskets and cheese platters or for sandwiches that require a fine assertive mustard. You can also team it up with a steaming bowl of your favorite soup and a crisp green salad for a satisfying and delicious meal.

This slow-rising bread takes eight to nine hours to make from start to finish, so it's best to start it early in the day. Also, be sure to make your Rye Sour Starter a day or two before you plan to make your dough, because you may have to feed the sour more than once to boost its leavening power.

This recipe will make one teddy bear. For instructions for shaping and baking a bear, see page 174.

Makes two 1¹⁄₄-pound round loaves

• •

Scant ¹⁄₃ cup (1¹⁄₂ ounces) flaxseed (sold at natural food stores)

1 cup (9 ounces) Rye Sour Starter (page 48)

1¹⁄₂ cups (12 ounces) cool water (75°F; see Step 2)

³⁄₄ cup (4 ounces) cracked rye (or cracked wheat)

Scant ¹⁄₃ cup (1¹⁄₂ ounces) sesame seeds

2¹⁄₂ cups (12¹⁄₂ ounces) high-gluten (bread) flour

1 tablespoon plus 2¹⁄₂ teaspoons kosher salt

1 to 1¹⁄₃ cups (5 to 7 ounces) coarse whole wheat flour

Additional cracked rye and sesame seeds for topping (about ¹⁄₂ cup
    of each; optional)

• •

1. Put the flaxseed in a small bowl and add enough warm water to cover them by ¹⁄₈ inch. Set aside to soak for at least 10 minutes.

continued

2. Combine the rye sour and water in the bowl of a heavy-duty electric mixer fitted with the dough hook. Stir briefly on low speed to break up the starter. (If necessary, adjust the temperature of the water to achieve a final dough temperature of 75° to 77°F. This is especially important with this dough, as it can become bitter-tasting if it is allowed to get over 80°F. For instructions on calculating dough temperature during mixing, see page 179.)

3. Add the cracked rye (or wheat), sesame seeds, flaxseed (along with any liquid) high-gluten (or bread) flour, and salt and mix on medium-low speed just until the ingredients are combined. Slowly add enough coarse whole wheat flour to make a pliable dough.

4. As soon as all of the flour has been moistened and a good dough mass has formed, take the dough out of the bowl and place it on a lightly floured surface. This

> *You must have a good, active Rye Sour Starter (see page 48) before you attempt to make this recipe because it uses no commercial yeast. The only leavening power comes from the sourdough rye starter. If you're concerned that your rye sour is not strong enough to leaven the dough properly, you may add just a pinch (no more than an eighth of a teaspoon) of active dry yeast when you are mixing the dough.*

dough is heavy and somewhat clay-like because of all of the coarse grains and seeds, and it will feel sticky because of the rye flour used in the sourdough starter. Don't be intimidated by its unusual texture; even though it is a heavy dough, it should still be wet enough to be soft and pliable without being so sticky that it's impossible to work with. If it feels too stiff, add a little more water 1 tablespoon at a time until you get a pliable dough. If the dough feels too soft and sticky, knead in a little more coarse whole wheat flour until you get a workable dough. Keeping your hands and the work surface lightly floured, knead the dough for about 5 minutes, or until it forms a soft, compact ball that feels somewhat springy and no longer sticks to the work surface.

5. Cover the dough with plastic wrap and let it rest on the work surface for 20 minutes. (This rest period is the autolyse.)

6. Scrape the dough mass up with a dough cutter, flour the work surface lightly, and knead the dough again for another minute or so.

7. Shape the dough into a loose ball and place it in a lightly oiled bowl. Turn to coat with oil and cover the bowl with oiled plastic wrap. Let the dough rise at room temperature (75° to 77°F) until doubled in volume. Check the dough temperature occasionally during this rise; it should be around 75° to 77°F. Absolutely don't let it go above 80°F for any length of time. If this happens, immediately refrigerate the dough until the temperature is in the desired range. This dough may take 4 to 5 hours to double the first time, depending on the strength of your rye starter and the temperature of the room.

8. Combine the cracked rye and sesame seeds for topping, if using, and spread on a flat dish or a baking pan. Turn the dough out onto a floured work surface and divide it into 2 equal pieces. Shape each piece into a compact boule (see page 26). Roll the tops of the boules in the cracked rye mixture. Dust a peel or the back of a baking sheet generously with coarse cornmeal. Place the loaves seam side down on the peel or sheet, leaving several inches between them so they won't grow into each other as they rise. Cover them with oiled plastic wrap and let rise at room temperature until they have almost doubled in volume (a finger pressed lightly into the dough will leave a slight indentation). This should take about $2^1/_2$ hours, but it could take longer if your starter is weak or the room is chilly.

9. Thirty minutes before baking, preheat the oven to 425° F. Place a baking stone in the oven to preheat and place an empty water pan directly below the stone.

10. When the loaves have almost doubled, cut an X on top of each one with a *lame*, a razor blade, or a very sharp knife. Shake the peel or pan slightly to be sure the loaves aren't sticking and slide them onto the baking stone. Quickly pour 1 cup of very hot water into the water pan and immediately shut the oven door. After 1 minute, using a plant sprayer, mist the loaves 6 to 8 times, then quickly shut the door. Repeat the misting procedure 1 minute later.

11. Bake for 20 minutes, then reduce the oven temperature to 400° F and bake for 18 to 25 minutes longer, until the loaves are dark golden brown and sound hollow when tapped on the bottom. Transfer the loaves to a rack and allow to cool before serving. This bread freezes well, wrapped tightly in aluminum foil and then in plastic wrap or a heavy-duty freezer bag.

Rye dough has a tendency to be very sticky, so we find it easier to start this dough out in a mixer, until a dough mass forms, and then finish the dough by hand. If you don't have a mixer with a dough hook, just dig in by hand and bear (no pun intended!) with the sticky mess until you get the dough going. Keeping your hands and the work surface lightly floured and using a dough scraper to lift and turn the dough will make it easier.

5

Sustenance
with
Substance

◆

Whole-Grain
Favorites

We love the textures and flavors of whole grains so much it's almost guaranteed we'll find a way to use them whenever we're developing new recipes. We've come a long way from the dull packaged "brown bread" our mothers made us eat when we were kids. "It's good for you," they always said. Well, Mom, here are a few basic good-for-you breads that you can put on your table or in the lunch box without hearing any complaints!

Organic Whole Wheat Sandwich Bread with Oats and Pecans

A sponge starter bread

Mildly sweet and slightly crunchy, our version of whole wheat oatmeal bread is great for tuna sandwiches. Cut in thick slices, it's perfect for French toast. Shape it into rolls for a dinner party or a family picnic. For variety, add one and a half cups (seven and a half ounces) of golden raisins to the dough and shape half of it into twists (see page117); crusty and delicious, they're good for breakfast-on-the-go and afternoon snacks. This versatile bread is sure to become one of your favorites.

Makes two 9 by 5-inch loaves

. . . .

1 teaspoon active dry yeast

¼ cup (2 ounces) very warm water (105° to 115°F)

3¾ cups (or more if needed) (18½ ounces) organic whole wheat flour

2¾ cups (12½ ounces) organic unbleached all-purpose flour

2 cups (6 ounces) organic old-fashioned rolled oats, plus additional

    for topping

2 tablespoons (¾ ounce) kosher salt

1½ cups (12 ounces) Sponge Starter (page 40)

2½ cups (20 ounces) cool water (75°F) *– 85° to 90° for cold starter*

3 tablespoons (1½ ounces) honey

2 tablespoons (1 ounce) molasses

2 tablespoons (1 ounce) canola or other vegetable oil

2 cups (8 ounces) pecan pieces, toasted (see box, page 68)

. . . .

Equipment: Two 9 by 5-inch loaf pans, oiled

1. Place the yeast and warm water in a large bowl and stir with a fork to dissolve the yeast. Let stand for about 3 minutes.

2. Whisk the whole wheat flour, unbleached flour, oats, and salt together in a medium bowl.

3. Add the sponge starter, cool water, honey, molasses, and oil to the yeast mixture. Mix with your fingers for 1 to 2 minutes, just long enough to break up the sponge. The mixture should look milky and be slightly foamy. Add the flour mixture to the bowl and stir with your fingers to incorporate the flour, scraping the sides of the bowl and folding the dough over itself until it gathers into a shaggy mass. Don't be concerned if the dough feels very sticky at this point.

4. Lightly flour a work surface with whole wheat flour. Remove the dough from the bowl and knead it for 6 to 8 minutes, until it becomes compact and elastic. It should be very moist but not mushy. If it feels too stiff to knead, add water 1 tablespoon at a time until you have a soft, malleable dough. If it's sloppy wet and impossible to knead, add another $1/4$ to $1/3$ cup ($1^1/4$ to $1^2/3$ ounces) of whole wheat flour. Shape the dough into a loose ball and let it rest, covered with plastic wrap, on the lightly floured work surface for 20 minutes. (This rest period is the autolyse.)

5. Flatten the dough and stretch it gently into a rectangle about an inch thick. Spread the pecans evenly over the dough. Fold the whole mass into an envelope (see page 23) and knead and fold it gently until the nuts are well distributed, about 2 to 3 minutes. If the dough resists, let it rest for 5 minutes and then continue kneading. Some of the nuts may pop out of the dough, but they can easily be incorporated again after the first rise, when the dough has softened.

6. Shape the dough into a loose ball and place it in a lightly oiled bowl, along with any loose nuts. Turn the dough to coat with oil and cover the bowl tightly with oiled plastic wrap. Let the dough rise at room temperature (75° to 77° F) until it has doubled in volume, about $2^1/2$ to 3 hours. (You can also refrigerate this dough overnight and shape it and bake it the next day: Let it rise for 1 hour at room temperature, or until it looks slightly puffy but has not doubled, before refrigerating. The next day, let it rise for 2 hours at room temperature before shaping it.)

7. When the dough has doubled, loosen it from the bowl with lightly floured hands and gently pour it onto a floured work surface. Press any loose pecans into the dough and divide it into 2 equal pieces. Shape each piece into a log (see page 22).

8. Spread the oats for topping on a flat plate or baking sheet. Use a pastry brush or a plant sprayer to lightly moisten the top of each log with water, then roll the tops of the loaves in the oats. Place each loaf seam side down in an oiled 9 by 5-inch loaf pan. Cover them with oiled plastic wrap and allow to rise for about 2 hours, or until they have doubled in size (a finger pressed gently into the dough will leave an indentation).

continued

9. Thirty minutes before baking, preheat the oven to 425° F. Place a baking stone in the oven to preheat and place an empty water pan directly below the stone.

10. When the loaves have doubled, place the pans on the baking stone. Quickly pour 1 cup of very hot water into the water pan and immediately shut the door. After 1 minute, using a plant sprayer, mist the loaves quickly 6 to 8 times, then shut the oven door. Repeat the misting procedure 1 minute later.

11. Bake for 15 minutes, then reduce the oven temperature to 375° F and bake for 20 to 25 minutes longer, until the loaves sound slightly hollow when tipped out of the pans and tapped on the bottom. The sides and bottom of the loaves should feel firm and slightly crusty. If the tops are browned but the sides are still somewhat soft, place the loaves directly on the stone to bake for 5 to 10 minutes longer. Transfer the loaves to a rack and allow to cool completely before slicing.

Fragrant Whole Wheat Dinner Rolls

A sponge starter bread

Flavored with earthy sesame seeds and sweet, toasty wheat germ, these fragrant whole wheat rolls will complement any menu. For large dinner parties, you can double the recipe and bake the rolls in a nine-by-thirteen-inch pan. You may want to do that anyway and freeze the leftovers for another meal. Wrap them in aluminum foil first, then in a heavy-duty freezer bag. Let them thaw at room temperature for an hour and reheat them in the oven just before serving. Voilà! Instant dinner rolls.

Makes 12 rolls

• •

1 teaspoon active dry yeast

¼ cup (2 ounces) very warm water (105° to 115°F)

1⅓ cups (6¾ ounces) organic whole wheat flour

1 cup (or more as needed) (4½ ounces) unbleached all-purpose flour

½ cup (3 ounces) cooked wheat berries (see box, page 67),
    coarsely chopped

⅓ cup (1¼ ounces) toasted wheat germ

¼ cup (1½ ounces) sesame seeds

1 tablespoon plus ½ teaspoon kosher salt

1¼ cups (10 ounces) Sponge Starter (page 40)

¾ cup (6 ounces) cool water (75°F)

1½ tablespoons honey

1 tablespoon canola oil (or other vegetable oil)

Additional sesame seeds, for topping

• •

Equipment: One 9-inch square baking pan, oiled

1. Place the yeast and warm water in a small bowl. Stir with a fork to dissolve the yeast and allow to stand for about 3 minutes.

2. Whisk the whole wheat flour, unbleached flour, wheat berries, wheat germ, sesame seeds, and salt together in a medium bowl.

continued

3. Add the sponge starter, cool water, honey, and oil to the yeast mixture. Mix the ingredients with your fingers for 1 to 2 minutes, just long enough to break up the sponge. The mixture should be foamy. Add the flour mixture and stir with your fingers to incorporate the flour, scraping the sides of the bowl and folding the dough over itself until it gathers into a shaggy mass.

4. Move the dough to a lightly floured surface and knead it for 5 to 6 minutes, until it becomes supple and elastic. The dough should be moist but not mushy. If it feels too wet, add another tablespoon or so of unbleached flour as you knead. If it feels too stiff to knead, add cool water 1 tablespoon at a time until you have a soft, malleable dough. Shape the dough into a loose ball and let it rest, covered with plastic wrap, on the lightly floured work surface for 20 minutes. (This rest period is the autolyse.)

5. Knead the dough again gently for 1 to 2 minutes, or until it is smooth and springy. Shape the dough into a loose ball and place it in a lightly oiled bowl. Turn to coat the dough with oil and cover the bowl tightly with oiled plastic wrap. Let the dough rise at room temperature (75° to 77° F) until it has doubled in volume, about $1^1/_2$ to 2 hours.

6. Place the sesame seeds for topping in a small bowl. Loosen the dough from the bowl with lightly floured hands and gently pour it onto a floured work surface. Divide it into 12 equal pieces (about $2^3/_4$ ounces each). Shape them into rolls (see page 27). Dip the top of each one into the sesame seeds, and place seam side down in an oiled 9-inch square pan, arranging them in three rows of 4 rolls each. Cover them with oiled plastic wrap and allow to rise for about 1 hour, or until they have doubled in size (a finger gently pressed into the dough will leave an indentation).

7. Thirty minutes before baking, preheat the oven to 425° F. Place a baking stone in the oven to preheat and place an empty water pan directly below the stone.

8. When the rolls have doubled, place the pan on the baking stone. Quickly pour 1 cup of very hot water into the water pan and immediately shut the oven door. After 1 minute, using a plant sprayer, mist the rolls 4 to 6 times and shut the oven door. Repeat the misting procedure 1 minute later.

9. Bake for 15 minutes, then reduce the oven temperature to 350° F and bake for 5 to 10 minutes longer, until the rolls are nicely browned and sound slightly hollow when tapped on the top. Tip them out of the pan and transfer them to a cooling rack. They can be served warm or at room temperature. To ensure that they stay moist, don't separate the rolls until just before serving.

Dense Rye Bread

An overnight yeast bread

Many people associate the flavor of rye with the taste of caraway because using caraway seeds in rye bread is a long-standing tradition in the baking industry. But rye doesn't taste like caraway at all. It has a wonderful earthy, rich, fruity flavor all its own. Rye also has a unique texture. Bread doughs made with a high percentage of rye flour are heavy, sticky, even a little bit slimy! Rye dough is much easier to work with if you include a lot of white flour to pump up the gluten content, but then much of the delicious rye flavor is lost. In this recipe, we opted for a moist, dense loaf that is packed with pure rye flavor. Working with this dough will challenge even the most experienced baker, but the final result is worth the effort. Let the loaf cool completely after baking, then slice it thin and savor it on its own or with your favorite cheese and paper-thin cold cuts. Try it with caraway Muenster!

Make this dough just before you go to bed and immediately put it into the refrigerator. It will overproof if you let it sit out first, . Try to shape it early the next day. It can overproof even if left too long in the refrigerator.

Flavor and nutrition booster: Save any liquid when you drain the cooked rye berries and use it as part of the water in the recipe.

The rye sour in this bread is used more for its taste than for its leavening power; it's okay to use some of the maintenance Rye Mother (page 47), straight from the refrigerator, providing you've fed it within the past three days.

Makes two 1-pound loaves

• •

1¼ *teaspoons active dry yeast*

¼ *cup (2 ounces) very warm water (105° to 115°F)*

3¼ *cups (14 ounces) organic rye flour*

1¼ *cups (6 ounces) clear flour*

1 *tablespoon plus 2 teaspoons kosher salt*

¼ *cup (2¼ ounces) Rye Mother (page 47) (see box, above)*

1⅔ *cups (13 ounces) cool water (75°F) plus reserved cooking liquid from*
   rye berries

½ *cup (2½ ounces) cooked rye berries (see box, page 67), coarsely chopped*
   (reserve the cooking liquid)

Additional rye flour for coating (about 1 cup)

• •

continued

1. Place the yeast and warm water in a small bowl and stir with a fork to dissolve the yeast. Let stand for about 3 minutes.

2. Whisk the rye flour, clear flour, and salt together in a medium bowl.

3. Combine the yeast, rye mother, and cool water/rye berry cooking liquid mixture in the bowl of an electric mixer fitted with a dough hook and mix briefly on medium speed to break up the starter. When the mixture starts to look slightly foamy, add the flour mixture and rye berries and mix on medium speed until combined. When all of the flour is moistened and a dough mass has formed, increase the speed to medium-high and knead the dough for 2^1/$_2$ minutes. If necessary, turn off the mixer occasionally and use your hand (moistened with water) to push the dough down into the bowl so it kneads more evenly. (If working the dough by hand, knead it for 4 to 5 minutes.)

4. Leaving the dough in the bowl, cover it with plastic wrap, or wrap a plastic shopping bag around the bowl and mixer. Let it rest for 20 minutes. (This rest period is the autolyse.)

5. Mix the dough on medium-high speed for 30 seconds. The dough will be very sticky with some "fluffiness" to it (imagine whipped modeling clay). Using a wet plastic dough scraper or your wet hand, scrape the dough from the sides of the bowl and gently shape it into a rough ball. Transfer the dough to a moistened surface (use a plant sprayer to mist the surface lightly). Keeping your hands and the table wet, use a light touch to knead the dough again for about 15 to 30 seconds, just long enough to work it into a compact ball. It should form a soft, compact ball, but it will still stick to a dry work surface. Don't be intimidated by the unusual texture of the dough. Even though it's a heavy dough, it should still be wet enough to be soft and pliable without being so mushy that it won't form a cohesive dough mass. If it feels too stiff and dry, add a little more water 1 tablespoon at a time until you get a pliable dough. If the dough feels too mushy, knead in a little more clear flour until you get a workable dough. (If you're working the dough by hand, knead it for about 1 minute after the autolyse, or until it reaches the texture described above.)

> *Rye dough has a tendency to be very sticky, so we find it easier to knead this dough in a mixer with a good dough hook. If you don't have a mixer with a dough hook, just dig in by hand and bear with the sticky mess until you get the dough going. Keeping your hands and the work surface lightly moistened with water and using a wet dough scraper to lift and turn the dough will make it easier.*
>
> *The kneading time for this high-percentage-rye dough is considerably shorter than the kneading time for our other doughs. When combined with water, the proteins in rye flour form a very weak gluten structure, so it's easy to damage this fragile network if you overwork the dough. Rye gluten is also easily damaged by overproofing, so we give this dough a cold first rise and a short second rise after the loaves are shaped.*

6. Shape the dough into a ball and place it in a lightly oiled bowl. Turn the dough to coat with oil, then smooth the top with your moistened hand. Cover the bowl tightly with oiled plastic wrap. Place the dough in the refrigerator to proof overnight. (This is when most of the flavor development takes place.)

7. Spread about 1 cup of rye flour on a flat dish or baking sheet. Remove the dough from the refrigerator. Working with this dough is a little like working with soft clay—handle it with a light touch, keep the table and your hands moistened with water, and use a scraper to help you lift the dough as you shape it. Divide it into 2 equal pieces.

8. Spread each piece into a 6-inch square. Fold the top third down and the bottom third up as if you were folding a business letter, then roll the dough into a 10-inch cylinder to form a log and smooth the surface of the log with wet hands. Lift each loaf gently and roll it in the rye flour until well coated. The flour makes the loaves easier to handle—once they are coated, you can smooth the shape. (As the loaves rise, cracks will form in the flour coating, giving a rough, rustic look to the bread.)

9. Dust a peel or the back of a baking sheet generously with coarse cornmeal. Gently place the loaves seam side down on the peel or sheet, leaving several inches between them so they won't grow into each other as they rise. Cover with oiled plastic wrap and allow to rise at room temperature (75° to 77° F) for 1 hour, or until almost doubled in size. This bread is best if baked when it's slightly underrisen; if you overproof it, you'll get flat loaves. They'll taste delicious, but they won't look as beautiful.

10. Thirty minutes before baking, preheat the oven to 425° F. Place a baking stone in the oven to preheat and place an empty water pan directly below the stone.

11. When the loaves have almost doubled, using a sharp serrated knife, cut ¼-inch-deep diagonal slashes at ¾-inch intervals on top of each loaf. Shake the peel or pan slightly to be sure the loaves aren't sticking and slide them onto the baking stone. Quickly pour 1 cup of very hot water into the water pan and immediately shut the oven door. After 1 minute, using a plant sprayer, mist the top and sides of the oven 6 to 8 times and shut the oven door. Repeat the misting procedure 1 minute later. (Avoid spraying the bread when misting, or the flour on the top will look blotchy and unappetizing.)

12. Bake for 20 minutes, then reduce the oven temperature to 400° F and bake for 20 to 25 minutes longer, until the loaves sound hollow when tapped on the bottom. Transfer the loaves to a rack and allow to cool completely before serving.

Toy's Anadama Bread

A sponge starter bread

Our version of traditional Anadama bread is made without any "white" flour. The attractive, dense loaf makes narrow slices that are perfect for snacks and hors d'oeuvres. Dark and flavorful with a crackly crust and the slightly sweet richness of molasses, it contains a secret ingredient to give it extra complexity! Let the bread cool completely to mellow the flavor, then serve it in thin slices with a strong, peppery French mustard, transparent slices of prosciutto or capocollo ham, and a glass of bold red wine.

Makes three 1-pound loaves

- $1\frac{1}{2}$ cups (12 ounces) cold water
- 1 tablespoon plus $2\frac{1}{4}$ teaspoons kosher salt
- $\frac{1}{4}$ cup ($1\frac{1}{2}$ ounces) canola oil (or other vegetable oil)
- 3 tablespoons ($2\frac{1}{4}$ ounces) molasses
- 1 cup (6 ounces) coarse cornmeal
- $2\frac{1}{4}$ teaspoons active dry yeast
- $\frac{1}{4}$ cup (2 ounces) very warm water ($105°$ to $115°F$)
- $3\frac{1}{2}$ cups ($17\frac{1}{2}$ ounces) organic whole wheat flour
- 1 cup (5 ounces) pumpernickel flour
- $\frac{2}{3}$ cup ($3\frac{1}{2}$ ounces) cooked rye berries (see box, page 67), coarsely chopped
- $1\frac{1}{2}$ teaspoons freshly ground black pepper
- 1 cup plus 2 tablespoons (9 ounces) cool water ($75°F$)
- 2 cups (16 ounces) cold whole wheat Sponge Starter (see box)
- Additional coarse cornmeal for coating (about 2 cups)

1. Combine the cold water, oil, molasses, and salt in a medium saucepan and bring to a boil. Reduce the heat to medium and gradually stir in the cornmeal. Cook for 1 minute, stirring constantly. Remove the saucepan from the heat and allow the cornmeal mixture to cool to warm ($90°$ to $100°F$).

2. Place the yeast and warm water in a large bowl and stir with a fork to dissolve the yeast. Let stand for about 3 minutes.

3. Whisk the whole wheat flour, pumpernickel flour, rye berries, and pepper together in a medium bowl.

4. Add the cool water and sponge starter to the yeast mixture. Mix the ingredients with your fingers for 1 to 2 minutes, just long enough to break up the sponge. The mixture should look milky and be slightly foamy. Add the cornmeal mixture and mix until well combined. Add the flour mixture and stir with your fingers to incorporate the flour, scraping the sides of the bowl and folding the dough over itself until it gathers into a shaggy mass.

5. Move the dough to a lightly floured surface and knead it for 4 to 5 minutes, until it becomes compact and somewhat springy. Keep your hands and the surface lightly floured and use a dough scraper to lift and turn the dough until it no longer sticks to the work surface. The dough should be moist but not mushy. If it feels too wet, add another tablespoon or 2 of whole wheat flour as you knead. If it feels too stiff to knead, add cool water 1 tablespoon at a time until you have a soft, malleable dough. Shape the dough into a loose ball and let it rest, covered with plastic wrap, on the lightly floured work surface for 20 minutes. (This rest period is the autolyse.)

6. Knead the dough gently for 1 to 2 minutes, or until it is smooth and springy. Shape the dough into a loose ball and place it in a lightly oiled bowl. Turn to coat the dough with oil and cover the bowl tightly with oiled plastic wrap. Let the dough rise at room temperature (75° to 77° F) until it has doubled in volume, about 1¹/₂ to 2 hours.

7. Spread about 2 cups of cornmeal on a flat dish or baking sheet. Loosen the dough from the bowl with lightly floured hands and gently pour it onto a floured work surface. Divide it into 3 equal pieces. (Handle this dough with a light touch because the gluten structure is fragile and can easily be damaged.) Shape each piece into a smooth log (see page 22) 9 to 10 inches long. Using a plant sprayer, moisten the surface of each loaf and gently roll in the cornmeal until evenly coated. (As the loaves rise, cracks will form in the cornmeal coating, giving a rough, rustic look to the bread.)

> ### Whole Wheat
> ### Sponge Starter
>
> *To make a whole wheat sponge starter, follow the procedure described on page 40, using these ingredients:*
>
> *1 cup (8 ounces) very warm water (105° to 115°F)*
>
> *¹/₃ teaspoon active dry yeast*
>
> *2 cups (10 ounces) organic whole wheat flour*
>
> *Make the sponge the day before you want to use it and store it in the refrigerator overnight. The sponge should be cold when you use it to make the dough. (Makes 18 ounces.)*

continued

8. Dust a peel or the back of a baking sheet generously with coarse cornmeal. Place the shaped loaves seam side down on the peel or sheet, leaving several inches between them so they won't grow into each other as they rise. (You may have to reform the loaves slightly after you've moved them.) Cover them with oiled plastic wrap and allow to rise at room temperature (75° to 77° F) for 45 minutes to 1 hour, until almost doubled in size. This bread is best if you bake it when it's slightly underrisen; if you overproof it, you'll get flat loaves. They'll taste delicious, but they won't look beautiful.

9. Thirty minutes before baking, preheat the oven to 425° F. Place a baking stone in the oven to preheat and place an empty water pan directly below the stone.

10. When the loaves have almost doubled, shake the peel or pan slightly to be sure they aren't sticking and slide them onto the baking stone. You may have to rearrange them carefully so they won't grow into each other as they expand during baking. Quickly pour 1 cup of very hot water into the water pan and immediately shut the oven door. After 1 minute, using a plant sprayer, mist the loaves 6 to 8 times and shut the oven door. Repeat the misting procedure 1 minute later.

11. Bake for 20 minutes, then reduce the oven temperature to 375° F and bake for 20 to 25 minutes longer, until the loaves sound hollow when tapped on the bottom. Transfer the loaves to a rack and allow to cool completely before serving. This bread freezes well, wrapped tightly in aluminum foil and then in plastic wrap or a heavy-duty freezer bag.

6

Sunny
Loaves

♦

Semolina Breads
from Our Hearth
to Yours

The natural golden yellow color of semolina
bread is beautiful and enticing. The appealing look
and flavor of semolina loaves come from flour that
has been ground from durum wheat, the hardest
variety of wheat. When the germ and bran are
stripped away, the inner part of the wheat may be
ground into semolina, a very coarse, gritty flour or
meal good for making pasta. Ground finer, the meal
becomes a silky golden flour, often labeled patent
durum flour. This flour is high in gluten and makes
for easy kneading and bouncy loaves. It is very
good for bread baking, especially when mixed with
a little unbleached flour to reduce the gluten
slightly. Do not substitute semolina flour for
durum flour–it is too coarse and will not make
good bread. If durum flour is not available in a
health food store in your area, buy it through a
mail-order source (see page 189).

Golden Italian Semolina Loaves

A straight dough bread

"Italian bread" has its own definition in New York City. When we first opened the bakery, people often came in and asked for Italian bread. We would say, "Our Semolina Black Sesame Bread is inspired by an Italian recipe, and we have this beautiful focaccia today." "NO, I want Italian bread," they would insist. Eventually we realized that the bread they wanted was a pointed white loaf with a soft, plain crumb and a medium-thick, golden crust. It has become a staple of local bakeries because of the large number of Italian immigrants in New York who grew up on this bread. It can be found in every area supermarket in a red, white, or green paper bag. We find that version of Italian bread cottony and uninteresting. Having traveled in Italy, we know that Italians make hundreds of kinds of breads based on centuries-old baking traditions. For us, these robust, sophisticated, and delicious semolina breads are *real* Italian bread. Our semolina version of the New York loaf is moist, chewy, and delightfully different from the supermarket variety.

Makes two 14-ounce loaves

- -

2 teaspoons active dry yeast

¼ cup (2 ounces) very warm water (105° to 115°F)

4 cups plus 1 tablespoon (18½ ounces) patent durum flour

2 teaspoons kosher salt

1¼ cups (10 ounces) cool water (75°F)

Sesame seeds for topping (optional)

- -

1. Mix the yeast and warm water together in a small bowl and stir with a fork to dissolve the yeast. Let the mixture stand for 3 minutes.

2. Mix the flour and salt together in a large mixing bowl. Add the yeast mixture and the cool water and, using your fingers, mix the dough into a shaggy mass.

3. Move the dough to a lightly floured work surface and knead for 4 minutes. If the dough feels stiff or dry, gradually knead in 1 to 2 tablespoons of water. The dough should feel slightly firm and very smooth and supple.

4. Place the dough on a clean spot on the work surface, cover with a towel, and let rest for 20 minutes. (This rest period is the autolyse.)

5. Very lightly flour the work surface and knead the dough for 5 to 7 minutes. At first the dough will be sticky, then it will become stretchy and supple. Don't be tempted to add extra flour; the dough will become soft and smooth without it.

6. Lightly dust a clean bowl with flour. Place the dough in it and cover with oiled plastic wrap or a towel. Allow the dough to rise at room temperature (75° to 77° F) for about 2 hours, until it has doubled in volume (an indentation made by poking your finger deep into the dough should not spring back).

7. Place the dough on a very lightly floured surface and gently deflate it. Divide it into 2 equal pieces and shape each piece into a bâtard (see page 24). If desired, mist or lightly brush the loaves with water and spread the sesame seeds on top.

8. Generously sprinkle a peel or the back of a baking sheet with cornmeal or line it with parchment paper. Place the loaves on the peel or pan, cover with oiled plastic wrap, and let rise at room temperature for about 1 hour, until they have almost doubled. These loaves should be baked slightly underproofed; if they begin to rise very quickly, place them in the refrigerator for 20 to 30 minutes to slow the rise.

9. Thirty minutes before baking, preheat the oven to 425° F. Place a baking stone in the oven to preheat and place an empty water pan directly below the stone.

10. Use a *lame* or a sharp razor blade to score each loaf gently three times from tip to tip, holding the blade at a 30-degree angle (cutting at this angle will result in a ridge on the edge of each cut as the loaves bake). Gently slide the loaves onto the baking stone. Pour 1 cup of very hot water into the water pan and immediately shut the oven door. After 1 minute, using a plant sprayer, quickly mist the loaves 6 to 8 times, then shut the oven door. Mist the loaves again after 1 minute.

11. Bake for 15 minutes, then reduce the oven temperature to 400° F and bake for about 25 minutes longer, until the loaves are a golden yellow-brown and sound hollow when they are tapped on the bottom. Place the loaves on a wire rack to cool. Serve with extra-virgin olive oil for dipping.

Semolina Beehive with Black Sesame Seeds

An overnight sponge starter bread

We make this beautiful golden loaf every day at the bakery. We shape the loaves we sell into a distinctive S shape but we also like this pretty, spiraled beehive coil. The yellow bread is studded with black sesame seeds, which provide an interesting textural contrast and a delicious nutty flavor. Of all of our breads, this is the favorite of several of our employees. It goes well with so many foods and is so easy that you will want to make it again and again.

Makes 2 large loaves

- -

1 teaspoon active dry yeast

¼ cup (2 ounces) very warm water (105° to 115°F)

1¼ cups plus 3 tablespoons (11½ ounces) cool water (75°F)

1¼ cups (10 ounces) Sponge Starter (page 40)

4 cups (18 ounces) patent durum flour

⅓ cup (2 ounces) coarse yellow cornmeal

¼ cup black sesame seeds

1 tablespoon plus 1 teaspoon kosher salt

- -

1. Combine the yeast and warm water in a medium bowl and stir with a fork to dissolve the yeast. Let the mixture stand for 3 minutes.

2. Add the cool water and sponge to the yeast mixture and mix with your fingers for about 2 minutes, breaking up the sponge. The mixture should look milky and slightly foamy.

3. Whisk the flour, cornmeal, 2 tablespoons of the sesame seeds, and the salt together in a large bowl. Pour the sponge mixture on top and mix with your fingers until the dough forms a sticky mass.

4. Move the dough to a lightly floured surface and knead for 5 to 7 minutes, until smooth and elastic, using as little additional flour as possible.

5. Shape the dough into a loose ball and place it in a lightly oiled bowl. Turn the dough to coat with oil, cover the bowl tightly with oiled plastic wrap, and let the dough rise at room temperature (75° to 77° F) for 1 hour, or until it looks slightly puffy but has not doubled.

6. Refrigerate the dough for at least 8 hours, or preferably overnight, to let the flavors develop and the dough relax.

7. Take the dough from the refrigerator and allow it to warm up and rise slowly, about 1 to 2 hours.

8. Divide the dough into 2 equal pieces. On a lightly floured surface, gently flatten one piece of dough into a rectangle, then shape it into a cylinder by rolling it up tightly from left to right, as if you were shaping a baguette (see page 26). Seal the seam well. Place both hands over the center of the cylinder and roll it back and forth from the center out to the ends to elongate it until you have a rope about 20 inches long. Roll the rope lightly in flour and shape it into a coil, following the instructions on page 171. Repeat with the second piece of dough.

9. Line a peel or the back of a baking sheet with parchment paper and generously sprinkle it with cornmeal. (If your baking stone is small, you may need both a peel and a pan for rising because these loaves are so large.) Place the loaves seam side down on the peel and/or baking sheet; if they are placed side by side, leave 3 to 4 inches between them for rising. With a plant mister, lightly spray a stream of water into the groove of each coil. Pour the remaining 2 tablespoons of black sesame seeds in a stream into the groove of each coil. Cover the loaves with oiled plastic wrap and allow them to rise for 1 to 2 hours, or until almost doubled in bulk but still slightly underproofed. (If you must bake the loaves in two batches, refrigerate one loaf after the first hour of rising to stop the rising process, then let the loaf finish rising at room temperature while the other one bakes.)

10. Thirty minutes before baking, preheat the oven to 425° F. Place a baking stone in the oven to preheat and place an empty water pan directly below the stone.

11. Gently slide the coils onto the baking stone. Pour 1 cup of very hot water into the water pan and immediately shut the oven door. After 1 minute, quickly mist the loaves 6 to 8 times, then quickly shut the oven door. Mist the loaves again 1 minute later.

12. Bake for 20 minutes, then reduce the oven temperature to 375° F and bake for 15 to 20 minutes longer, until the loaves are golden yellow and sound slightly hollow when tapped on the bottom. Transfer the bread to a rack to cool completely before slicing. (If necessary, let the baking stone heat for 5 minutes, then bake the second loaf.)

Semolina Bread with Apricots and Sage

An overnight sponge starter bread

This lovely, golden bread is both sweet and savory. Apricots sweeten the loaves and chopped fresh sage adds an earthy, grassy flavor. The bread is shaped like a sunflower and looks impressive on a buffet table. It also makes a unique gift. We like to serve it with fish or poultry and we've even diced the bread to add to Thanksgiving turkey stuffing. With its crunchy cornmeal crust and dense, almost cake-like interior, this bread is sure to please.

Makes three 1-pound round loaves

1½ cups (8 ounces) dried apricots, diced

1 teaspoon active dry yeast

¼ cup (2 ounces) very warm water (105° to 115°F)

1½ cups plus 1 tablespoon (12½ ounces) cool water (75°F)

1¼ cups (10 ounces) Sponge Starter (page 40)

4 cups plus 1 tablespoon (18 ounces) patent durum flour

1 cup (6 ounces) coarse yellow cornmeal

1 tablespoon plus 2 teaspoons kosher salt

3 tablespoons fresh sage leaves, chopped

1. Place the apricots in a large measuring cup or deep bowl, and add warm water to come just below the top of the fruit. Set aside to soak.

2. Combine the yeast and warm water in a medium bowl and stir with a fork to dissolve the yeast. Let the mixture stand for 3 minutes.

3. Add the cool water and sponge to the yeast mixture and mix with your fingers for about 2 minutes, breaking up the sponge. The mixture should look milky and slightly foamy.

4. Whisk 4 cups of the flour, ½ cup of the cornmeal, and the salt together in a large bowl. Pour in the sponge mixture and mix with your fingers until the dough forms a sticky mass. If the dough feel too stiff, add 1 tablespoon of water.

5. Move the dough to a very lightly floured surface and knead for 5 to 8 minutes, until smooth, elastic, supple, and somewhat resilient. The dough will still be somewhat firm. Flatten the dough out slightly and cover it with a towel. Let rest for 10 minutes.

6. Drain the apricots and toss them with the remaining 1 tablespoon flour. Add the sage and toss again. Stretch the dough into a rectangle and spread the apricot mixture evenly over it. Press the fruit into the dough, then fold the dough in thirds like a business letter. Knead the dough for about 1 minute to distribute the apricots. Don't worry if some pop out; they can easily be incorporated after the dough has rested.

7. Shape the dough into a loose ball and place it in a lightly oiled bowl, along with any loose apricots. Turn the dough to coat with oil, cover the bowl tightly with oiled plastic wrap, and let the dough rise at room temperature (75° to 77° F) for 1 hour, or until it looks slightly puffy but has not doubled.

8. Refrigerate the dough for at least 8 hours, or preferably overnight, to let the flavors develop and the dough relax.

9. Take the dough from the refrigerator and gently dump it onto a work surface to deflate it. Gently fold the dough in half, then in half again, and then again to incorporate all the apricots, and reshape it into a ball. Place it in the bowl, cover with oiled plastic wrap, and let sit at room temperature for $1^1/_2$ to 3 hours, until it warms up and begins to rise.

10. Place the dough on a lightly floured surface. Divide it into 3 equal pieces (about 18 ounces each). Shape each piece into a boule (see page 26).

11. Spread the remaining $^1/_2$ cup cornmeal in a shallow pan. Using a plant mister, spray each loaf generously, then roll the loaves in the cornmeal, coating them completely. Place the loaves on the work surface and press down to flatten them into disks about 8 inches in diameter. Let rest for 10 minutes.

12. Line a peel and a baking sheet with parchment paper and sprinkle with cornmeal. Place one disk on the peel and the others on the baking sheet. Place an inverted mug or glass with a 2- to 3-inch opening in the center of one disk. Press it gently into the dough, and use a dough cutter to cut the dough into 4 wedges, starting at the edge of the glass. Cut those wedges in half, then in half again, so you have 16 segments. Give each cut segment a quarter-turn so a cut side is facing upward (see photograph, page 98). Remove the glass, leaving an uncut area in the center of the loaf. Repeat the procedure with the other 2 disks. Let the loaves rise at room temperature for 1 to $1^1/_2$ hours, until they have almost doubled in volume.

continued

13. Thirty minutes before baking, pre-heat the oven to 425° F. Place a baking stone in the top third of the oven to preheat and position a rack below the baking stone for the baking sheet.

14. Loosen the loaf from the peel and gently slide it onto the stone. Place the pan of bread on the rack below. Using the plant sprayer, mist the loaves and the oven walls 8 to 10 times, then quickly shut the oven door. About 1 minute later, mist the loaves again. Repeat the misting procedure 1 minute later.

15. Bake for 10 minutes, then reduce the oven temperature to 350° F and bake for 10 to 15 minutes longer, until the loaves are a golden yellow-brown and sound hollow when tapped on the bottom. The crust should be firm but not too dark; watch the bread carefully–it will brown quickly during the last few minutes of baking. Place the loaves on wire racks and let cool before serving.

Semolina with Apricots and Sage

Demonstration of shaping and cutting the sunflower

Note: If you want to use this bread for sandwiches, as we recommend in our sandwich section (page 133), it is best to shape the loaves into logs instead of the round sunflower shape. Or you could shape two sunflowers and one log, and enjoy them both.

7

Flat and Flavorful

◆

Pizza and Focaccia

Take a piece of bread dough and flatten it, spread it with a few toppings, and bake it to crusty golden perfection. Do you have pizza or focaccia? These flatbreads are so similar it's often difficult to tell them apart. We like our pizza thin and crisp, more crust than bread, and we like our focaccia thick, moist, and tender, more bread than crust. And we like both of them dressed with only the best fresh seasonal ingredients to complement, not overpower, the flavor and texture of the bread. It's easy to see the bread part of pizza and focaccia as secondary to the topping. But at the bakery we put just as much effort into developing these recipes as we put into creating our signature breads, because even the most exquisite topping won't hide a crust of inferior quality. If you start out with an incredible crust, you can create a masterpiece by adding even the simplest fresh topping.

A Versatile Pizza Crust with Tempting Toppings

A straight dough bread

In Manhattan, pizza is practically a way of life. You can't walk two blocks without seeing at least one "famous" quick-service establishment where you can run in (we're always running in Manhattan) and buy fresh hot pizza by the slice. Long-time New Yorkers experience culture shock when they find themselves in a town where the only way they can get a slice of pizza is to purchase an entire pie!

At the bakery, the staff likes to spread leftover dough on an oiled sheet pan, top it with whatever cooked vegetables are on hand, and sprinkle on a little fresh rosemary and Parmesan cheese. Throw it in the deck oven to bake and voilà! A simple-to-make and simply delicious pizza treat for the entire staff.

Making pizza in your own kitchen can be just as easy. All you need is good-quality bread dough for the crust, a selection of vegetables and/or meat, a little cheese, and some herbs for extra flavor. Sauce is optional. Instead of tomato sauce, we like to use sliced or diced ripe fresh tomatoes when they're in season. The secret to great pizza is to use fresh ingredients and to use them sparingly. Keep it simple and try to keep it small. While the idea of creating a big, beautiful sixteen-inch pizza is appealing, the reality is often a culinary disaster if you're inexperienced or lack all the necessary professional equipment. We've found the easiest size to work with in a home kitchen is a disk no larger than ten inches in diameter or a twelve-by-seventeen-inch rectangle to fit a baking sheet. (It doesn't matter whether or not the baking sheet has a rim when making pizza.) A baking stone is mandatory if you want to achieve that satisfying crackly crust.

> ### Fresh Tomato Sauce
>
> *To make fresh tomato sauce, peel and seed 5 medium ripe tomatoes. Coarsely chop them and puree in a blender or food processor with 1 or 2 cloves of garlic. Heat the puree briefly, 5 to 10 minutes, in a small saucepan, just to soften the intensity of the raw garlic and reduce some of the liquid. Season with salt and pepper to taste. Store, refrigerated in an airtight container, for up to 5 days. Use on pizza or pasta. (Makes 1½ to 2 cups.)*

This is one of our favorite recipes for pizza crust. It includes a little coarse cornmeal for extra crunch. You can vary the recipe by using different vegetables and herbs to complement the flavors of the topping ingredients you choose. Try adding minced onion, finely diced red bell pepper, or chopped imported olives to the dough. Or simply leave it plain. In this version we use garlic and oregano to complement the eggplant topping.

• •

Dough

1⅔ cups (13½ ounces) very warm water (105° to 115°F)

1 tablespoon active dry yeast

4½ cups (20¼ ounces) unbleached all-purpose flour

⅓ cup (2 ounces) coarse cornmeal

1 tablespoon olive oil

1 tablespoon garlic, minced, or 1 teaspoon dried
   minced garlic

2½ teaspoons dried oregano

1 tablespoon plus 2 teaspoons kosher salt

1 teaspoon cayenne pepper (optional)

Savory Eggplant Sauté (recipe follows)

Olive oil for brushing

Jalapeño pepper slices, fresh or canned (optional)

3 cups (10½ ounces) mozzarella cheese, shredded

1 cup (4 ounces) Parmesan cheese, grated

> *Almost any good-quality plain or savory dough can be stretched to make a pizza crust. Try using the dough for our Golden Whole Wheat Bread (page 55), The Baguette (page 59), Coarse Cracked Corn with Four Peppers (page 72), or Semolina Beehive with Black Sesame Seeds (page 94). It takes about 9 ounces of dough for one 10-inch disk, or 18 ounces for one 12 by 17-inch rectangle.*

• •

Equipment: Two 12 by 17-inch baking sheets, lined with
parchment paper and lightly oiled with olive oil,
if making rectangular pizzas

1. For the dough: Combine all of the ingredients in a large bowl and stir vigorously with your hand for 1 to 2 minutes, until all the flour is moistened and a shaggy dough mass has formed. (Note: This is a very warm dough, so it's not necessary to dissolve the yeast in water first to give it a head start.)

2. Move the dough to a lightly floured work surface and knead until it is smooth and supple, about 7 minutes. This dough should not be too dry, or it will be difficult to stretch when you're shaping the pizza. If necessary, add water 1 tablespoon at a time until you have a soft, pliable, but not mushy dough. (Note: If you are using fresh garlic, it may give the dough a somewhat sticky texture; handle the dough gently and keep your hands and the work surface lightly floured.)

continued

3. Gently shape the dough into a loose ball. Put it in a lightly oiled bowl, turn to coat with oil, and cover it with oiled plastic wrap. Let it rise at room temperature (75° to 77° F) until it has doubled in volume, about 1 hour.

4. Preheat the oven to 425°F and place a baking stone in the oven to preheat for at least 30 minutes.

5. When the dough has doubled, loosen it from the bowl with lightly floured hands and gently pour it

This recipe makes enough dough for four 10-inch pizzas, but you probably won't be able to bake more than two at once in your oven. If you're making pizza for a group, we recommend that you use the dough to make two large rectangular pizzas. On the other hand, if you use only half the dough, you can freeze the other half for later use. Without allowing the dough to rise, wrap it in aluminum foil, then place it in a heavy-duty plastic freezer bag and freeze. The day before you're going to use it, move it to the refrigerator to thaw. Let the dough sit at room temperature for about 3 hours, or until doubled in volume. Start with Step 4 to make pizza.

onto a floured work surface. Divide it into 4 equal pieces if making round pies or 2 equal pieces if making large rectangular pizzas. Shape each piece into a loose ball, cover it with plastic wrap, and let rest on the work surface for 10 minutes. (This allows the dough to relax so it's easier to shape.)

6. To make round pies: Place a dough ball on a lightly floured work surface and press down to flatten slightly. From the center, with your fingers gently press the dough out to a 10-inch circle of uniform (about ¼ inch) thickness. Do not to tear the dough; you may have to lift the edges gently and shake the dough slightly to encourage the stretching. (You can also use a rolling pin; flour the table and the top of the dough lightly and lift and turn the disk frequently as you roll to be sure the dough doesn't stick.) If the dough resists stretching, let it rest again for 2 to 5 minutes–or until it will let you stretch it again. Keep letting the dough rest as necessary until you achieve the size you want.

Dust a peel or the bottom of a baking sheet generously with coarse cornmeal. Gently move the dough onto the peel or sheet. Shake the peel or pan gently to be sure the dough is not sticking to the surface (add more cornmeal if necessary) and repeat the process with a second ball of dough. (If you are making 4 pies, assemble and bake them in two batches; don't start shaping and topping the second batch until the first one is in the oven.)

To make rectangular pizzas: Line two 12 by 17-inch baking sheets with parchment and brush a little olive oil over the parchment and the sides of the pans. Place one of the dough balls on a lightly floured work surface and press down to flatten it slightly. Gently press and stretch the dough into a 9 by 12-inch rectangle of uniform thickness; you can lift the dough gently up off the worktable and hold it by one end to let gravity help you with some of the stretching. Be careful not to tear the dough. Place the rectangle in the center of one of the prepared pans and continue stretching it gently until it fills the pan. Try to keep the thickness of the dough uniform. If the dough resists stretching, let it rest for 2 to 5 minutes before continuing (see instructions for making round pies). Repeat with the remaining dough.

7. Lightly brush each round or rectangle of dough with olive oil, being sure to brush the edges. Using 1 cup of the eggplant topping for each 10-inch pie and 2 cups for each rectangular pizza, spread the topping evenly over the dough, leaving a $^3/_4$-inch border around the edges. If you are using jalapeño peppers, spread as many slices as you like evenly over the filling. Sprinkle $^3/_4$ cup (generous $2^1/_2$ ounces) of the mozzarella cheese and $^1/_4$ cup (1 ounce) of the Parmesan evenly over the top of each 10-inch pie, or double the amount for each rectangle.

8. For the round pies: Shake the peel or baking sheet to be sure the dough isn't sticking, then slide it onto the baking stone. If only one disk fits on your stone, bake the second pie on a parchment-lined pan on an oven rack above the baking stone. Once the crust has set, about halfway through the baking time, rotate the 2 pizzas so each bakes for some time on the baking stone; this has to be done very carefully, and is best done using a peel. Slide the pizza on the stone onto the peel and set it out of harm's way while you slide the second pizza off the baking pan and onto the stone. Then use the peel to slide the first pizza directly onto the oven rack above the stone.

9. For the rectangular pizzas: Put one pan on the baking stone and one on a rack above it. Watch the pan on the stone carefully to be sure the crust doesn't burn on the bottom. You may want to rotate the pans from top to bottom halfway through the baking time. (If you are baking just one pizza, you can put the pan directly on the baking stone or place it on the oven rack above the stone; the stone gives a crisper crust, but you must watch carefully so the bottom doesn't burn.)

Bake the 10-inch pizzas for about 10 to 13 minutes, the 12 by 17-inch pizzas for 20 to 25 minutes, or until the crust is crisp and golden and the cheese is completely melted and bubbly but not browned. Too much browning will make the cheese stringy and tough.

10. Use the peel or a flat baking sheet to remove each round pizza from the oven and slide it onto a cutting surface. Using a pizza wheel or a long chef's knife, cut each pie into 4 wedges.

Or let the pan pizzas cool in the pans on a rack for about 5 minutes. Use a sturdy metal spatula to loosen the crust of each pizza from the edges of the pan, then slide the spatula under the parchment, pick up one end, and slide the pie out of the pan onto a cutting surface, parchment and all. Slide the parchment out from under the pie and discard it, and use a pizza wheel or a long chef's knife to cut the pizza into 8 to 10 pieces.

continued

Savory Eggplant Sauté

This is a generous recipe and you won't need all of it to top your pizzas. But the topping is delicious by itself and can be served in a variety of different ways. Make a meal of the leftovers with some steamed brown rice, toss them with a little cooked pasta, stuff them into a pita bread pocket, use them on focaccia, or simply freeze them for your next pizza.

Makes enough topping for four 10-inch or two 12 by 17-inch pizzas, with leftovers

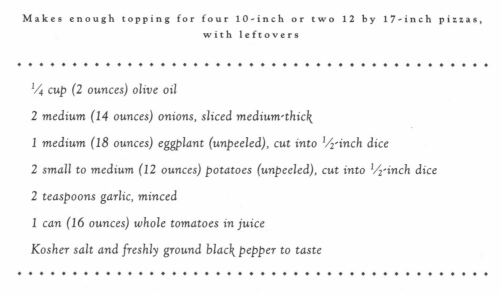

¼ cup (2 ounces) olive oil

2 medium (14 ounces) onions, sliced medium-thick

1 medium (18 ounces) eggplant (unpeeled), cut into ½-inch dice

2 small to medium (12 ounces) potatoes (unpeeled), cut into ½-inch dice

2 teaspoons garlic, minced

1 can (16 ounces) whole tomatoes in juice

Kosher salt and freshly ground black pepper to taste

1. Heat the olive oil in a large nonstick pan over medium heat. Add the onions, eggplant, potatoes, and garlic and cook, stirring occasionally, until lightly browned, about 10 minutes.

2. Pour the tomatoes into a bowl and crush them with a fork or your fingers. Add them, along with their juice, to the vegetables and stir to combine. (Or just crush the tomatoes between your fingers directly into the pan.) Season with salt and pepper to taste. Turn the heat to low, cover the pan, and simmer, stirring occasionally, for about 15 to 20 minutes, until the potatoes are tender but not mushy. Remove the pan from the heat, uncover it, and let cool before using to top pizza. Refrigerate or freeze any leftovers.

Rich Focaccia with Basil Oil

A sponge starter bread

Unlike our pizza dough, this includes a little milk to keep it tender and moist, and it is allowed a second rise to get a thicker, more bread-like texture. Just before baking, the dough is given the traditional "dimpling." The dimples, made by firmly pressing your fingertips into the dough, help flavor and moisten the bread by capturing some of the olive oil that is brushed over the surface; they also keep the dough from puffing up and forming a domed center as it bakes. Traditionally, only a single ingredient is used as a topping for focaccia, spread sparsely over the top or sprinkled in a decorative pattern. The bread is the focal point, the topping an accent.

Focaccia can be eaten like pizza, or you can split it in half and stuff it to make an unusual sandwich. It can be served warm or at room temperature, but it is best eaten the same day it is baked.

Makes two 8-inch square breads or one 12 by 17-inch bread

* *

1/2 teaspoon active dry yeast

1 3/4 cups plus 2 tablespoons (15 ounces) warm water (85° to 90°F)

1 1/2 cups (12 ounces) Sponge Starter (page 40)

4 1/2 cups (22 1/2 ounces) high-gluten (bread) flour

1 tablespoon plus 1 1/4 teaspoons kosher salt

2 tablespoons plus 1 1/2 teaspoons (1 1/4 ounces) olive oil

2 tablespoons plus 1 1/2 teaspoons (1 1/4 ounces) milk

Sliced tomatoes, sautéed onions, or pitted imported olives (whole, sliced, or in chunks) for topping

1/2 cup (4 ounces) Basil Oil (recipe follows)

Additional olive oil and kosher salt for topping

Fresh basil leaves for garnish

* *

Equipment: Two 8-inch square baking pans, or one 12 by 17-inch baking sheet, lined with parchment paper and lightly oiled with olive oil

1. Place the yeast and warm water in a large bowl. Stir with a fork to dissolve the yeast and allow to stand for about 3 minutes.

continued

2. Add the sponge to the yeast mixture and mix with your fingers for 1 to 2 minutes to break up the sponge. The mixture should be foamy. Add the flour and mix it in with your hand, lifting the wet mixture over the flour to incorporate it. When the dough becomes a shaggy mass, knead it in the bowl until it becomes smooth and somewhat elastic, about 5 minutes. Cover it with plastic wrap and let rest for 20 minutes. (This rest period is the autolyse.)

3. Add the salt to the dough and knead briefly to incorporate it. Gradually add the oil and milk and knead gently until all the liquid has been incorporated.

4. Move the dough to a lightly floured work surface and knead until it is very smooth, silky, and elastic, about 7 to 10 minutes. The dough will be sticky, so you will need to keep the work surface and your hands lightly floured, but don't overdo it–the dough should be wet but supple and springy.

5. Put the dough in a lightly oiled bowl, turn it to coat with oil, and cover it tightly with oiled plastic wrap. (At this point, the dough can be refrigerated until the next day.) Let the dough rise at room temperature (75° to 77°F) until almost doubled in volume, about $2^1/_2$ hours. (If you refrigerate the dough, it may rise adequately overnight; if not, let it rise at room temperature until doubled.)

6. Line two 8-inch square pans or one 12 by 17-inch baking sheet with baking parchment. Brush the parchment and the sides of the pan(s) generously with olive oil.

7. When the dough has risen, loosen it from the bowl with lightly floured hands and gently pour it onto a floured work surface. If using two pans, cut it into 2 equal pieces. Place half the dough in the center of each square pan, or place all the dough in the center of the rectangular baking sheet, and press on it gently to stretch it evenly out to the edges of the pan(s). Be careful not to tear the dough. If the dough resists stretching, let it rest for 2 to 5 minutes, or until it becomes supple enough to stretch again. (If the dough is dry, you may have to repeat the resting/stretching procedure several times.) Brush the top of the dough lightly with olive oil, cover with lightly oiled plastic wrap, and let rise for 1 to 2 hours, or until the dough has doubled and fills the pan(s) (a finger pressed into the dough will leave an indentation).

8. Thirty minutes before baking, preheat the oven to 425°F and place a baking stone in the oven to preheat.

9. Arrange the tomatoes, sautéed onions, or olives in a decorative random or symmetrical pattern on the dough, being careful not to deflate it. With your fingertips, randomly press dimples all over the dough, making deep impressions that go all the way down to the pan bottom(s)–one every 2 to 3 inches is enough. Don't press too vigorously, or you may make holes in the dough or deflate it. Stir the basil oil and lightly brush it over the dough, allowing it to pool in the dimples. Sprinkle with kosher salt.

10. If you are using two pans, put one on the baking stone and one on a rack above. For just one focaccia, put the pan directly on the baking stone or on the rack above the stone; the stone gives a crisper bottom crust but you must watch carefully so the bottom doesn't burn. Using a plant sprayer, mist the focaccia 6 to 8 times, then quickly shut the oven door. Repeat the misting procedure after 1 minute, then again 1 minute later.

11. Bake for 15 minutes, then reduce the oven temperature to 350° F and bake for 15 to 25 minutes longer, or until golden brown and crusty but still very soft inside. If using two pans, watch the pan on the stone carefully to be sure the focaccia doesn't burn on the bottom, and rotate the pans halfway through the baking time.

12. Remove the focaccia from the oven and immediately brush it lightly with basil oil. Cool in the pan(s) 10 minutes, then carefully slide it onto a cooling rack. Remove the parchment (to prevent steam from softening the bottom crust) and let cool. Serve warm or at room temperature, with a few basil leaves and cut into squares.

Basil Oil

Makes about 1 cup

. . . .

1 large bunch fresh basil

$\frac{1}{8}$ teaspoon, or to taste, kosher salt

$\frac{3}{4}$ cup (6 ounces) extra-virgin olive oil

. . . .

1. Prepare an ice water bath in a large bowl. Bring a medium saucepan of water to a boil. Blanch the basil leaves in the boiling water for 30 seconds. Drain them in a strainer and immediately put them in the ice water bath to cool.

2. Drain the basil and squeeze out the excess moisture. Place the blanched leaves in a food processor or a blender and add the salt. Turn on the machine and slowly pour in the olive oil. Continue processing to a smooth puree.

3. Transfer the basil oil to a container and put a piece of plastic wrap directly on the surface to help preserve the bright green color. The oil will keep for about 2 weeks in the refrigerator as long as the plastic wrap stays in contact with the surface. Use the basil oil and pureed basil as a topping for focaccia, on cooked pasta, or in a salad dressing.

More Topping
Suggestions

The sky is the limit when it comes to creating combinations of ingredients for topping pizza or focaccia. Often you can put together a delicious concoction with what is on hand in your refrigerator. Fresh raw vegetables or leftover cooked vegetables (as long as they're not mushy), cooked meats, fresh herbs, and almost any kind of cheese, such as mozzarella, Monterey Jack, Fontina, Parmesan, or Romano, or even goat cheese, blue cheese, and Brie can be used. Herbed oils, vinaigrettes, and of course tomato sauces can be used to add flavor and moistness. Below are some of our favorite combinations. These can be used with equal enjoyment on either pizza or focaccia. In general, use the toppings sparingly on focaccia and somewhat more generously on pizza.

◆ **Portobello mushrooms and onions with fresh sage and grated imported Parmesan cheese.** Slice mushrooms and onions about $1/4$ inch thick and sauté them briefly, about 5 minutes, in a little extra virgin olive oil. Let cool. Slice a generous number of fresh sage leaves diagonally into $1/4$-inch-wide strips and toss them lightly with the cooled vegetables (if they were just sprinkled on top of the vegetables, the leaves would burn during baking). Spread the vegetables over the dough, season with salt and pepper, sprinkle lightly with grated Parmesan, and bake. Note: If portobello mushrooms are unavailable, any type of wild or cultivated exotic mushroom can be used, such as shiitakes, oyster mushrooms, porcini (cèpes), and/or chanterelles.

◆ **Pesto sauce and fresh plum tomatoes.** Use 2 to 3 tablespoons pesto sauce for each 10-inch pizza or 9-inch focaccia, 6 tablespoons for each 12 by 17-inch pizza or focaccia.

Spread the pesto evenly over the dough and top with slices of ripe plum tomatoes (thin slices for focaccia, slightly thicker slices for pizza). Brush the tomatoes lightly with olive oil or basil oil and sprinkle on salt and pepper, and a little Parmesan cheese if you wish. After baking, garnish with a few fresh basil leaves. Note: For a variation, make the pesto sauce with arugula instead of basil and toasted walnuts instead of pine nuts; use small arugula leaves for garnish.

◆ **Quattro stagione with olives, prosciutto, mushrooms, and artichoke hearts.** This topping is really better suited to pizza than focaccia because the distinct flavors of the individual ingredients are more noticeable on a thinner crust. Also, the ingredients are best layered generously, which is undesirable for focaccia. *Quattro stagione* means "four seasons," for the four main ingredients of the topping. Spread a thin layer of fresh tomato sauce over the pizza dough. Mentally divide it into quarters and fill one quarter with sliced fresh mushrooms, one quarter with olives (the Italians use them whole, pits and all), one quarter with artichoke hearts, and the last quarter with two or three thin slices of prosciutto, arranged in soft accordian folds, like loops of ribbon. Sprinkle a little olive oil and some herbs over if you like, and bake.

◆ **Red potatoes, sautéed leeks, and herbed goat cheese.** This is a great way to use up leftover potatoes. We prefer the texture of red potatoes, but any whole cooked potato will serve. Slice the potatoes about $1/4$ inch thick (they are easier to slice when cold), and toss them with a little of your favorite vinaigrette. Slice the white part of a leek into $1/4$-inch-thick slices, rinse well, and drain. Heat a little olive oil in a small skillet and sweat the leeks just until they're slightly softened; let cool. Spread the leeks and potatoes over the dough, season with salt and pepper to taste, and crumble herbed goat cheese lightly over all. Bake and enjoy!

Country Sourdough Boule

Tempting loaves in the retail store

Toy and Amy with their "daily bread"

Cooling loaves, fresh from the oven

Big Beautiful White Pan Loaf

Cinnamon Raisin Bread

Clockwise from lower left:
Golden Whole Wheat Bread,
Amy's Crusty Italian Loaf (whole and slices),
The Baguette

Garlic and walnuts

Left to right: *Coarse-Grained Whole Wheat
with Toasted Walnuts, Coarse Cracked Corn
with Four Peppers, Grainy Whole Wheat and
Seeds with Apricots, Prunes, and Raisins*

ABOVE
Toy's Anadama Bread

FACING PAGE
Left to right: *Dense Rye Bread, Fragrant Whole Wheat
Dinner Rolls, Organic Whole Wheat Sandwich Bread with
Oats and Pecans*

Apricots and sage

Semolina Bread with Apricots and Sage

Left to right: *Tangy Twenty-Four-Hour Sourdough,*
Wand of Walnut Scallion Bread, Rustic Round of
Black Olive and Sweet Red Pepper

Toasty Seeded Bread Twists

Left to right: *Fresh Rosemary Bread with Olive Oil, Amy's Organic Rye with Caraway and Mustard Seeds*

Clockwise from center:
Chewy Pumpernickel, Onion and Parmesan Loaf with Caraway, Lentil Rolls

Pecan Sticky Buns

ABOVE
Clockwise from left: *Hot Cross Buns, Chocolate Peanut Butter Buns,*
Suze's Buttermilk Oatmeal Scones, Maple Walnut and Fig Bread,
Autumn Pumpkin Bread with Pecans

FOLLOWING PAGE
Clockwise from lower left: *Toy's Teddy Bread, braided loaf,*
knot-shaped loaf, string-tied loaf, snail-shaped loaf

8

From Stretchy to Crispy

◆

Bread Sticks for Snacks and Parties

Bread sticks can be soft and chewy or thin and crispy. Either way they are easy to pick up and munch on the run. There are several different kinds of bread sticks here, one from our very popular line of sourdough bread twists. Let any savory dough rise once, then simply flatten it, cut it into thin strips, and stretch the sticks to the length you want. For soft, chewy bread sticks, leave them short; for thin and crispy sticks, stretch them further. Place them on a baking sheet, let them rise, and bake.

Specific instructions have been given for how to cut and stretch the bread sticks and we recommend that you follow them carefully. Because of the dough's gluten formation, it can be stretched only to a certain length. And stretch the dough and sticks in the same direction each time to get the longest sticks possible.

Chewy Olive and Thyme Sticks

An overnight sponge starter bread

These bread sticks are soft and chewy. They are about eight inches long and can be stood up in a short crock or a basket for an inviting party display. They are great dipped in a little extra virgin olive oil or served with ratatouille or roasted garlic. We recommend them as an accompaniment to a crisp vegetable salad in summer, or serve with a hot winter soup, such as one of potatoes and leeks or white beans and Swiss chard. They are great warm from the oven–and may not even make it to your party table!

Makes twenty-four 8-inch sticks

. . . .

1 teaspoon active dry yeast

¼ cup (2 ounces) very warm water (105° to 115°F)

1¼ cups (10 ounces) cool water (75°F)

1¼ cups (10 ounces) Sponge Starter (page 40)

4 cups (18 ounces) unbleached all-purpose flour

1 tablespoon kosher salt

½ cup (3½ ounces) imported black olives, pitted and chopped (see Note)

1 tablespoon plus 1 teaspoon fresh thyme leaves, chopped

Olive oil for brushing

. . . .

Equipment: Two 12 by 17-inch baking sheets, lined with parchment paper and sprinkled with cornmeal

1. Combine the yeast and warm water in a large bowl and stir with a fork to dissolve the yeast. Let stand for 3 minutes.

2. Add the cool water and sponge to the yeast mixture and mix with your fingers for 2 minutes, breaking up the sponge until it looks milky and slightly foamy.

3. Add the flour and salt and mix with your fingers to incorporate the flour, scraping the sides of the bowl and folding the dough over onto itself until it gathers into a mass.

4. Move the dough to a lightly floured surface and knead for 4 minutes, then return the dough to the bowl, place the olives and thyme on top of the dough, and let rest for 3 minutes. Mix with your fingers for 1 to 2 minutes, until the olives and herbs are well incorporated. The dough will be wet and slightly sticky.

5. Return the dough to the lightly floured surface and knead for 3 to 4 minutes, until smooth and elastic, using as little additional flour as possible. The dough will look a little bumpy from the olives and it should be slightly sticky.

6. Shape the dough into a loose ball and place it in an oiled bowl. Turn the dough to coat with oil, then cover the bowl tightly with oiled plastic wrap. Let the dough rise at room temperature (75° to 77° F) for 1 hour, or until it looks slightly puffy but has not doubled.

7. Refrigerate the dough overnight to let it relax and become more flavorful. (You can make the bread sticks the same day by allowing the dough to rise until doubled, about 2 hours, but it develops a better flavor and texture if refrigerated overnight.)

8. Take the dough from the refrigerator and let rise for $1^1/_2$ to $2^1/_2$ hours, until doubled in volume (a finger poked into the dough should leave a deep indentation).

9. Lightly flour the work surface. Gently loosen the dough from the bowl, then carefully turn the bowl upside down to release the dough in a flat mass, without folding it over itself. Stretch the dough into a 10 by 14-inch rectangle, then fold it in thirds as if you were folding a business letter. Pat the dough into a long narrow rectangle about 18 inches long and 6 inches wide. Lightly flour an 8 by 20-inch area on the work surface and sprinkle it with cornmeal. Set the dough on top and brush with a little olive oil. Using a dough cutter or bench scraper, cut the dough crosswise into 24 strips about $^3/_4$ inch wide.

10. Line two 12 by 17-inch baking sheets with parchment paper and sprinkle lightly with cornmeal. Lift each stick, stretch it to about $8^1/_2$ inches long, leaving it nice and plump, and place on the prepared pans, leaving $^1/_2$ inch between the sticks for rising. Cover the pans loosely with oiled plastic wrap and let the sticks rise for 30 to 45 minutes, until they are slightly puffy but have not doubled.

11. While the sticks are rising, preheat the oven to 425° F and position the oven racks in the middle and lower part of the oven.

12. Place the baking sheets in the oven and, using a plant sprayer, mist the sticks 8 to 10 times, then quickly shut the oven door. Spray the bread sticks again 1 minute later.

13. Bake for 10 minutes, then rotate the pans and reduce the oven temperature to 375° F. Bake for 15 to 20 minutes longer, until the sticks have browned on the bottom, the tops are light golden brown, and the crust is still soft. You may need to flip the sticks over on the pans partway through baking so they brown on both the top and bottom. Place the sticks on racks to cool slightly. These are great warm from the oven.

Note: We use Kalamatas or other large full-flavored black olives.

Aromatic Twigs with Anise, Coriander, and Mustard Seed

A straight dough bread

Everyone loves these bread sticks. They are loaded with flavor and are delicious on their own or served with boldly flavored dishes from the Mediterranean. Try them, for example, with whole fish braised with tomato and fresh fennel or with a clear vegetable soup accented with lemon and garlic. They are great served with beer or wine and are delicious dipped in hummus. Almost eighteen inches long, they make an eye-catching centerpiece displayed in a tall crock or a large glass vase. Be careful, though, because they can be fragile and may break if you try to transport them.

Makes 40 long twigs

. . . .

1¾ teaspoons active dry yeast

¼ cup (2 ounces) very warm water (105° to 115°F)

1 tablespoon plus 2 teaspoons mustard seeds

1 tablespoon plus 2 teaspoons anise seeds

1¾ cups (14 ounces) lukewarm water (85° to 90°F)

1½ tablespoons barley malt syrup (see Note)

⅓ cup plus 1 tablespoon (3 ounces) extra virgin olive oil

5¾ cups plus 1 tablespoon (26½ ounces) unbleached all-purpose flour

1 tablespoon plus 2 teaspoons ground coriander

3 tablespoons sesame seeds

Scant 2 tablespoons, plus extra for sprinkling, kosher salt

Olive oil for brushing

. . . .

Equipment: Three 12 by 17-inch baking sheets, lined with parchment paper and sprinkled with cornmeal

1. Combine the yeast and very warm water in a medium mixing bowl and stir with a fork to dissolve the yeast. Let stand for 3 minutes.

2. If you have a spice grinder, briefly pulse the mustard seeds and anise seeds to chop them slightly; do not grind them to a fine powder. You can also crush the spices using a mortar and pestle. Or spread then on a work surface, cover with a thin towel, and crush them with the bottom of a heavy pot.

3. Add the lukewarm water, barley malt, and olive oil to the yeast mixture and mix with a wire whisk until well combined.

4. Combine the flour, the mustard, anise, and coriander seeds, the sesame seeds, and salt in a large bowl. Pour the yeast mixture over the dry ingredients and mix with your fingers to blend well, scraping the sides of the bowl and folding the dough over onto itself until it gathers into a mass. The dough will be moist.

5. Move the dough to a lightly floured surface and knead for 5 to 8 minutes, until the dough becomes smooth and elastic, using as little additional flour as possible. The dough should be slightly firm, bouncy, and supple.

6. Pat the dough into a rectangle. Brush it on both sides with olive oil and place it on an oiled spot on your work surface. Cover it with plastic wrap and let it rise at room temperature (75° to 77° F) for 1 to 1$^1/_2$ hours, or until not quite doubled in volume.

7. Lightly flour a 12 by 22-inch area on the work surface and sprinkle it with fine cornmeal. Keeping the dough flat, gently move it to the cornmeal-sprinkled area and stretch and pat it to form a narrow rectangle about 20 inches long and 6 inches wide.

8. Line three 12 by 17-inch baking sheets with parchment paper and sprinkle them lightly with cornmeal. Brush the dough with a little olive oil and sprinkle it lightly with kosher salt. Using a dough cutter, cut the rectangle crosswise into 4 equal pieces. Cut each piece crosswise into 10 strips about $^1/_2$ inch wide. Lift each stick and carefully stretch it as evenly as possible until it is 14 to 18 inches long (the length of your baking sheets). Place the sticks on the prepared baking sheets, leaving $^1/_2$ inch between them for rising. Cover the pans loosely with oiled plastic wrap. Let the sticks rise for about 30 minutes, just until they are slightly puffy but not fully risen.

9. While the sticks are rising, preheat the oven to 425° F. Position the oven racks in the middle and lower parts of the oven.

continued

10. Place two of the baking sheets in the oven. (Leave the third pan of sticks at room temperature to bake when the oven is empty.) Using a plant sprayer, mist the sticks 6 to 8 times, then quickly shut the oven door. Spray the bread sticks again 2 minutes later.

11. Bake for 10 minutes, then rotate the pans and reduce the oven temperature to 400° F. Bake for 10 to 15 minutes longer, until the sticks are light brown and the thinner parts are crisp. Watch them carefully, because the thin parts brown quickly near the end of the baking time. (It's OK if the fatter parts are still slightly soft.) Place the sticks on racks to cool. Preheat the oven to 425° F again, then bake the remaining pan of bread sticks. These sticks can be served as soon as they cool slightly, but they will get crunchier over time and are very good served the next day.

Note: Buy barley malt in a natural food store. It is a sweet syrup made from barley, with a consistency like honey and a mild flavor all its own.

Moist Potato-Rye Wands with Dill

A sourdough bread

These moist potato-rye wands are chewy and satisfying. They are flavored with onion and dill seed and go well with hearty winter soups and stews. Try them with split pea soup with ham or with a German dish like cabbage and leek soup, studded with bits of bacon and splashed with vinegar. Of course they are great for vegetarian meals too, because they make a filling side dish. We made them for a fund-raising benefit, where they were served with just beer and wine. They received raves from many happy eaters!

Makes twenty 8-inch wands

- -

1 large potato (6 ounces), peeled and quartered

1 teaspoon active dry yeast

$\frac{1}{4}$ cup (2 ounces) very warm water (105° to 115°F)

1 cup (9 ounces) Rye Mother (page 47) (see box, page 85)

1 cup (8 ounces) cool water (75°F)

$\frac{1}{2}$ cup (2$\frac{1}{4}$ ounces) organic rye flour

3 cups (13$\frac{1}{2}$ ounces) unbleached all-purpose flour

1 tablespoon, plus extra for sprinkling, kosher salt

Scant $\frac{3}{4}$ cup (3$\frac{1}{2}$ ounces) medium onion, cut into small dice

1 teaspoon dill seed

Olive oil for brushing

Extra virgin olive oil for brushing (optional)

- -

Equipment: Two 12 by 17-inch baking sheets, lined with
parchment paper and sprinkled with cornmeal

1. Place the potato in a pot and add enough water to almost cover it. Salt the water, bring to a simmer, and cook until the potato is tender but still slightly firm. Drain, reserving the water for a future batch of dough if desired–yeast loves to feed on potato water! Let cool, then cut into $\frac{1}{4}$-inch dice.

2. While the potato is cooking, combine the yeast and warm water in a large bowl and stir with a fork to dissolve the yeast. Let stand for 3 minutes.

continued

3. To make a sponge, whisk the rye mother, cool water, and rye flour into the yeast mixture and whisk until it is free of lumps. Cover the bowl with plastic wrap and let rest for 30 minutes, or until the sponge begins to bubble.

4. Add the unbleached flour and salt to the sponge and mix with your fingers to form a sticky, gluey mass. Knead the dough in the bowl for 2 minutes, then move to a lightly floured surface and knead for 5 to 6 minutes longer, until an elastic dough has formed. If the dough feels too firm, knead in additional water a tablespoon at a time. The dough should feel slightly tacky but firm and supple. Dust the work surface lightly with flour and pat the dough into a rectangle. Let it rest, covered with oiled plastic wrap, for 20 minutes. (This rest period is the autolyse.)

5. Combine the diced potato, onion, and dill seed in a small bowl and set aside.

6. Gently stretch the dough into a larger rectangle. Spread the potoatoes and onions evenly over the dough and gently press them into it. Fold the dough in thirds, as if you were folding a business letter, and knead very gently until the potatoes and onions are well distributed, 1 to 3 minutes.

7. Shape the dough into a loose ball and place it in an oiled bowl, turning the dough to coat with oil. Cover the bowl tightly with oiled plastic wrap and let the dough rise at room temperature (75° to 77°F) for $1\frac{1}{2}$ to $2\frac{1}{2}$ hours, until doubled in volume.

8. Lightly flour an 8 by 22-inch area on the work surface and sprinkle it with cornmeal. Gently loosen the dough from the bowl and carefully turn the bowl upside down to release the dough in a flat mass; don't let it fold over onto itself. Gently stretch and pat the dough into a thick rectangle about 20 inches long and 6 inches wide.

9. Line two 12 by 17-inch baking sheets with parchment paper and sprinkle lightly with cornmeal. Brush the top of the dough with a little olive oil. Using a dough cutter, cut the rectangle crosswise into 4 equal pieces. Then cut each piece crosswise into 5 strips about 1 inch wide. Lift each stick and gently stretch it until it is $8\frac{1}{2}$ inches long, leaving it nice and plump. Place 10 sticks on each prepared baking sheet, leaving about $\frac{3}{4}$ inch between them for rising. Cover the pans loosely with oiled plastic wrap and let the sticks rise for 50 to 60 minutes, until slightly puffy but not fully risen.

10. While the sticks are rising, preheat the oven to 425°F and position the oven racks in the middle and lower part of the oven.

11. Sprinkle the sticks with a little kosher salt. Place the pans in the oven. Using a plant sprayer, mist the sticks 8 to 10 times and quickly shut the oven door. Spray the bread sticks again 2 minutes later.

12. Bake for 15 minutes, then rotate the pans and reduce the oven temperature to 375° F. Bake for 10 to 15 minutes longer, until the sticks are browned on the bottom and golden brown on top but still soft to the touch. (If the sticks are browning unevenly, rotate the pans once more.) Place the sticks on racks to cool. If you would like to make them a bit richer, brush the sticks with a little extra-virgin olive oil while they are still very hot. These need to cool enough so that they are not sticky inside, but they taste great warm. They are best eaten the day they are baked.

Toasty Seeded Bread Twists
A sourdough or straight dough bread

Seeded bread twists are one of the most popular snack items at the bakery. We like the combination of the delicious toasty seeds and the rich olive oil. We use our country sourdough to make the twists, which gives them a tangy, chewy dimension. You can use either the Country Sourdough Boule or the White Pan Loaves as your base. These twists are quite substantial and make a nice addition to a light meal of a salad or pasta. Some people even cut them in half lengthwise to make funny, narrow sandwich rolls. Spread a twist with some Brie or Camembert, add leafy lettuce and a tomato slice, and you may be surprised with a new kind of sandwich!

Makes twelve 6-inch twists

* *

1 recipe (2 pounds) Country Sourdough Boule (page 141), prepared through

Step 4 or White Pan Loaves (page 52), prepared through Step 5

⅓ cup (3 ounces) sesame seeds

¼ cup (2 ounces) poppy seeds

3 to 4 tablespoons (1½ to 2 ounces) extra virgin olive oil

Kosher salt for sprinkling

* *

Equipment: One 12 by 17-inch baking sheet, lined with
parchment paper and oiled

1. If using the country sourdough, knead the dough for 2 to 3 minutes, until it is smooth and supple. If using the white pan dough, proceed to Step 2.

continued

2. Dust your work surface with flour and place the kneaded dough on it. Cover the dough with oiled plastic wrap and allow it to rise at room temperature (75° to 77° F) for 1 hour. The dough will be soft but will not have doubled.

3. Combine the sesame and poppy seeds in a small bowl. Pat the dough into a 12-inch square. Sprinkle the dough lightly with about one third of the seed mixture. Fold the dough in thirds like a business letter, folding the top third of the square down and the bottom third up over the middle, to make a 12 by 4-inch rectangle. Gently pinch the open ends of the rectangle to seal. Using a plant sprayer, generously mist the dough. Coat both sides of the dough completely with the remaining seed mixture; make sure there are no bare spots. Gently brush the dough on both sides with olive oil and sprinkle it with kosher salt.

4. Line a 12 by 17-inch baking sheet with parchment paper and oil the paper. Place the seeded dough rectangle on the pan and cover it with oiled plastic wrap. If using the country sourdough, let it rise at room temperature for 1¹/₂ hours; if using the white pan dough, let it rise for 40 minutes in the refrigerator. The dough should be soft but will not have doubled.

5. Lightly oil a 12 by 4-inch area on the work surface. Place the dough on the oiled area, brush the top with a little olive oil, and sprinkle it lightly with kosher salt. Using a dough cutter, cut the dough crosswise into twelve 1-inch-wide strips. Lift each stick, stretch it slightly so it's 6 inches long, and twist it, then lay it back on the baking sheet. Place the twists side by side with no space between them. You want them to touch each other as they rise and to bake together. Let rise for 30 minutes for the white pan dough, or up to 1 hour for the sourdough, until slightly puffy but not quite fully risen.

6. Thirty minutes before baking, preheat the oven to 425° F. Place a baking stone in the oven to preheat and place an empty water pan directly below the stone.

7. Place the pan of bread on the baking stone. Quickly pour 1 cup of very hot water into the water pan and immediately shut the oven door. After about 1 minute, use a plant sprayer to mist the twists with water 6 to 8 times, then quickly shut the oven door. Mist again after 1 more minute.

8. Bake for 15 minutes, then reduce the oven temperature to 375° F and bake for 10 to 15 minutes longer, until the twists look golden brown and sound slightly hollow when tapped on the bottom but are still soft inside. (The white pan twists will bake for a few minutes less than the sourdough.) Brush the hot bread twists with a little olive oil if desired, transfer them to a rack, and let cool for at least 15 minutes before serving. Leave the twists connected until ready to serve, then pull them apart.

9

Flavor Powerhouses

◆

Breads to Impress Your Guests

In our travels to other bakeries, we are always on the lookout for flavorful and innovative breads. Sometimes we hear fellow bakers, or food purists, asserting that adding certain ingredients to bread makes the loaves trendy or flashy, or unappetizing. Although we agree that some mixtures just don't work, we like breads that include tasty additions.

Our philosophy is to make good dough first, using the highest-quality ingredients and careful methods to make a basic dough the best it can be. But then we often like to add other top-notch products to the dough to make the bread taste even better. Our specialty breads show up at fancy dinner parties and hors d'oeuvre buffets, on classy restaurant tables, and in brown paper lunch bags. We hope that you will enjoy these breads too. We think they are both very sophisticated and wonderfully delicious.

Fresh Rosemary Bread with Olive Oil

An overnight sponge starter bread

Fresh rosemary is a pungent and sturdy herb that is well suited for bread making. Some herbs turn black and lose their potency when chopped and heated, but rosemary stays green and flavorful throughout the baking process. We make lots of rosemary bread at the bakery and are still surprised by its versatility. We love it toasted for breakfast and served with orange marmalade. Then it reminds Amy of a trip to Capri, where she picked wild rosemary and saw citrus trees full of bright fruit. It is also delicious toasted and rubbed with fresh garlic, then drizzled with a little more extra virgin olive oil. The beauty of this bread is that it tastes great with a fresh green salad, or with a pasta dish, or simply by itself.

Makes two 20-ounce round loaves

• •

1 teaspoon active dry yeast

¼ cup (2 ounces) very warm water (105° to 115°F)

¾ cup plus 1 tablespoon (6½ ounces) cool water (75°F)

3 tablespoons (1½ ounces) extra virgin olive oil

¼ cup (½ ounce) fresh rosemary leaves, chopped

2 cups (16 ounces) Sponge Starter (page 40)

3 cups (13½ ounces) unbleached all-purpose flour

½ cup (2½ ounces) organic whole wheat flour

2 tablespoons kosher salt

Extra virgin olive oil for brushing

• •

1. Combine the yeast and warm water in a large bowl and stir with a fork to dissolve the yeast. Let stand for 3 minutes.

2. Add the cool water, olive oil, rosemary, and sponge to the yeast mixture and mix with your fingers for about 2 minutes, breaking up the sponge. The mixture should look milky and slightly foamy.

3. Add both flours and the salt and mix with your fingers to incorporate the flour, scraping the sides of the bowl and folding the dough over itself until it gathers into a mass. When sticky strands of dough begin to cling to your fingers, gather the dough into a ball and move it to a lightly floured surface. If the dough feels too firm, add 1 tablespoon of water.

4. Knead the dough for about 5 minutes, until it becomes smooth and supple. Allow the dough to rest on the work surface, covered with plastic wrap, for 15 minutes. (This rest period is the autolyse.)

5. Knead the dough again for 2 to 3 minutes, until it becomes smooth and stretchy, using as little additional flour as possible. Shape the dough into a loose ball and place it in a lightly oiled bowl. Turn the dough to coat with oil, cover the bowl tightly with oiled plastic wrap, and let the dough rise at room temperature (75° to 77° F) for about 1 hour, or until it looks slightly puffy but has not doubled.

6. Refrigerate the dough for at least 8 hours, or preferably overnight.

7. Take the dough from the refrigerator and let it warm up until it begins to rise again, $1^1/_2$ to 2 hours.

8. Sprinkle a peel or the back of a baking sheet generously with cornmeal or line it with parchment paper. Place the dough on a well-floured surface and divide it into 2 equal pieces (about 23 ounces each); the dough may be quite sticky. Shape each piece into a boule (see page 26). Don't work the dough too long or make the ball too tight, or the skin will tear; you want surface tension, but you also want to leave some of the medium air holes in the dough. Flour the seam of each boule and place the loaves seam side down on the peel or pan, leaving 3 to 4 inches between them for rising. These loaves are moist and will spread. Cover with oiled plastic wrap and let rise for $1^1/_2$ to 2 hours, or until doubled in bulk.

9. Thirty minutes before baking, preheat the oven to 450° F. Place a baking stone in the oven to preheat and place an empty water pan on the shelf directly below the stone.

10. Using a *lame* or a razor blade, cut a shallow tic-tac-toe pattern on the top of each loaf (see page 177), being careful not to tear the dough. Gently slide the bread onto the stone. Pour 1 cup of very hot water into the water pan and immediately shut the oven door. After about 1 minute, quickly mist the loaves 6 to 8 times, then shut the oven door. Mist the loaves again after 1 minute.

11. Bake for 20 minutes, then reduce the oven temperature to 400° F and bake for 10 to 15 minutes longer, until the loaves are light golden brown and sound hollow when tapped on the bottom. Brush the loaves with olive oil. Place them on a rack to cool, and enjoy them while they're still slightly warm and crusty!

Rustic Rounds of Black Olive and Sweet Red Pepper

An overnight sponge starter bread

On a trip to Italy, Amy and her sister Sally spent some time in Venice. Since they were on a limited budget, they feasted on treats from the local food shops. One morning, as they were buying provisions for a picnic, they passed a bakery window where they saw a chewy-looking white bread that was studded with olives and stripes of bright red peppers. The loaf looked so tempting they bought a wedge. After hiking along twisting alleyways, they came to some docks on the far edge of town, where they spread their feast: Yes, the cheeses were tasty, the salami good, and the wine pleasant, but the bread! It was the best thing they had ever tasted. The crust was hard and crunchy, the inside chewy and moist. The olives were robust and, in true Italian style, came complete with their pits. But the best part of the loaf was the sweet, tender strips of fresh red pepper. The soft bread around each strip was filled with sweet juices that perfectly balanced the salty olives. That loaf lives on in our memory, but this version is a close approximation. Buon appetito!

Makes 3 round loaves

. . . .

¾ teaspoon active dry yeast

¼ cup (2 ounces) very warm water (105° to 115°F)

1 cup (8 ounces) cool water (75°F)

1½ cups (12 ounces) Sponge Starter (page 40)

3¾ cups (17 ounces) unbleached all-purpose flour

1 tablespoon plus 1 teaspoon kosher salt

1 cup (6 ounces) imported black olives (see Note)

1 large (5½ ounces) red bell pepper

. . . .

1. Combine the yeast and warm water in a large bowl and stir with a fork to dissolve the yeast. Let stand for 3 minutes.

2. Add the cool water and sponge to the yeast mixture and mix with your fingers for 2 minutes, breaking up the sponge. The mixture should look milky and slightly foamy.

3. Add the flour and salt and mix with your fingers to incorporate the flour, scraping the sides of the bowl and folding the dough over itself until it gathers into a mass. The dough will be sticky, with long strands hanging from your fingers.

4. Move the dough to a lightly floured surface and knead for about 5 minutes, until the dough becomes smooth, supple, and elastic, using as little additional flour as possible. The dough should feel slightly firm. Sprinkle a little flour on the work surface and pat the dough gently into a rectangle. Cover the dough with a towel and let rest for 15 minutes. (This rest period is the autolyse.)

5. Meanwhile, drain the black olives well on paper towels. Pit them (crush them gently with your hand to loosen the pits) and roughly chop them. Cut the red pepper in half lengthwise, then in quarters, and remove the core and seeds. Place the pepper quarters skin side down and, using a serrated knife, cut crosswise into very thin strips. It is important to cut the strips as thin as possible, or they will steam inside the bread, leaving open air pockets.

6. Stretch the rectangle of dough slightly wider. Place the olives and red pepper pieces evenly on the dough and press them into it. Dust the dough lightly with flour, to absorb some of the moisture, roll it up into a loose cylinder, and knead very gently until the olives and peppers are distributed throughout the dough, 1 to 2 minutes. The dough may become very slippery; don't worry if some of the olives and peppers pop out. They can easily be incorporated after the first rise.

7. Shape the dough into a loose ball and place it in a lightly oiled bowl, along with any loose olives or peppers. Turn the dough to coat with oil. Cover the bowl tightly with oiled plastic wrap and let the dough rise at room temperature (75° to 77°F) for about 1 hour, or until it looks slightly puffy but has not doubled.

8. Refrigerate the dough overnight to let it relax and become more manageable.

9. Take the dough from the refrigerator and let it warm up until it begins to rise again, $1^{1}/_{2}$ to 2 hours.

10. Gently dump the dough onto a well floured surface and spread it into a rectangle, then fold it in thirds, as if you were folding a business letter, making sure the peppers and olives are evenly distributed. The dough will be very sticky. Divide it into 3 equal pieces (about 16 ounces each). Place each piece on a lightly floured surface, gently press out the large air bubbles, and form it into a boule (see page 26). Generously sprinkle a peel and the back of a baking sheet with cornmeal or line with parchment paper. (These loaves spread, so you will need to place 2 on the peel and 1 on a separate pan.) Dust the seams of the loaves with flour and place the loaves seam side down on the prepared surface. Sprinkle some flour on top of the loaves (this will give them a rustic appearance), cover with oiled plastic wrap, and allow to rise for $1^1/_2$ to 2 hours, or until doubled in bulk.

11. Thirty minutes before baking, preheat the oven to 450° F. Place a baking stone in the oven to preheat and position an oven rack below the baking stone.

12. Gently slide 2 of the breads onto the stone and place the third loaf on the baking pan on the rack below. Using a plant sprayer, spray the oven walls and the loaves 8 to 10 times, being careful not to spray the floured area on top of the loaves, then quickly shut the door. After about 1 minute, mist the loaves 6 to 8 times, then quickly shut the oven door. Mist the loaves again after 1 minute.

13. Bake for 15 minutes, then rotate the loaves from one shelf to the other and reduce the oven temperature to 400° F. Bake for 10 to 15 minutes longer, until the loaves sound slightly hollow when tapped on the bottom. Transfer the bread to a rack to cool for at least 45 minutes before serving. (This bread is rather sticky if cut too soon.) These loaves are still very nice the second day.

Note: We use fleshy black olives such as Kalamatas or other large full-flavored black olives.

Wands of Walnut Scallion Bread
An overnight sponge starter bread

This is a delicious bread that is much loved by our customers and even more so by our employees. When we make it as a special for our retail store, people stock up on it, buying one loaf to eat right way and one to freeze. And whenever we happen to make a loaf that is not well formed and can't be sold in the store, it seems to disappear magically before our eyes. Try it warm from the oven on its own, or with a soft, mild cheese. We like it as an appetizer with thinly sliced prosciutto and wedges of ripe cantaloupe. How about walnut scallion bread with Caesar salad? We know you'll find lots of pleasing combinations of your own.

Makes three 12-ounce loaves

½ teaspoon active dry yeast

2 tablespoons (1 ounce) very warm water (105° to 115°F)

¾ cup plus 2 tablespoons (7 ounces) cool water (75°F)

1 cup (8 ounces) Sponge Starter (page 40)

1 tablespoon plus 1½ teaspoons (¾ ounce) walnut oil

1 tablespoon (½ ounce) honey

2¾ cups (13 ounces) unbleached all-purpose flour

1 tablespoon kosher salt

¾ cup (1 bunch) scallions, thinly sliced

1½ cups (6 ounces) walnut pieces, toasted (see box, page 68)

Equipment: One 12 by 17-inch baking sheet, lined with parchment paper and sprinkled with cornmeal

1. Combine the yeast and warm water in a large bowl and stir with a fork to dissolve the yeast. Let stand for 3 minutes.

2. Add the cool water, sponge, walnut oil, and honey to the yeast mixture and mix with your fingers for 2 minutes, breaking up the sponge. The mixture should look milky and slightly foamy.

3. Add the flour and salt and mix with your fingers to incorporate the flour, scraping the sides of the bowl and folding the dough over itself until it gathers into a mass. The dough will be wet and sticky, with long strands hanging from your fingers.

4. Move the dough to a lightly floured surface and knead for 5 to 6 minutes, until it becomes supple and elastic, using as little additional flour as possible. If the dough feels too stiff, knead in 1 tablespoon more water. It should still be somewhat sticky. Sprinkle a little flour on the work surface and pat the dough gently into a rectangle. Allow the dough to rest, covered with a towel, for 15 minutes. (This rest period is the autolyse.)

5. Stretch the dough into a larger rectangle. Spread the scallions and walnuts evenly over the dough and gently press them into it. Dust the dough lightly with flour and fold it in thirds, as if you were folding a business letter. Roll up the dough and gently knead for 1 to 2 more minutes to incorporate the nuts and scallions. Some may pop out of the dough, but they can easily be incorporated after the dough has rested.

continued

6. Shape the dough into a loose ball and place in a lightly oiled bowl, along with any loose nuts or scallions. Turn the dough to coat with oil. Cover the bowl tightly with oiled plastic wrap and let the dough rise at room temperature (75° to 77°F) for about 1 hour, or until it looks slightly puffy but has not doubled.

7. Refrigerate the dough overnight to allow the flavors to develop and the walnuts to color the dough.

8. Remove the dough from the refrigerator and gently fold it over onto itself in the bowl. Cover the bowl again and let the dough sit at room temperature for $1^1/_2$ to 2 hours, until it is soft and beginning to rise again.

9. Gently dump the dough onto a lightly floured surface pressing in any loose nuts or scallions. Divide the dough into 3 equal pieces (about 13 ounces each). Gently flatten each piece of dough into a rectangle and shape it into a rough-looking cylinder or wand about the length of a baking sheet, as if you were shaping a baguette (see page 26). These loaves look nice when left a bit irregular in shape.

10. Line a 12 by 17-inch baking sheet with parchment paper and dust it generously with cornmeal. Place the loaves side by side on the pan, leaving at least 3 inches between them. Sprinkle the loaves with a little flour to give them a rustic appearance, then cover with oiled plastic wrap and allow to rise for $1^1/_2$ to 2 hours, or until doubled in bulk.

11. Meanwhile, preheat the oven to 425°F and place an empty water pan directly below the rack where the loaves will bake.

12. Gently place the pan of bread in the oven. Quickly pour 1 cup of very hot water into the water pan and immediately shut the oven door. After about 1 minute, using a plant sprayer, mist the loaves 6 to 8 times, then quickly shut the oven door. Mist the bread again after 1 minute.

13. Bake for 15 minutes, then reduce the oven temperature to 375°F and bake for 15 to 20 minutes longer, until the loaves are a glossy purple brown and sound slightly hollow when tapped on the bottom. After the first 20 minutes, you may need to flip the loaves over so they brown evenly on the top and bottom. Transfer the bread to a rack to cool slightly before serving. This bread tastes delicious when it's still warm from the oven. It freezes well too, wrapped tightly in aluminum foil and then in a heavy-duty freezer bag.

Amy's Organic Rye with Caraway and Mustard Seeds

An old dough bread

This is a wonderfully chewy, tangy, and very flavorful loaf that goes well with cured or smoked meats, poultry, or fish. Amy first came up with this recipe when she was working with chef Tom Colicchio at Mondrian. He was making an untraditional squab pastrami and wanted the perfect bread to accompany it. His goal was to make a hearty, "manly," flavorful sandwich that was easy to eat while standing, and it had to taste great with beer—it would be served at the Taste of the NFL, a hunger-relief benefit held in conjunction with the Super Bowl. The bread was supposed to echo the tastes of New York's favorite deli sandwich, pastrami piled high on caraway rye spread with mustard. Amy developed a dense, chewy rye made tangy with mustard and caraway seeds mixed right into the dough. This bread has a tight crumb because it is made with a high proportion of rye flour, which is low is gluten, and so doesn't rise high in the oven. It tasted great with Tom's delicious squab pastrami and cabbage slaw, and we hope you'll enjoy it too.

Makes three 14-ounce round loaves

1½ teaspoons active dry yeast

¼ cup (2 ounces) very warm water (105° to 115°F)

2¾ cups (11½ ounces) organic rye flour

1 cup (5 ounces) high-gluten (bread) flour

Scant 2 tablespoons (scant ¼ ounce) caraway seeds

2 tablespoons (½ ounce) mustard seeds

½ cup (2½ ounces) cooked organic rye berries (see box, page 67)

1 tablespoon plus ½ teaspoon kosher salt

1¼ cups (10 ounces) cool water (75°F)

1 recipe (14½ ounces) Old Dough Starter (page 42), at room temperature

continued

1. Combine the yeast and warm water in a small bowl and stir with a fork to dissolve the yeast. Let stand for 3 minutes.

2. Combine the two flours, the caraway and mustard seeds, rye berries, and salt in a large mixing bowl. Pour in the cool water and the yeast mixture and stir with your fingers to combine. Bring the dough together into a rough mass and knead and fold it over onto itself for 3 minutes. If the dough seems too stiff, knead in up to 3 tablespoons of water a tablespoon at a time. (The dough should be very sticky and gloppy, almost like clay, through most of the kneading process.)

3. Place the dough on a floured work surface and flatten it into a rough rectangle. Place the old dough on top of the rye dough, stretching it to cover the rye dough. Fold the whole mass up like a business letter, folding the top third of the rectangle down and the bottom third up over it, then gently knead to blend the two doughs together. Continue to knead until the dough becomes smooth and supple, about 4 minutes total. Cover the dough with a cloth or plastic wrap and let it rest for 20 minutes. (This rest period is the autolyse.)

4. Loosen the dough from the work surface with a bench scraper, lift it up, and lightly flour the work surface. Knead the dough for 2 to 3 minutes, until it feels gluey, airy, and supple. It should still feel slightly firm, almost like aerated modeling clay.

5. Shape the dough into a loose ball and place it in a lightly oiled bowl. Turn the dough to coat with oil. Cover the bowl tightly with oiled plastic wrap and let the dough rise at room temperature (75° to 77°F) for $1^1/_2$ to 2 hours, or until doubled in bulk. (This dough will not develop and rise as well at cooler temperatures.)

6. Generously sprinkle a peel or the back of a baking sheet with cornmeal or line it with parchment paper. Place the dough on a lightly floured surface and divide it into 3 equal pieces (about 16 ounces each). Shape each piece of dough into a boule (see page 26). Place the loaves seam side down on the peel or pan, leaving 2 to 3 inches between them for rising. These loaves are small, so they should all fit on one baking stone. Cover them with oiled plastic wrap and allow to rise at room temperature for $1^1/_2$ to 2 hours, or until doubled in bulk. (Rye bread lacks gluten and the dough has the tendency to crack. If the loaves start to split or tear, they have become too acidic and have overrisen, and they should to be baked right away. Don't worry–they will still be good but will have a tangier flavor.)

7. Thirty minutes before baking, preheat the oven to 425°F. Place a baking stone in the oven to preheat and place an empty water pan directly below the stone.

8. Sprinkle a little rye flour on top of each loaf, then cut the top of each loaf with a razor blade making three lines that connect at one end like the prongs of a fork. Gently slide the loaves onto the stone. Quickly pour 1 cup of very hot water into the water pan and immediately shut the oven door. After about 1 minute, using a plant sprayer, mist the loaves 6 to 8 times, then quickly shut the oven door. Mist again after 2 more minutes.

9. Bake for 20 minutes, then reduce the oven temperature to 400° F and bake for 15 to 20 minutes longer, until the loaves are a rich reddish brown and sound hollow when tapped on the bottom. Transfer the bread to a rack to cool completely. (Make sure the loaves are completely cool before slicing, or they will be gummy inside.) This bread is great on the second day.

Tangy Twenty-Four-Hour Sourdough
An overnight sourdough starter bread

This tangy bread is similar to a San Francisco sourdough. The sharp, sour flavor is achieved by making a sourdough sponge that is allowed to develop for several hours and by giving the bread a long, slow fermentation. We have also made this bread without the long fermentation, resulting in a mild, chewy sourdough loaf. At one time we called the mild version Church Bread. Not long after the bakery opened, a local Catholic church asked Amy if she could make a communion bread that would be more substantial than the usual communion wafer. The bread was to be made from only the most basic ingredients, used in the first breads thousands of years ago. Commercial yeast wasn't available then, of course, so bakers would mix an ancient form of ground wheat and water together into a paste and let it ferment on the hearth near a warm fire. The

> *This bread contains no commercial yeast. Its only leavening is the sourdough starters, so be sure the White Sourdough Mother and Rye Sour Starter are fresh and active before you make this recipe. We use the white sourdough mother, rather than a levain starter, because we want a moister starter for this bread. Instructions for building and maintaining the starters can be found on pages 43–49.*

fermented mass was mixed into the next batch of bread to make it rise, much the way a sourdough starter is used today. We came up with our version of bread made only from flour, water, and starter, and the church liked it.

Amy mixed the loaves by hand every Friday night. It was very pleasing to knead this small batch of special bread on our table after making all the other doughs in a large industrial mixer. The bread was shaped into rounds, risen, baked, and delivered on Saturday morning for the weekend masses. Many people knew that the bread came from our bakery and would often come to our store to say that they had tried our bread in church. Several parishioners also sheepishly reported, "I feel guilty because I find myself concentrating on how good the bread is instead of on communion!" We hope you will try both the mild and the tangy versions of our sourdough.

Makes three 12-ounce round loaves

• •

Sponge

2 cups (14½ ounces) White Sourdough Mother (page 49)

¼ cup (2¼ ounces) Rye Sour Starter (page 48)

1¼ cups (10 ounces) very warm water (105° to 115°F)

1¾ cups (9 ounces) high-gluten (bread) flour

Dough

¾ cup (3½ ounces) organic whole wheat flour

2 cups (9 ounces) unbleached all-purpose flour

1 tablespoon plus 2 teaspoons kosher salt

• •

Equipment: One deep 2-quart clear plastic container

1. For the sponge: Place the white sourdough mother and rye sour in a medium bowl. Add the warm water and mix with your fingers, breaking up the starter into smaller pieces and letting it start to dissolve in the water. Let the mixture rest for 5 minutes, then mix it again to break up the pieces even more.

2. Add the high-gluten flour and stir rapidly about 2 minutes to make a thick, batter-like mixture. Scrape it into a deep 2-quart clear plastic container. Mark the level of the sponge, and the time, with a marker or tape. Cover with plastic wrap and let sit at warm room temperature (77° to 78°F) 2½ to 4 hours to mature. When the sponge is bubbly and has almost doubled its original height, it is ready to be used in the dough.

3. Taste the sponge: It should be slightly sweet with a tangy aftertaste. This is the moment to use it, even if you want a very tangy bread. If the sponge tastes very sour and sharp with no hint of sweetness, either your starters were too mature or your sponge has aged too long. You can still use the sponge, but it may take longer to get the bread to rise and the loaves will be denser than usual.

4. For the dough: Scrape the sponge into a large mixing bowl. Add the flours and salt and mix to form a rough, shaggy mass. Knead the dough for about 2 minutes, until the wet and dry ingredients are well combined.

5. Move the dough to a lightly floured surface and knead for about 4 minutes, until an elastic dough has formed. If the dough feels too firm, knead in additional water 1 tablespoon at a time. Let the dough rest, covered with a cloth or plastic wrap, for 20 minutes. (This rest period is the autolyse.)

6. Knead the dough for 3 to 4 minutes, until it is very smooth and supple. Place the dough in a floured bowl, cover it with oiled plastic wrap, and let it rise at room temperature (75° to 77° F) for about $1^1/_2$ hours, until the dough looks slightly puffy but has not doubled.

7. Put the dough in the refrigerator to chill for at least 12 hours, or preferably overnight. From the beginning of the sponge stage through the final rise, this dough should age for at least 18 to 24 hours before baking.

8. Remove the dough from the refrigerator and let it sit at room temperature for about 2 hours, until it has warmed up, feels soft, and is beginning to rise again.

9. Place the dough on a lightly floured surface and divide it evenly into 3 pieces. Shape each piece into a boule (see page 26), and place on a heavily floured dish towel on a spread/baking sheet, leaving 3 inches between the loaves for rising. Cover the loaves with oiled plastic wrap and let rise for 2 to 4 hours, until the loaves have almost doubled in volume and feel fairly light and airy when gently lifted. This bread rises best at about 78° F in a draft-free place; it is important to check the room temperature and the dough temperature to make sure you are in the optimal range. If the dough is warmer than 78° F, chill it briefly, then let it rise again at room temperature. If your room and dough are too cool, move the bread to a warm place in the sun or near a radiator to get it moving.

10. Thirty minutes before baking, preheat the oven to 475° F. Place a baking stone in the oven to preheat and place an empty water pan directly below the stone. If you can fit only 2 loaves on your baking stone, you will have to bake the third on a pan on the rack below. In this case, you won't have room for a water pan.

11. When ready to bake, sprinkle a peel and/or baking sheet generously with cornmeal or line with parchment paper. Gently lift the loaves from the towel and place them seam side down on the peel and/or pan, allowing 2 to 3 inches between them for rising. Score each loaf with a *lame* or a sharp razor blade, making three parallel cuts about $^1/_4$ inch deep across each loaf. Slide the bread gently onto the stone. If necessary, place the baking sheet with the third loaf on the rack below. If using a water pan, quickly pour 1 cup of very hot water into the pan and immediately shut the oven door. Without a water pan, using a plant sprayer, spray the surface of the loaves 8 to 10 times, then quickly shut the door. In either case, after 1 minute, mist the loaves again 6 to 8 times, then quickly shut the oven door. Mist again after 1 more minute.

12. Bake for 15 minutes, then reduce the oven temperature to 400° F and bake for 17 to 22 minutes longer, until the loaves are a deep golden brown with a glossy, bubbly crust. They should sound hollow when tapped on the bottom. Place the loaves on a wire rack to cool completely before serving.

Note: To make a less sour dough, shorten the fermentation time of the sponge to 2 hours or less. Don't refrigerate the dough: After mixing the dough, let it take a full first rise until doubled, 2 to 4 hours. Divide and shape the loaves, let them rise again for 3 to 4 hours, and bake according to the directions above.

Sample Timing Schedule for Tangy Twenty-Four-Hour Sourdough

Mix the sponge	15 minutes	4:15 P.M.
Rise	2½ to 4 hours	8:15 P.M.
Knead dough	6 minutes	8:21 P.M.
Autolyse	20 minutes	8:41 P.M.
Knead dough	4 minutes	8:45 P.M.
Rise	1½ hours	10:15 P.M.
Chill overnight	12 hours	10:15 A.M.
Rise	2 hours	12:15 P.M.
Shape loaves	5 minutes	12:20 P.M.
Rise	2 to 4 hours	4:20 P.M.
Bake	35 minutes	4:55 P.M.
Cool	45 minutes	5:40 P.M.
Eat!		5:45 P.M.

10

Sandwich Distractions

◆

Is the Bread Better Than the Filling?

Most of the bakery's wholesale clients are well-known Manhattan restaurants. They're always eager to include our rolls and twists in their bread baskets. Encouraging them to use our loaves for lunchtime sandwiches, however, is sometimes a different story. More than once we've encountered chefs who love the taste of our breads so much they say they couldn't possibly use them for sandwiches–the bread would detract from their own creative fillings! Fortunately, you don't have to worry about such things in your own kitchen where you're both the baker and the chef. Here are some of our best-loved sandwich breads to get your creative energy going.

Onion and Parmesan Loaf with Caraway

A sponge starter bread

This wonderful savory bread has a dense but light-textured crumb and a rich, deep cheese flavor that can only be achieved if you use a high-quality imported Parmesan, such as Parmigiano-Reggiano. Mild, prepackaged cheese will produce disappointing results. The onions in the dough release their juices while the bread is baking, adding moistness as well as flavor. This bread may not even last long enough to make sandwiches out of it, but if it does, try a "fresh green salad" filling: Moisten mixed baby lettuces (mesclun) with your favorite vinaigrette and pile between two pieces of Parmesan bread along with some thin slices of ripe tomato. A delicious way to eat your greens!

Makes two 9 by 5-inch loaves

- -

$1^{1}/_{2}$ teaspoons active dry yeast

$^{1}/_{4}$ cup (2 ounces) very warm water (105° to 115°F)

3 cups ($13^{1}/_{2}$ ounces) unbleached all-purpose flour

$2^{1}/_{2}$ cups ($10^{1}/_{2}$ ounces) rye flour

1 cup plus 2 tablespoons ($4^{1}/_{2}$ ounces) imported Parmesan cheese, grated

$1^{1}/_{2}$ teaspoons caraway seeds

$1^{1}/_{2}$ tablespoons kosher salt

$2^{1}/_{4}$ cups (18 ounces) Sponge Starter (page 40)

$1^{3}/_{4}$ cups (14 ounces) cool water (75°F)

$1^{1}/_{4}$ cups (5 ounces) onions, cut into $^{1}/_{4}$-inch dice

$^{1}/_{2}$ cup (4 ounces) cold water

$1^{1}/_{4}$ teaspoons cornstarch

- -

Equipment: Two 9 by 5-inch loaf pans, oiled

1. Place the yeast and warm water in a medium bowl and stir with a fork to dissolve the yeast. Allow to stand for about 3 minutes.

2. Whisk the unbleached flour, rye flour, Parmesan cheese, caraway seeds, and salt together in a medium bowl. Set aside.

3. Add the sponge and cool water to the yeast mixture. Mix the ingredients with your fingers for 1 to 2 minutes, just long enough to break up the sponge. The mixture should be foamy. Add the flour mixture and stir with your fingers to incorporate the flour, scraping the sides of the bowl and folding the dough over itself until it gathers into a shaggy mass.

4. Move the dough to a lightly floured surface and knead it for 7 to 10 minutes, until it becomes supple and elastic. The dough will feel somewhat sticky because it contains rye flour; it should be moist but not mushy. If it feels too stiff to knead, add cool water 1 tablespoon at a time until you have a soft, malleable dough. Shape the dough into a loose ball and let it rest, covered with plastic wrap, on the work surface for 20 minutes. (This rest period is the autolyse.)

5. Flatten the dough and stretch it gently with your fingers to form a rectangle about an inch thick. Spread the diced onions evenly over the rectangle. Fold the whole mass into an envelope (see page 23) and knead and fold it gently until the onions are well distributed, about 2 to 3 minutes. If the dough resists, let it rest for 5 minutes and then continue kneading it again. Some of the onions may pop out of the dough, but they can easily be incorporated again after the first rise, when the dough has softened.

6. Shape the dough into a loose ball and place it in a lightly oiled bowl, along with any loose onions. Turn to coat the dough with oil and cover the bowl tightly with oiled plastic wrap. Let the dough rise at room temperature (75° to 77° F) until it has doubled in volume, about $2^1/_2$ to 3 hours.

7. When the dough has doubled, loosen it from the bowl with lightly floured hands and gently pour it onto a floured work surface. Press any loose onions into the dough, and divide it into 2 equal pieces. Shape each piece into a log (see page 22), and place each one seam side down in an oiled 9 by 5-inch loaf pan. Cover them with oiled plastic wrap and allow to rise for about 2 hours, or until they have doubled in size (a finger pressed into the dough will leave an indentation).

8. Thirty minutes before baking, preheat the oven to 425° F. Place a baking stone in the oven to preheat and place an empty water pan directly below the stone.

continued

9. While the bread is proofing, make a cornstarch wash: Put the cold water in a small saucepan and whisk in the cornstarch. Bring to a boil, stirring frequently until it thick-ens. Remove from the heat and cover to keep a skin from forming. Set aside to cool.

10. When the loaves have doubled, place the pans on the baking stone. Quickly pour 1 cup of very hot water into the water pan and immediately shut the door. After 1 minute, using a plant sprayer, mist the loaves quickly 6 to 8 times, then shut the oven door. Repeat the misting procedure 1 minute later.

11. Bake for 20 minutes, then reduce the oven temperature to 375°F and bake for 15 to 20 minutes longer, until the crust is lightly browned and the bread sounds slightly hollow when tipped out of the pans and tapped on the bottom. The sides and bottoms of the loaves should also feel firm and slightly crusty; if the tops are browned but the sides are still slightly soft, set the loaves directly on the stone to bake for about 5 to 10 minutes longer. Transfer the loaves to a rack and brush the tops with the cornstarch wash. Allow to cool completely before slicing.

Chewy Pumpernickel

An overnight sponge starter bread with sourdough added

In our version of a dark pumpernickel rye bread the rye sour is used more for its taste than for its leavening power. You don't really need to "build a sour"; it's okay to use maintenance Rye Mother (see page 47) from the refrigerator, providing you've fed it in the past three days. Traditionally coffee, molasses, cocoa powder, or caramel color gives pumpernickel its characteristic dark brown color. We tried them all and finally decided the caramel color achieved the almost-black bread we desired–but we left all the others in for the depth of flavor they added. (The caramel color can be made well ahead of time and stored.) An overnight proofing in the refrigerator and sunflower seeds give this bread its pleasantly chewy texture.

Makes two 9 by 5-inch loaves

. . . .

1 teaspoon active dry yeast

¼ cup (2 ounces) very warm water (105° to 115°F)

3 cups (13½ ounces) unbleached all-purpose flour

2¼ cups (11¼ ounces) pumpernickel flour

1½ tablespoons unsweetened cocoa powder

1 tablespoon plus 1 teaspoon kosher salt

1½ cups (12 ounces) Sponge Starter (page 40)

½ cup (4½ ounces) Rye Mother (page 47)

1¼ cups (10 ounces) cool water (75°F)

¼ cup plus 2 tablespoons (3 ounces) brewed coffee

2 tablespoons (1½ ounces) honey

1½ tablespoons (1 ounce) molasses

2 tablespoons (1 ounce) Caramel Color (recipe follows)

1 cup (5 ounces) raw sunflower seeds

½ cup (4 ounces) cold water

1¼ teaspoons cornstarch

. . . .

Equipment: Two 9 by 5-inch loaf pans, oiled

continued

1. Combine the yeast and warm water in a large bowl and stir with a fork to dissolve the yeast. Let stand for about 3 minutes.

2. Whisk the unbleached flour, pumpernickel flour, cocoa powder, and salt together in a medium bowl. Set aside.

3. Add the sponge, rye mother, cool water, coffee, honey, molasses, and caramel color to the yeast mixture. Mix the ingredients with your fingers for 1 to 2 minutes, just long enough to break up the sponge. The mixture should be foamy. Add the flour mixture and stir with your fingers to incorporate the flour, scraping the sides of the bowl and folding the dough over itself until it gathers into a shaggy mass.

4. Move the dough to a lightly floured surface and knead it for 5 to 6 minutes, until it becomes supple and somewhat elastic. The dough will have a heavy, sticky consistency because of the pumpernickel flour in it, but it should not be hard to knead. If necessary, add additional cool water 1 tablespoon at a time until you have a soft but not mushy, malleable dough. If it feels too wet and mushy, add another tablespoon or two of unbleached flour as you knead. Shape the dough into a loose ball and let it rest, covered with plastic wrap, on the lightly floured work surface for 20 minutes. (This rest period is the autolyse.)

> ### Raisin Pumpernickel Rolls
>
> *For variety, add 1¾ cups dark raisins (8¾ ounces dry weight), soaked in warm water for 20 minutes and drained, to the pumpernickel dough. Shape the dough into 2½-ounce rolls (see page 27) instead of loaves. Put the rolls on parchment-lined baking sheets and let them rise until doubled. Brush them lightly with the cornstarch wash and bake in a 400°F oven for 20 to 25 minutes, or until they sound slightly hollow when tapped on the bottom. The recipe makes about 30 rolls, so you may want to freeze some of them, or bake half the dough in a 9 by 5-inch loaf pan. At the bakery, we've got regular customers whose kids will choose our raisin pumpernickel rolls over cookies every time!*

5. Use a dough cutter to lift up the dough mass and lightly flour the work surface again. Flatten the dough and stretch it slightly with your fingers to form a rectangle about an inch thick. Spread the sunflower seeds evenly over the rectangle. Fold the whole mass into an envelope (see page 23) and knead and fold it gently until the seeds are well distributed, about 2 to 3 minutes. Some of the seeds may pop out of the dough, but they can easily be incorporated again after the first rise, when the dough has softened.

6. Shape the dough into a loose ball and place it in a lightly oiled bowl, along with any loose sunflower seeds. Turn the dough to coat with oil, and cover the bowl tightly with oiled plastic wrap. Let the dough rise at room temperature (75° to 77° F) for 1 hour, or until it looks slightly puffy but has not doubled.

7. Refrigerate the dough overnight to allow the flavors of the ingredients to combine and mellow.

8. Remove the dough from the refrigerator and allow it to rise at room temperature for 2 hours.

9. Gently remove the dough from the bowl and place it on a lightly floured work surface, pressing in any loose sunflower seeds. Divide it into 2 equal pieces. Shape each piece into a log (see page 22) and place each log seam side down in an oiled 9 by 5-inch loaf pan. Cover them with oiled plastic wrap and allow the loaves to rise for about 2 to 2½ hours, or until they have doubled in size (a finger pressed into the dough will leave an indentation).

10. Thirty minutes before baking, preheat the oven to 425° F. Place a baking stone in the oven to preheat and place an empty water pan directly below the stone.

11. While the bread is proofing, make a cornstarch wash: Put the cold water in a small saucepan and whisk in the cornstarch. Bring to a boil, stirring frequently until it thickens. Remove from the heat and cover to keep a skin from forming. Set aside to cool.

12. When the loaves have doubled, use a pastry brush to paint the tops with the cornstarch wash; brush gently so you don't deflate the dough. (Cover the remaining cornstarch wash and set aside.) Place the baking pans directly on the baking stone. Quickly pour 1 cup of very hot water into the water pan and immediately shut the door. After 1 minute, using a plant sprayer, mist the top and sides of the oven 6 to 8 times, then immediately shut the oven door. Repeat the misting procedure 1 minute later.

13. Bake for 20 minutes, then reduce the oven temperature to 375° F and bake for 20 to 25 minutes longer, until the loaves sound slightly hollow when tipped out of the pan and tapped on the bottom. The sides and bottoms of the loaves should feel firm and slightly crusty; if the tops are browned but the sides are still somewhat soft, place the loaves directly on the stone to bake for 5 to 10 minutes longer. Transfer the loaves to a rack and brush the tops again with the cornstarch wash. Allow to cool completely before slicing.

continued

Caramel Color

Makes about $1/3$ cup

• •

1½ tablespoons (¾ ounce) cold water

4½ tablespoons (2 ounces) granulated sugar

Pinch cream of tartar

¼ cup (2 ounces) boiling water

• •

1. Combine the cold water and sugar in a small heavy saucepan and heat over medium-low heat, stirring with a wooden spoon until the sugar has almost dissolved. Increase the heat to medium-high and bring the syrup to a full boil. Use a pastry brush moistened with water to wash down any sugar crystals sticking to the sides of the pan.

2. Boil for about 2 minutes. Using a clean wooden spoon, stir in the cream of tartar. Continue boiling the syrup until it is almost black in color—don't be afraid to let it get really dark. It will begin to smoke because the sugar is actually burning.

3. Take the pan from the heat and allow it to cool slightly, about 2 to 3 minutes. Gradually add the boiling water, stirring to dissolve the caramel. Be very careful, because the syrup will bubble up and splatter. Let cool completely, then store in an airtight container at room temperature. It will last indefinitely.

Country Sourdough Boule
An overnight sourdough bread

This is a scaled-down version of the basic country sourdough recipe we use at the bakery. The big beautiful loaves that burst open when we bake them in our steam-injected deck oven are so crusty and flavorful that we were sure we'd never be able to come close to getting the same results in a home oven. But when we tested this recipe in an apartment kitchen, the loaves of bread were so satisfying and delicious we couldn't stop eating them. You may be amazed to find you can produce a basic bread this good out of your own oven. At the bakery it's our best seller, partly because it's good for lots of other things as well as sandwiches. We love it plain, but for variety, you can knead toasted nuts, chopped fruit and raisins, or imported olives into the dough, or shape it into triangles, or beehives, or logs for a whole new look.

Makes two 1¹/₂-pound round loaves

• •

³/₄ teaspoon active dry yeast

¹/₄ cup (2 ounces) very warm water (105° to 115°F)

5¹/₃ cups (24 ounces) unbleached all-purpose flour

1 cup (5 ounces) pumpernickel flour

Scant 2 tablespoons (³/₄ ounce) kosher salt

1 cup (7¹/₂ ounces) Levain Starter (page 50)

2¹/₄ cups plus 2 tablespoons (19 ounces) cool water (75°F)

• •

Equipment: Two round baskets about 7¹/₂ to 8¹/₂ inches
in diameter (see Step 8)

1. Place the yeast and warm water in a medium bowl and stir with a fork to dissolve the yeast. Allow to stand for about 3 minutes.

2. Whisk the unbleached flour, pumpernickel flour, and salt together in a bowl. Set aside.

3. Add the *levain* starter and cool water to the yeast mixture and mix with your fingers for 2 to 3 minutes, just long enough to soften the *levain* and break it up into small pieces. Add the flour mixture and stir with your fingers to incorporate the flour, scraping the sides of the bowl and folding the dough over itself until it gathers into a shaggy mass.

continued

4. Move the dough to a lightly floured surface and knead for 6 to 8 minutes, until it becomes supple and somewhat elastic. The dough will be very sticky at first; keep your hands and the work surface lightly floured, using a dough scraper if necessary to prevent the dough from sticking and building up on the work surface. As you continue kneading, the dough will become more elastic and easier to handle. Shape the dough into a loose ball, return it to the bowl, and cover it with plastic wrap. Let it rest for 20 minutes. (This rest period is the autolyse.)

5. Knead the dough again on the lightly floured surface for about 2 to 3 minutes, or until it becomes very smooth and springy. Shape the dough into a loose ball and place it in a lightly oiled bowl. Turn the dough to coat with oil and cover the bowl tightly with oiled plastic wrap. Let rise at room temperature (75° to 77°F) for 1 hour, or until it looks slightly puffy but has not doubled.

6. Refrigerate the dough overnight to allow the flavors of the ingredients to combine and mellow.

7. Remove the dough from the refrigerator and allow it to rise at room temperature for 2 hours.

8. Line two round baskets with well-floured cloths (see page 28); if you don't have baskets, use two round-bottomed (not flat-bottomed) bowls or colanders. Gently remove the dough from the bowl and place it on a lightly floured work surface. Divide it into 2 equal pieces. Shape each piece into a boule (see page 26), being careful not to tear the outer surface of the loaf by exerting too much pressure during shaping. Place the boules seam side down in the prepared baskets. Cover them with oiled plastic wrap and let rise for about 3 to 4 hours, or until they have almost doubled in volume.

9. Thirty minutes before baking, preheat the oven to 450°F. Place a baking stone in the oven to preheat and place an empty water pan directly below the stone.

> *This bread is easy to make, but you need to start planning for it several days in advance. Make the levain starter a day or two before you make the dough because you have to feed the levain more than once to boost its leavening power. (If your levain starter doesn't quite double within 8 hours, you can still use it, but your bread may take longer to rise and it may not achieve as much volume; although the recipe includes a small amount of commercial yeast, the levain is its primary leavener.) This slow-rising bread takes 3 to 4 hours to rise after it has been shaped, so it's best to shape it early in the day.*

10. Dust a peel or the back of a baking sheet generously with coarse cornmeal. Quickly but carefully tip the loaves out of the baskets onto the prepared peel or baking sheet. (If the floured cloths have stuck to the loaves, gently peel them away.) Shake the peel or pan gently to be sure the loaves aren't sticking and slide them onto the baking stone, leaving at least 2 inches between them to allow for oven spring. (If your stone isn't large enough to accommodate both loaves, cover one loaf with plastic wrap and refrigerate it until the first loaf has finished baking, then bake the second loaf.) Quickly pour 1 cup of very hot water into the water pan and immediately shut the door. After 1 minute, using a plant sprayer, quickly mist the top and sides of the oven 6 to 8 times, then immediately shut the oven door. (Avoid spraying the bread when misting, or the flour on the top will look blotchy and unappetizing.) Repeat the misting procedure 1 minute later.

11. Bake for 20 minutes, then reduce the oven temperature to 400° F and bake for 20 to 25 minutes longer, until the loaves are a deep golden brown and sound hollow when tapped on the bottom. Transfer them to a rack and allow to cool before serving.

Lentil Rolls

An overnight old dough plus sourdough bread

This is an adaptation of a recipe Toy brought back from France after she spent a week at École Francaise Boulangerie in Aurillac. The recipe has a lot of steps, but the result is worth the effort. These light, fine-textured rolls have the subtle flavor of the green lentils that are grown in south-central France, in the region around Aurillac. For a crusty lunch treat, toast them whole, split them, and fill them with tuna salad and fresh butter lettuce. Or shape the dough into four baguettes, flatten them slightly, and place a spicy sausage (such as andouille) in the center of each one. Fold the dough over to cover the sausages completely, seal the seams securely, and let rise. Bake for 25 to 30 minutes. Cut into slices for an unusual and attractive hors d'oeuvre.

Makes 12 large rolls

• •

Scant $\frac{1}{3}$ cup plus generous $\frac{1}{2}$ cup ($5\frac{1}{4}$ ounces) green lentils

   (see Steps 1 and 3)

$1\frac{1}{3}$ cups ($10\frac{1}{2}$ ounces) cold water

$2\frac{3}{4}$ teaspoons kosher salt

$1\frac{1}{4}$ teaspoons active dry yeast

$\frac{1}{4}$ cup (2 ounces) very warm water (105° to 115°F)

3 cups plus 2 tablespoons (14 ounces) unbleached all-purpose flour

Scant $\frac{1}{4}$ cup (1 ounce) whole wheat flour

1 teaspoon freshly ground black pepper

1 recipe ($14\frac{1}{2}$ ounces) Old Dough Starter (page 42), at room temperature

Generous $\frac{1}{2}$ cup ($4\frac{1}{4}$ ounces) Levain Starter (page 50)

2 tablespoons plus 2 teaspoons ($1\frac{1}{4}$ ounces) olive oil

$1\frac{1}{4}$ cups (10 ounces) cool water including reserved lentil cooking

   water (75°F)

$\frac{1}{2}$ cup (4 ounces) cold water

$1\frac{1}{4}$ teaspoons cornstarch

• •

Equipment: Two 12 by 17-inch baking sheets, lined with
parchment paper

1. Put the $^1/_3$ cup ($1^3/_4$ ounces) lentils, the cold water, and $^1/_4$ teaspoon of the salt in a small saucepan and bring to a boil. Reduce the heat and simmer for about 15 to 20 minutes, or until the lentils are cooked through but still firm. Drain, saving the liquid to use as part of the cool water in the dough, and set the lentils aside to cool.

2. Place the yeast and warm water in a large bowl. Stir with a fork to dissolve the yeast and allow to stand for about 3 minutes.

3. Grind the remaining $^1/_2$ cup ($3^1/_2$ ounces) lentils in a coffee grinder or a grain mill until the consistency of coarse cornmeal. Place in a medium bowl, add the unbleached flour, whole wheat flour, the remaining $2^1/_2$ teaspoons salt, and the pepper, and stir to combine. Set aside.

4. Cut the old dough into 6 to 8 pieces. Add the old dough, *levain* starter, olive oil, and cool water/lentil cooking liquid to the yeast mixture and mix with your hand for 2 to 3 minutes, just long enough to soften the old dough and the *levain* and break them up into small pieces. The mixture should be slightly foamy. Add the flour and stir with your fingers to incorporate the flour, scraping the sides of the bowl and folding the dough over itself until it gathers into a shaggy mass.

5. Move the dough to a lightly floured surface and knead for about 6 minutes, until it becomes supple and somewhat elastic. Use as little additional flour as possible; the dough should be moist, pliable, and very easy to knead. If necessary, add more water 1 tablespoon at a time to achieve the proper consistency. Let the dough rest for 5 minutes.

6. Flatten the dough and stretch it gently with your fingers to form a rectangle about an inch thick. Spread the cooked lentils evenly over the rectangle. Fold the dough into an envelope (see page 23) and knead gently for 3 to 4 minutes, until the dough is uniform in color and the lentils are evenly distributed. Shape the dough into a loose ball, cover it with plastic wrap, and let it rest on the work surface for 20 minutes. (This rest period is the autolyse.)

7. Knead the dough gently for 2 minutes, or until it is smooth and springy to the touch. Shape it into a ball, place it in a lightly oiled bowl, and turn to coat the dough with oil. Cover the bowl tightly with oiled plastic wrap. Let the dough rise at room temperature (75° to 77°F) for 1 hour, or until it looks slightly puffy but has not doubled.

8. Refrigerate the dough overnight to combine the flavors of the ingredients.

9. Remove the dough from the refrigerator and allow it to rise at room temperature for 2 hours.

continued

10. Line two 12 by 17-inch baking sheets with parchment paper. Loosen the dough from the bowl with lightly floured hands and gently pour it onto a floured work surface. Divide it into 12 equal pieces (each weighing about 4 ounces). Shape the pieces into rolls (see page 27). Dip the bottom of each roll into a little flour so it won't stick to the parchment and place 6 rolls on each prepared baking sheet, leaving several inches between them for rising. Cover the pans with oiled plastic wrap and let the dough relax for 15 minutes.

11. Flour your hands and, using your palms and fingers, gently but firmly flatten each roll into a disk about $4^1/_2$ inches in diameter. Cover them with oiled plastic wrap and let rise for about 1 hour, until doubled.

12. While the bread is proofing, make a cornstarch wash: Put the cold water in a small saucepan and whisk in the cornstarch. Bring to a boil, stirring frequently until it thickens. Remove from the heat and cover to keep a skin from forming. Set aside to cool.

13. Place one oven rack in the top third of the oven and another in the bottom third, and preheat the oven to 425° F.

14. When the rolls have doubled, place one pan on each oven rack. Using a plant sprayer, immediately mist the rolls 6 to 8 times and quickly close the oven door. After 1 minute, mist again and immediately close the door.

15. Bake the rolls for 20 to 25 minutes, or until they are golden brown and sound slightly hollow when tapped on the bottom. Rotate the pans from top to bottom and front to back halfway through the baking time. Remove from the oven and use a pastry brush to paint the top of each roll quickly and evenly with the cornstarch wash. Transfer the rolls to a rack and allow them to cool.

16. Slice the rolls in half with a serrated knife, fill them with your favorite sandwich filling, and enjoy! These rolls also freeze extremely well if double-wrapped in heavy-duty freezer bags.

Sandwich Suggestions: Great Combinations of Bread and Fillings

Most of our breads make super sandwiches. Even some of the specialty breads with fruits and nuts can be used for delicious and creative combinations. Here are some of our favorites:

Country Sourdough Boule, grilled or lightly toasted, layered with sautéed fresh spinach and thinly sliced smoked salmon, and sprinkled with a squeeze of fresh lemon juice.

Semolina Bread with Apricots and Sage, spread lightly with mayonnaise and layered with sliced roast turkey breast, thin red onion slices, and red leaf lettuce.

Coarse-Grained Whole Wheat with Toasted Walnuts, spread with honey mustard, filled with sliced rare roast beef and roasted red peppers, and watercress.

Amy's Crusty Italian Loaf, cut in half and the center scooped out, spread with garlic mayonnaise, and filled with sautéed asparagus spears, hard-boiled egg slices, and thick slices of ripe tomato.

Amy's Organic Rye with Caraway and Mustard Seeds, layered with capocollo ham and provolone cheese and garnished with a mesclun salad tossed in a Dijon mustard vinaigrette.

Rich Focaccia, split in half, spread lightly with pesto sauce, filled with grilled eggplant and zucchini, and garnished with fresh basil leaves and thin slices of tomato.

Walnut Scallion Bread, layered with thinly sliced prosciutto and grilled chicken breast and garnished with freshly ground black pepper and arugula.

Lentil Rolls, warmed, split, spread with mayonnaise, and topped with a veggie burger, red onion slices, tomato slices, and radish sprouts.

11

Breakfast Treats and Other Sweet Delights

The mornings are a busy time of day at our retail store. When we first opened the bakery in 1992, we offered our morning customers a variety of healthy and delicious little breads, but only one "sweet"–Amy's irresistible sticky buns. It didn't take us long to find out that coffee and sweet baked breakfast treats are the name of the game for busy New Yorkers. Now in addition to the sticky buns, our morning menu includes quick breads, coffee cakes, muffins, scones, and, for the dedicated sugar addicts, a selection of cookies and our award-winning double chocolate brownies. Customers have even placed special orders to be picked up on the way to the airport so they could take our scones to Russia or our brownies to France! In addition, we've also created a number of richer yeast breads that include butter and eggs as well as honey, maple syrup, or sugar. So, even though our first love is for breads that are high in nutrition and low in fat, we sympathize with that craving for sweet delights. Here are a few we think you'll enjoy.

Chocolate Peanut Butter Buns
A straight dough bread

These moist, plump, glossy little treats were inspired by the recipe for chocolate bread in Carol Field's wonderful book *The Italian Baker*. For variety, you can replace the peanut butter chips with chocolate chips and have a double chocolate experience, or be really decadent and try a peanut butter chip–chocolate chip combination! These take about four hours from start to finish. If you're an early riser, you can have them warm from the oven in time for a mid-morning coffee break or weekend brunch. They are also great in picnic baskets and lunch boxes. Don't overbake them, or their flavor will be diminished.

Makes 12 buns

. . . .

2 teaspoons active dry yeast

¼ cup (2 ounces) very warm water (105° to 115°F)

Scant ⅓ cup plus ¼ teaspoon (2 ounces) granulated sugar

3 cups plus 2 tablespoons (14 ounces) unbleached all-purpose flour

¼ cup unsweetened cocoa powder

1½ teaspoons kosher salt

1 cup (8 ounces) warm brewed coffee (90°F)

1 large egg yolk

2 teaspoons unsalted butter, softened

⅔ cup (4 ounces) peanut butter chips

½ cup (4 ounces) cold water

1¼ teaspoons cornstarch

. . . .

Equipment: Two 12 by 17-inch baking sheets, lined with parchment paper

1. Place the yeast, warm water, and $1/4$ teaspoon sugar in a large bowl. Stir with a fork to dissolve the yeast and allow to stand for about 3 minutes.

2. Whisk the unbleached flour, cocoa powder, the remaining scant $1/3$ cup sugar, and the salt together in a medium bowl. Set aside.

3. Using a wooden spoon or your hand, stir the coffee, egg yolk, and butter into the yeast mixture. Gradually add the flour mixture, stirring until a shaggy mass forms and all of the flour is moistened.

4. Move the dough to a lightly floured surface and knead for about 7 to 8 minutes, until it is silky-smooth and elastic. This dough should be nice and moist, so add flour sparingly as you work. Shape the dough into a loose ball, cover it with plastic wrap, and let it rest for about 10 minutes to relax the gluten strands.

5. Flatten the dough and stretch it gently with your fingers to form a rectangle about an inch thick. Spread the peanut butter chips evenly over the rectangle. Fold the dough into an envelope (see page 23) and knead gently for 2 to 3 minutes, until the chips are well distributed. The dough should be

> *If you want to sleep in a little later in the morning, make the dough the night before: Put it in a lightly oiled nonmetal bowl, cover the bowl tightly with oiled plastic wrap, and let the dough sit out at room temperature (75° to 77°F) for 1 hour, or until it looks slightly puffy. Then refrigerate it overnight. First thing in the morning, take it out, divide it, and shape it into rolls. Let the rolls rise, as described in the recipe, until they have completely doubled in volume, about 2 hours, then bake them. The only difference is that the buns will be a little more densely textured than they would be if you made them all in one day.*

soft, smooth, and springy. If it resists, let it rest for 5 minutes and then continue kneading it. Some of the chips may pop out of the dough, but they can easily be incorporated again after the first rise, when the dough has softened.

6. Shape the dough into a loose ball and place it in a lightly oiled bowl, along with any loose chips. Turn to coat the dough with oil, and cover the bowl tightly with oiled plastic wrap. Let rise at room temperature (75° to 77° F) until the dough has doubled in volume, about 2 hours.

7. Line two 12 by 17-inch baking sheets with parchment paper. Gently pour the dough onto the floured work surface, pressing any loose peanut butter chips into the dough. Flour your hands lightly and divide the dough into 12 equal pieces (each weighing about $2^{1}/_2$ ounces). Shape the pieces into rolls (see page 27) and place 6 buns on each prepared baking sheet, leaving several inches between them so they won't grow together as they rise. Cover loosely with oiled plastic wrap and let them rise at room temperature until doubled in volume, about 45 minutes to 1 hour.

continued

8. While the bread is proofing, make a cornstarch wash: Put the cold water in a small saucepan and whisk in the cornstarch. Bring to a boil, stirring frequently until it thickens. Remove from the heat and cover to keep a skin from forming. Set aside to cool.

9. About 15 minutes before you're ready to bake, place one oven rack in the top third of the oven and another in the bottom third, and preheat the oven to 400°F.

10. When the buns have doubled, use a pastry brush to paint them with a thin coating of the cornstarch wash. Brush gently so you don't deflate them. (Cover the remaining cornstarch wash and set aside.) Place one pan on each oven rack. Using a plant sprayer, immediately mist the top and sides of the oven 6 to 8 times, and quickly close the oven door. Repeat this misting procedure two more times at 1-minute intervals.

11. Bake for 10 minutes, then reduce the oven temperature to 350°F and rotate the pans from top to bottom and front to back to ensure even baking. Bake for 10 to 15 minutes longer, or until the tops of the buns feel firm but not hard when you press them slightly and the bottoms are very lightly browned. These rolls should have a thin soft covering, not a hard crunchy crust. Remove from the oven and use the pastry brush to paint the top of each bun quickly and evenly with the cornstarch wash. Transfer the rolls to a rack and allow them to cool before serving. These are best eaten the day they are baked.

Suze's Buttermilk Oatmeal Scones

A quick bread

These are the scones that went to Russia with one of our customers. They're rustic-looking crunchy golden breakfast biscuits filled with fruit and nuts. We can't imagine what they must have tasted like after traveling all that way, but our customer reported that her Russian friends were immediately hooked on them and insist that she bring them every time she visits.

In this recipe we've used golden raisins and toasted walnuts because that version is Toy's personal favorite. However, Suze Kantor, who developed this recipe for us at the bakery, is a creative free spirit who loves to surprise us with all kinds of wondrous fruit and nut combinations. Try fresh plums and toasted pecans, or chopped dried apricots and toasted almonds. Don't be afraid to experiment. Use up to two cups (total) of any flavoring ingredient(s) you choose; we guarantee you won't be disappointed.

Makes 12 large scones

• •

$2\frac{2}{3}$ cups (13 ounces) unbleached all-purpose flour

$\frac{1}{3}$ cup ($2\frac{1}{4}$ ounces) granulated sugar

$1\frac{1}{2}$ teaspoons baking powder

$\frac{3}{4}$ teaspoon baking soda

$\frac{3}{4}$ teaspoon ground cinnamon

1 teaspoon kosher salt

$\frac{1}{2}$ cup plus 2 tablespoons (5 ounces) cold unsalted butter, diced

$2\frac{2}{3}$ cups (8 ounces) old-fashioned rolled oats

$\frac{3}{4}$ cup ($3\frac{3}{4}$ ounces) golden raisins

$\frac{3}{4}$ cup (3 ounces) walnut pieces, toasted (see box, page 68)

$1\frac{1}{3}$ cups (11 ounces) buttermilk

1 large egg

• •

Equipment: Two 12 by 17-inch baking sheets, lined with parchment paper

continued

If you like to sweeten with honey instead of sugar, substitute ¼ cup honey for the sugar and dissolve it in the buttermilk/egg mixture before you add it to the dry ingredients.

1. Position one rack in the top third and one in the bottom third of the oven, and preheat the oven to 400° F. Line two 12 by 17-inch baking sheets with parchment paper.

2. In a food processor fitted with the metal blade, combine the unbleached flour, sugar, baking powder, baking soda, cinnamon, and salt and process until just combined. With the motor running, add the diced cold butter and process until the mixture looks like coarse meal. (If you don't have a food processor, mix the dry ingredients in a large bowl with a wire whisk and cut the cold butter in with a pastry blender, or rub it into the flour by hand.) Transfer the dough to a large bowl and stir in the oats, golden raisins, and walnuts.

3. In a small bowl, mix the buttermilk and egg thoroughly with a whisk. Remove ¼ cup of this mixture and set it aside. Pour the remaining mixture over the dry ingredients and lightly and briefly stir everything together, just until all the flour is moistened. Don't overmix, or your scones will be heavy and doughy. This dough won't be a single cohesive mass; it should look more like moistened clumps of flour and fruit.

4. Using your hands, drop free-form blobs of dough about 3½ inches in diameter (about 4 ounces each) onto the prepared baking sheets. Don't try to press them down or squeeze the blobs of dough together—they should look like irregular mounds or clumps. Using a pastry brush, dab the reserved buttermilk/egg mixture all over the tops of the scones.

5. Place one pan on each oven rack and bake for 20 minutes. Reduce the oven temperature to 375° F and bake for 10 to 15 minutes longer, until the scones are a deep golden brown on both the top and bottom. Remove them from the pans and let cool on a wire rack. Serve slightly warm or at room temperature. Store any leftovers in a plastic bag or freeze them, wrapping them first in aluminum foil and then in a heavy-duty plastic freezer bag.

Pecan Sticky Buns

A straight dough bread

Sticky buns seem to be one of those special things that most people believe originated in their own part of the country. When we first offered sticky buns in our retail store, customers would say, "Amy must be from Philadelphia, because that's where sticky buns are from." Or, "Amy must be from Ohio, because that's where sticky buns are from." Some of our friends even offered us their personal sticky bun recipes. They all contained eggs, milk, butter, and sugar in the dough plus more butter and sugar in the topping. These certainly were favorite regional versions, but they were not what we wanted. Amy wanted to make sticky buns the way her mother makes them back in Minnesota. She starts with a lean dough made from flour, water, yeast, and salt, then puts all of the sugar, butter, and other rich goodies in the topping. Incidentally, these buns are known as "sweet rolls" or "caramel rolls" where Amy comes from. Our sticky buns, based on a Midwestern recipe, have gathered quite a following in New York City. Who knows? Maybe you'll be converted too!

Makes 9 large buns

. . . .

2$\frac{1}{4}$ teaspoons active dry yeast

$\frac{1}{4}$ cup (2 ounces) very warm water (105° to 115°F)

5$\frac{1}{3}$ cups (24 ounces) unbleached all-purpose flour

2$\frac{1}{4}$ teaspoons kosher salt

2 cups (16 ounces) warm water (90°F)

9 tablespoons (4$\frac{1}{2}$ ounces) unsalted butter

$\frac{1}{2}$ cup plus 1 tablespoon (5 ounces) dark brown sugar, firmly packed

4 tablespoons (2 ounces) unsalted butter, softened

$\frac{2}{3}$ cup plus 1 tablespoon (2$\frac{3}{4}$ ounces) pecan pieces, toasted (see box, page 68)

$\frac{1}{3}$ cup plus 1 tablespoon (2$\frac{1}{2}$ ounces) granulated sugar

1 teaspoon ground cinnamon

. . . .

Equipment: One 9-inch square baking pan, preferably nonstick;
one baking sheet lined with aluminum foil

continued

1. Place the yeast and warm water in a small bowl and stir with a fork to dissolve the yeast. Allow to stand for about 3 minutes.

2. Mix the flour and salt together in a large bowl. Add the yeast and the warm water mixture and stir with your fingers to moisten the flour, scraping the sides of the bowl and folding the dough over itself until it gathers into a shaggy mass.

3. Move the dough to a lightly floured surface and knead for 5 minutes. This is a soft, moist dough. If the dough seems too stiff and hard to knead, add extra warm water 1 tablespoon at a time until you get a nice malleable dough. Gently shape the dough into a loose ball, cover it with plastic wrap, and let it rest on the table for 20 minutes. (This rest period is the autolyse.)

4. Gently knead the dough on the lightly floured surface for 1 to 2 more minutes, or until it becomes smooth, supple, and elastic but not too firm. The texture of the dough should be soft but springy. Shape the dough into a loose ball, place it in a lightly oiled bowl, and turn to coat with oil. Cover it tightly with oiled plastic wrap and let it rise at room temperature (75° to 77° F) until it has doubled in volume, about $1^1/_2$ to 2 hours.

5. While the dough is rising, combine the 9 tablespoons butter and the dark brown sugar in a small saucepan over low heat and heat, stirring occasionally, until the butter has melted and the sugar is completely moistened (it won't be dissolved). Then whisk until the mixture looks silky and a little lighter in color. Remove from the heat. Use 1 tablespoon of the softened butter to grease the sides of a 9-inch square pan, then pour in the caramel, tilting the pan slightly so the mixture spreads evenly over the bottom of the pan. Sprinkle the toasted pecans over the warm caramel and press them down slightly. Put the pan in the refrigerator to cool the caramel; be sure the pan's on a level surface.

6. Put the granulated sugar and cinnamon in a small bowl and stir until evenly mixed. Set aside.

7. When the dough has doubled, gently pour it out of the bowl onto the floured work surface. Flatten the dough and stretch it with your fingers to form a 13 by 10-inch rectangle, with a long side facing you. Work gently so you don't tear the dough. The dough should stretch easily at this point, but if it resists, let it rest for 5 minutes and resume stretching. Check to be sure the dough isn't sticking to the work surface and flour the table again if necessary.

8. Spread the remaining 3 tablespoons softened butter evenly over the dough, leaving a $^1/_2$-inch strip unbuttered along the top edge. Sprinkle the cinnamon/sugar mixture generously and evenly over the butter, again leaving the top $^1/_2$ inch of the rectangle bare. Starting with the bottom edge, roll up the dough jelly-roll fashion into a long log; if the dough sticks to the table as you're rolling, use a dough scraper to loosen it gently. Pinch gently but firmly along the seam to seal it. If necessary, gently shape the roll so it is a nice uniform log.

9. Cut the log of dough into 9 equal pieces. (It's easiest to mark the roll first to show where you're going to make the cuts–a slight indentation with the knife edge will do–then use a sharp serrated knife to cut completely through the dough.) Lay the pieces cut side down on top of the cooled caramel in the baking pan. Don't worry if it's a tight fit. Let rise, uncovered, at room temperature until the dough has almost doubled, about 1 to $1^1/_4$ hours. The rolls should fill the pan and extend $^1/_2$ to $^3/_4$ inch above the sides.

10. In the meantime, position a rack in the center of the oven and preheat the oven to 375°F.

11. Put the pan of sticky buns on a foil-lined baking sheet and place it in the oven. Bake for 10 minutes, then reduce the oven temperature to 350°F and bake for 30 to 40 minutes longer, until the tops of the buns are golden brown and crusty. It's important to bake the buns long enough so the dough is cooked all the way through and the caramel topping develops properly.

12. Set the pan of buns on a rack to cool for 5 minutes. Then quickly but carefully turn the pan upside down and release the sticky buns onto a large flat heatproof plate. Immediately scrape out any hot caramel remaining in the bottom of the pan and spread it on the tops of the buns, filling in any bare spots. Let them cool until just warm before serving. (Clean the pan by soaking it in very hot water to dissolve the caramel.) Store any leftovers covered with plastic wrap at room temperature.

Maple Walnut and Fig Bread
A quick bread

At the bakery we make a dozen different kinds of quick bread, taking advantage of seasonal ingredients and changing the selection throughout the week to offer our customers variety. This one is Amy's personal favorite, and a favorite of many of our regular customers too. One woman gets quite upset when she sees that we've used our figs to make something other than her beloved maple walnut bread! The recipe was created in the winter when Amy wanted to make a breakfast bread that was homey and comforting, with the goodness of dried fruit, maple syrup, and oatmeal. Eat it plain, lightly toasted, or spread with a thin layer of cream cheese.

Makes two 9 by 5-inch loaves

• •

1¾ cups (10½ ounces) dried figs, diced

½ cup (4 ounces) warm water (85° to 90°F)

2⅔ cups (12 ounces) unbleached all-purpose flour

1⅔ cups (6½ ounces) cake flour

1¾ cups (5¼ ounces) old-fashioned rolled oats

2 tablespoons baking powder

½ teaspoon kosher salt

1⅓ cups (11 ounces) maple syrup

1⅓ cups (11 ounces) milk

4 large eggs, lightly beaten

2 large egg yolks

¾ cup (6 ounces) canola oil

2 cups (8 ounces) walnut pieces, toasted (see box, page 68)

Additional maple syrup for glazing

• •

Equipment: Two 9 by 5-inch loaf pans, oiled

1. Position a rack in the center of the oven and preheat the oven to 350° F.

2. Put the diced figs in a medium bowl and add the warm water. Let soak until softened.

3. Whisk the unbleached flour, cake flour, oats, baking powder, and salt together in a large bowl. Set aside.

4. Put the maple syrup, milk, eggs, egg yolks, and canola oil in a medium bowl and stir with the whisk to combine. Add the mixture to the dry ingredients, stirring with a spoon just until all of the flour is moistened. This should be a wet batter, because the oats absorb a lot of the liquid during baking.

5. Fold the walnuts and figs into the batter (the figs do not need to be drained). Divide the batter evenly between two oiled 9 by 5-inch loaf pans. Bake for about 1 hour, until a toothpick inserted in the center comes out clean. (If your oven bakes unevenly, rotate the pans from left to right and front to back about halfway through the baking time.)

6. Remove the pans from the oven and use a pastry brush to glaze the tops of the loaves with maple syrup. Set them on a rack to cool for about 10 minutes. Turn the loaves out of the pans and set them on the rack to cool completely before serving. Wrap any leftovers tightly in plastic wrap and store at room temperature. They may also be frozen, wrapped first in aluminum foil and then in plastic wrap or a heavy-duty freezer bag.

Hot Cross Buns
A straight dough bread

One of our traditions is to make at least one special bread to celebrate each holiday throughout the year. For Easter we always make hot cross buns. These little currant-filled rolls are slightly sweet, mildly spicy, and richly tender with milk and eggs. In the pre-Christian era, these buns were served to honor the goddess of spring. Later, the cross was cut in the top to symbolize the Christian religion. Hot cross buns are traditionally sold in England on Good Friday. We sell them on Good Friday and the following Saturday too as a special treat for our customers' Easter Sunday breakfasts. Don't wait until Easter to try this recipe, however–once you've made them, you'll want them all year round. Be careful not to overbake them, or their delicate flavor will be lost.

Makes 18 small buns

- -

1 tablespoon plus ¾ teaspoon active dry yeast

½ cup (4 ounces) very warm water (105° to 115°F)

¼ cup (2 ounces) warm milk (90°F)

½ cup (3¾ ounces) canola oil

⅓ cup (2¼ ounces) granulated sugar

1½ teaspoons plus a pinch kosher salt

3½ to 4 cups (16 to 18 ounces) unbleached all-purpose flour

½ teaspoon ground cinnamon

½ teaspoon grated nutmeg

3 large eggs, lightly beaten

⅔ cup (3 ounces) dried currants

1 large egg white

¾ cup (3 ounces) powdered sugar

¼ teaspoon vanilla extract

- -

Equipment: Two 12 by 17-inch baking sheets, lined with parchment paper

1. Place the yeast and warm water in a large bowl and stir with a fork to dissolve the yeast. Allow to stand for about 3 minutes.

2. Add the warm milk, canola oil, granulated sugar, and the $1^1/_2$ teaspoons salt to the yeast mixture and stir with a whisk to combine.

3. Mix 1 cup ($4^1/_2$ ounces) unbleached flour, the cinnamon, and nutmeg and add to the liquids, stirring with a whisk until the ingredients are well combined. Add the eggs and whisk again. Gradually stir in $2^1/_2$ to 3 cups ($11^1/_2$ to $13^1/_2$ ounces) unbleached flour, just enough to make a very soft, pliable dough.

4. Move the dough to a lightly floured surface and knead for 5 to 7 minutes. This is a wet dough and it will be sticky at first, but it becomes easier to work with as the gluten forms to make it springy and give it strength. Return the dough to the bowl, cover it with plastic wrap, and let it rest for 20 minutes. (This rest period is the autolyse.)

5. Knead the dough on the lightly floured surface for about 1 to 2 minutes, or until it becomes smooth, supple, and elastic but not too firm. The texture of the dough will be soft but springy. Keeping the work surface and your hands lightly floured to prevent sticking, gently flatten the dough and spread it into a rectangle about an inch thick. If it resists, let it rest for 5 to 10 minutes, until you can stretch and spread it easily.

6. Spread the dried currants evenly over the rectangle. Fold the whole mass into an envelope (see page 23) and knead it gently until the currants are well distributed, about 2 to 3 minutes. Some of the currants may pop out of the dough, but they can easily be incorporated again after the first rise, when the dough has softened.

7. Shape the dough into a loose ball and place it in a lightly oiled bowl, along with any loose currants. Turn to coat the top of the dough with oil and cover the bowl tightly with oiled plastic wrap. Let the dough rise at room temperature (75° to 77° F), until doubled in volume, about $1^1/_2$ to 2 hours. (You can also refrigerate the dough, without letting it rise, and let it double slowly overnight. Take it out first thing in the morning and continue with the next step.)

8. Line two 12 by 17-inch baking sheets with parchment paper. When the dough has doubled, gently pour it out of the bowl onto the floured work surface, pressing in any loose currants. Flour your hands lightly and divide the dough into 18 equal pieces (each weighing about 2 ounces). Shape them into rolls (see page 27) and place them on the prepared pans, leaving a 1-inch space around the edges and 2 inches between the rolls so they won't grow together as they rise. Cover them loosely with oiled plastic wrap and let them rise at room temperature until almost doubled in volume, about 45 minutes to 1 hour. (If the dough has been refrigerated overnight, it will take about twice as long for the rolls to rise.)

continued

9. While the bread is proofing, make an egg wash: In a small bowl, whisk the egg white with the pinch of salt. Cover with plastic wrap and set aside.

10. About 15 minutes before you're ready to bake, place one oven rack in the top third of the oven and another in the bottom third, and preheat the oven to 400° F.

11. When the buns have doubled, use a *lame,* a razor blade, or a small sharp knife to cut a shallow cross on the top of each one. Lightly brush the buns with the egg wash, being careful not to deflate them. (Reserve the remaining egg wash.) Place one pan on each oven rack. Using a plant sprayer, immediately mist the top and sides of the oven 6 to 8 times and quickly close the oven door. After 3 minutes, mist again.

12. Bake for 10 minutes, then reduce the oven temperature to 350° F and bake for 5 to 10 minutes longer, or until the buns have turned a nice golden brown and the surface feels slightly firm but not hard when you press it lightly. These rolls should have a thin soft covering, not a hard crunchy crust. Transfer the rolls to a rack and let them cool for 5 minutes.

13. Meanwhile, make the frosting: In a small bowl, combine the powdered sugar with the reserved egg wash and the vanilla and whisk to mix well.

14. White the rolls are still warm, use a pastry bag fitted with a small plain tip, or a tea-spoon, to make an X of frosting over the cross on each bun. The frosting will harden somewhat as the buns cool. These are best eaten the same day they are baked. If you have any leftovers, you can store them at room temperature in a plastic bag, but they will retain their flavor better if you freeze them, wrapped in aluminum foil and then a heavy-duty freezer bag. Thaw at room temperature before serving, and frost again if necessary.

Autumn Pumpkin Bread with Pecans

A straight dough bread

The Indians of the Taos Pueblo in New Mexico use their beehive-shaped outdoor adobe ovens to make wonderful addictive little yeast breads they call pumpkin cookies. Toy loved these so much she wanted to duplicate their simple, fresh pumpkin flavor in a larger loaf that could be sold in the retail store during the fall/winter holiday season. Somehow, as the testing progressed, what started out as a relatively plain bread became almost cake-like instead. The pumpkin-gold loaf, flecked with bits of toasty pecans, is shaped in a knot, which makes it especially attractive for gift-giving. Be sure you make enough to eat at your own holiday table too, because the buttery rich, spicy aromas that fill the house when this bread is baking will drive your family wild.

Makes two 1¼-pound loaves

. . . .

1 tablespoon plus 1 teaspoon active dry yeast

¼ cup (2 ounces) very warm water (105° to 115°F)

½ cup (6 ounces) honey

1 cup (8¼ ounces) pumpkin puree (unsweetened)

½ cup (4 ounces) milk, at room temperature

2 large egg yolks, at room temperature

⅓ cup less 2 teaspoons (1½ ounces) coarse cornmeal

4 cups (19¾ ounces) high-gluten (bread) flour

1 teaspoon ground cinnamon

½ teaspoon ground ginger

½ teaspoon ground cloves

2½ teaspoons kosher salt

8 tablespoons (4 ounces) unsalted butter, melted

1 cup (4 ounces) pecan pieces, toasted (see box, page 68)

½ cup (4 ounces) cold water

1¼ teaspoons cornstarch

. . . .

Equipment: One baking sheet

continued

1. Place the yeast and warm water in a large bowl and stir with a fork to dissolve the yeast. Allow to stand for about 3 minutes.

2. Add the honey, pumpkin puree, milk, egg yolks, cornmeal, and $1^2/_3$ cups (8 ounces) of the high-gluten flour to the yeast mixture. Stir briskly with a whisk until the ingredients are well combined. Let this sponge stand for at least 15 minutes but no longer than 30 minutes.

3. In a medium bowl, whisk the remaining $2^1/_3$ cups ($11^3/_4$ ounces) high-gluten flour, the cinnamon, ginger, cloves, and salt together to mix well. Add to the sponge and stir with your fingers to incorporate the flour, scraping the sides of the bowl and folding the dough over itself until it gathers into a shaggy mass. Knead the dough in the bowl until it becomes smooth and somewhat elastic, about 5 minutes. Gradually add the melted butter, kneading it in gently until well incorporated.

4. Move the dough to a lightly floured work surface and knead until it is very smooth, silky, and elastic, about 5 minutes. The dough will be sticky, so keep the work surface and your hands lightly floured, but don't overdo it. The dough should be soft, supple, and springy. Shape the dough into a loose ball, cover it with plastic wrap, and let it rest for 20 minutes. (This rest period is the autolyse.)

5. Flatten the dough and stretch it gently with your fingers to form a rectangle about an inch thick. Spread the toasted pecans evenly over the rectangle. Fold the whole mass into an envelope (see page 00) and knead it gently until the nuts are well distributed, about 2 to 3 minutes. If the dough resists, let it rest for 5 minutes and then continue kneading it. Some of the pecans may pop out of the dough, but they can easily be incorporated again after the first rise, when the dough has softened.

6. Shape the dough into a loose ball and place it in a lightly oiled bowl, along with any loose pecans. Turn to coat the dough with oil, then cover the bowl tightly with oiled plastic wrap. Let the dough rise at room temperature (75° to 77° F) until it has doubled in volume, about 2 hours.

7. While the bread is rising, make a cornstarch wash: Put the cold water in a small saucepan and whisk in the cornstarch. Bring to a boil, stirring frequently until it thickens. Remove from the heat and cover to keep a skin from forming. Set aside to cool.

8. When the dough has doubled, gently pour it out of the bowl onto the floured work surface, pressing in any loose nuts. Flour your hands lightly and gently divide the dough into 2 equal pieces (each weighing about 24 ounces). Shape each piece into a knot (see page 172).

9. Generously dust a peel or the bottom of a baking sheet with flour or coarse corn-meal. Carefully place the shaped loaves on the peel or sheet, leaving several inches between them so they won't grow into each other as they rise. Cover the dough with oiled plastic wrap and allow it to rise at room temperature until it has just doubled in volume, about $1^1/_2$ to 2 hours.

10. Thirty minutes before baking, preheat the oven to 425° F. Place a baking stone in the oven to preheat and place an empty water pan directly below the stone.

11. When the loaves have doubled, use a pastry brush to paint each loaf with the cornstarch wash. Brush gently so you won't deflate the loaves. (Reserve the remaining cornstarch wash.) Shake the peel or pan gently to be sure the loaves aren't sticking and slide the dough onto the baking stone. Quickly pour 1 cup of very hot water into the water pan and immediately shut the door. After 1 minute, using a plant sprayer, mist the top and sides of the oven 6 to 8 times, then immediately shut the oven door. Repeat the misting procedure 1 minute later.

12. Bake for 15 minutes, then reduce the oven temperature 350° F and bake for 20 to 25 minutes longer, until the loaves are golden brown and the surface feels firm but not hard when you press it lightly. These should have a thin soft crust, not a hard crunchy one. Transfer the loaves to a rack and paint them again with the cornstarch wash. Allow to cool completely before serving. This bread is best eaten the day it is baked, but it also freezes exceptionally well if you wrap it in aluminum foil and then a heavy duty-plastic freezer bag. Thaw at room temperature before serving.

12

Techniques and Terminology

◆

Information for Advanced Bakers

Sourdough Information

◆

Sourdough is a subject of considerable debate among serious bakers and not one that lends itself to definitive answers. Our purpose in this section is merely to pass along some of the more detailed information we have been able to accumulate from our own experience.

A LITTLE BIT OF CHEMISTRY

Baking consistently excellent bread using sourdough as the leavener is the ultimate challenge for the passionate bread baker. Getting consistent results with commercially produced yeast is relatively easy because there are almost two hundred billion yeast cells in just a tablespoon of active dry yeast. With that many little microbes madly multiplying, your chances for success are pretty good! On the other hand, a whole cup of sourdough culture often contains well under one billion wild yeast cells. The trick to using a sourdough starter is to coerce those wild yeast cells into a reproductive frenzy so their strength will be equal to that of commercial yeast.

Yeasts are not the only important microbes in sourdough. The unique taste of sourdough bread comes from a variety of organic acids, primarily lactic acid and acetic acid, that are produced by bacteria called *lactobacilli*. These bacteria have a symbiotic relationship with the type of wild yeasts found in sourdough cultures. Unlike commercially processed yeasts, the wild yeasts that thrive in an acid environment cannot metabolize maltose, one of the complex sugars found in flour. The lactobacilli, on the other hand, can't survive without maltose, so you would be unlikely to find them growing in a dough made only with commercial yeast, because the commercial yeasts would have metabolized the maltose. In mature sourdough cultures, these same lactobacilli apparently produce an antibiotic that protects the starter from being contaminated by other harmful bacteria. This partially explains why there are sourdough starters that have been around for decades–perhaps even for centuries!

Once you get a good strong sourdough starter going, as long as it is either refrigerated or dehydrated, it's pretty difficult to kill it. When their food and water supply has been consumed and/or they are subjected to cold temperatures, yeast cells go into a dormant state by forming spores. These spores can survive until they encounter favorable conditions for reactivation of the yeast. That's why you can leave a mature starter in the refrigerator without feeding it for weeks. We don't recommend it, but just about every baker has done it. A gray liquid will accumulate on the top of the starter, but you can just pour it off, discard half the starter, feed it with flour and water, and let it sit at room temperature until the bubbling starts all over again (see the section on sourdough starters in Chapter 2, pages 43–47). You may have to feed it two or three times to really get it going, but it will work. As long as the starter isn't some unnatural color–green, pink, orange, purple, or black–it's safe to reactivate it. If you have any doubts, though, discard it and start from scratch.

If you're going on a long vacation or you know you won't be baking with sourdough for an extended period of time, you can dehydrate or freeze your starter. To dehydrate it, spread about half a cup of the "mother" in a very thin layer on a parchment paper–lined baking sheet. Leave it out at room temperature until it has completely dried out, then crumble it into chips and store it at room temperature in a waterproof, airtight container, such as a heavy-duty plastic freezer bag with a zip-up closure. It will last indefinitely. To reactivate it, soak the chips in half a cup of cool water (75° to 77° F) to soften and dissolve them, then begin refreshing the mixture with flour and water as described in Chapter 2. Or you can sim-

> *There are many different strains and combinations of yeast and lactobacilli throughout the world, and that's why the sourdough starters cultivated in different regions produce breads that have unique flavors and textures. Chicago sourdough bread is different from San Francisco sourdough and Parisian pain au levain. In fact, there is some question about whether or not you can maintain the integrity of a San Francisco starter if you take it to New York City, where it will be exposed to Big Apple microbes over an extended period of time. We haven't found the answer to that one yet but we'll keep on trying!*

ply freeze your starter, without dehydrating it. Stored in an airtight container, it will retain its potency for at least six months. Thaw it in the refrigerator and feed it as usual to reactivate it.

TO YEAST OR NOT TO YEAST

Sourdough purists cringe at the idea of adding commercial yeast to sourdough breads. At Amy's Bread, we do add about a pinch of yeast to most of our naturally leavened doughs, though the sourdough starters themselves are free of any commercial yeast. Many noted French bread bakers believe that you can add up to 0.2 percent of its weight in yeast to a sourdough–either the starter or the dough made from the starter–without destroying its flavor or the nature of the controlling microorganisms. Some also feel that this tiny bit of yeast produces a thinner, though still crunchy, crust and a lighter, more chewable crumb. We also use it because it helps us maintain the consistency with our sourdough breads from one day to the next. Performance of sourdough starters can be affected by changes in temperature and humidity. In the bakery, where we don't have an artificially controlled environment, we are often at the mercy of the weather and sea-sonal changes. So we use commercial yeast to "kick start" our natural starter. We are convinced that by the time the dough has fully matured, the properties of the commer-cial yeast have dissipated and only the qualities of the natural leavener remain. If you are curious, perform your own experiments with and without added yeast to create the sourdough loaf that gives you the most satisfaction.

DIFFERENT WAYS TO START A CULTURE

In Chapter 2 we explain how to make a starter using just rye flour and spring water. However, if you are a born experimenter, you will want to try some of the variations below. Each produces a starter with unique flavor and fermentation characteristics.

- ◆ Prepare the Dynamite Sourdough Starter (page 44), adding 1 tablespoon of milk to the rye flour and water mixture in Step 1 of Stage 1.

- ◆ Place $^1/_2$ cup of organic raisins in a covered container, add room-temperature water to cover, and let sit at room temperature for several days, until you begin to see some bubbling action. Drain the raisins, reserving the liquid (discard the raisins). Use this liquid to prepare the sourdough starter, combining it with an equal measure (by volume) of flour in Step 1 of Stage 1 and proceed from there.

- ◆ Use orange juice from a carton (squeezed or reconstituted) as the liquid instead of water in Step 1, Stage 1. We have also had interesting results using Apple and Eve cranberry/apple juice instead of water. Any fruit juice you try should be free of added sugar and preservatives.

- ◆ Use potato water for the liquid in Step 1, Stage 1.

- ◆ Add 1 tablespoon of mashed ripe banana or mashed potatoes along with the flour in Step 1, Stage 1.

- ◆ Add 1 teaspoon of honey, maple syrup, or barley malt syrup to the flour and water mixture in Step 1, Stage 1.

You will discover that some mixtures ferment more quickly than others, so the resulting starters will need to be refreshed more often than our basic sourdough starter.

SOME WORDS OF ENCOURAGEMENT

Don't be discouraged if your first attempts at creating a sourdough culture fail miserably. Flours vary dramatically in quality, and the concentration of yeast cells in the air of your home can't compare to the concentration of yeast cells in a commercial bakery. Try different brands and types of flour until you find one that likes to ferment readily. If you don't see any activity within the time frame we describe in Chapter 2, don't be afraid to let the mixture sit a little longer, and keep feeding it. As long as it's not moldy or discolored, chances are you'll eventually get a culture that will double in eight hours. Patience, persistence, and careful attention to detail are the keys to success with sourdough.

Suggestions for Bread Shapes

♦

At the bakery we form all our loaves by hand. Besides being gentler on the dough, hand-shaping allows you to leave more air bubbles in the dough, producing lighter, open-holed loaves. Although our loaves are sometimes irregular, our hand-shaped bread is beautiful and more rustic-looking than bread shaped by a machine.

Shaping bread takes repetition and practice, and it's hard to get that kind of experience when working with recipes that yield only two loaves. Here are some guidelines that should help you get better results without the experience of shaping hundreds of loaves a day: Start by gently patting the piece of dough into a small rectangle, lightly pressing out some of the bubbles but leaving some so you'll end up with irregular air holes in the bread. When forming the loaf, your goal is to pull the outer "skin" of the loaf tight without tearing it and without deflating the bubble formation too much. Then seal the seam of the bread very well so it doesn't unroll. The tight skin is important, because it holds in the carbon dioxide gas released as soon as the bread goes into the hot oven. A loaf with a loose skin or an unsealed seam will spread and flatten into a broad flat mass in the oven. Here we describe some of the more unusual shapes we like.

COIL, BEEHIVE, OR SNAIL

Shape a baguette following the instructions on page 26. Then elongate the rope further, placing your palms over the middle of the loaf, pushing down slightly, and rolling it back and forth. Work your hands from the middle out to the ends of the rope. If the dough springs back, let it rest for up to 5 minutes before elongating it further. When the rope is about 30 inches long, taper the ends slightly and coat the loaf lightly with flour. Hold one end of the rope between your thumb and forefinger to anchor it and form a snail, working from the inside out and coiling the rope of dough around itself. To complete the look of a snail, pull the outside end of the coil outward and flatten it slightly. Cut a 2-inch slit in the tip and separate the cut into antennae. (See photograph in color insert.)

If you want to garnish the loaf with sesame or poppy seeds, lightly spray a stream of water into the groove of the coil with a plant mister. Drop the seeds in a stream into the moistened groove. It's best to let the loaf rise on parchment paper dusted with cornmeal, because this shape is likely to stick to the peel. Bake the coil when it is slightly under-proofed so that it will maintain its definition.

BRAID

Divide the dough to be shaped into three equal pieces. (It is hard to shape a braid with pieces of dough that weigh less than 4 ounces each.) Shape each piece of dough into a baguette (see page 26). Then elongate the ropes slightly and taper the ends by pushing down on them as you roll them back and forth. The ropes should all be the same length. Place the ropes side by side, leaving an inch between them. Gather the ropes together at one end and press to seal them. Braid the ropes together into a loaf and press the other ends of the ropes together to seal them. Gently lift the braid onto a cornmeal-dusted peel or pan and let rise. (It's best not to lift a braided loaf after it has risen.) The braid shape is especially nice for challah or semolina bread. (See photograph in color insert.)

KNOT

Shape the dough into a baguette (see page 26). Elongate the baguette slightly so the rope is at least 25 inches long. Roll it lightly in flour, then tie a knot in the middle of the rope. Bring one of the long ends around one side of the knot and tuck it under the loaf, then bring the other end around the other side and tuck it under the loaf. Choose the most attractive side of the knot (the one where the rounded loops protrude) for the top of the loaf. Place the knot on a baking sheet lined with parchment paper, so you won't have to move it when it's ready to be baked. Bake it when it's slightly underproofed so it keeps its definition. (See photograph in color insert.)

CROWN OR COURONNE

Use a piece of dough that weighs at least 12 ounces to make a crown. Shape it into a short baguette (see page 26), but don't taper the ends. To determine the length you need, make the loaf into a donut shape with a 4- to 5-inch center opening. If the two ends don't meet, straighten the rope and roll it under your hands to elongate it further. Form the rope into a donut, overlap the two ends slightly, and press them together to seal, trying not to flatten the seal too much. Just before baking, use scissors to cut one of two patterns into the loaf: To create a spiky effect, make small snips around the entire ring, lifting up the points with the scissors as you cut them. Or make longer cuts (about 2 inches) on the top of the ring, and pull alternating cut pieces of dough in opposite directions to resemble leaves on a branch. Place the crown on a parchment-lined peel or pan to rise.

EPI

An epi is a loaf of bread cut like the top of a blade of wheat. Form the dough into a baguette (see page 26) and let it rise on a well-floured cloth. When the loaf is still slightly underproofed, move it to a baking sheet lined with parchment paper and generously sprinkled with cornmeal. Using sharp scissors, begin at the end of the baguette farthest away from you. Make a shallow 2-inch-long cut on top of the loaf with the point of the flap of dough facing toward you. Lift the cut open and pull the flap of dough to one side. Now make another 2-inch cut in front of the last one. Pull that flap of dough in the opposite direction. Continue to make cuts up the entire baguette, alternately folding the cut dough left and right, until you reach the top. Leave the top bulb-shaped piece straight, like the tip of a shaft of wheat. Bake the loaf immediately.

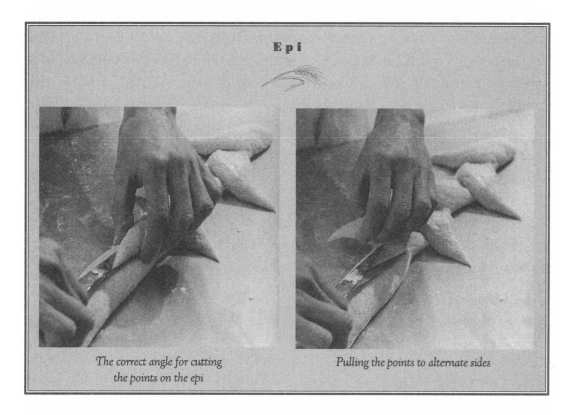

Epi

The correct angle for cutting the points on the epi

Pulling the points to alternate sides

FOUGASSE

A plain dough can be shaped and cut into a fougasse or the dough can be filled, then shaped and cut. Use a light white dough such as our baguette (page 59) or focaccia (page 105) for fougasse. Place the dough on a lightly floured surface and pat it into a long narrow rectangle. If you want to fill it, spread a filling such as chopped imported black olives, fresh herbs, or chopped anchovies, over the dough, leaving a 1-inch border around the edge. Sprinkle the topping lightly with flour. Fold the dough in thirds like a business letter, the top third down over the middle of the dough and

Fougasse

Cutting and stretching the openings on the fougasse

the bottom third over that, completely overlapping the two. Press the three open sides of the fougasse tightly shut.

Let the plain or filled dough rise until doubled in bulk. Then sprinkle a peel or upside-down baking sheet generously with cornmeal and place the fougasse on top, stretching it slightly to make it into a square. Cut a decorative pattern, such as a leaf or a ladder, into the dough with a dough cutter. Stretch the loaf until the cuts form large open holes, then gently slide the fougasse onto a baking stone and bake.

STRING-TIED LOAF

We saw this interesting shape at Greg Mistell's bakery, The Neighborhood Baking Company, in Portland, Oregon. Shape 1 pound of dough into a boule (see page 26). Sprinkle a little flour on the loaf for decoration, then wrap a piece of butcher's string around the middle of the loaf and tie a bow on the top. Let the dough rise; it will puff up around the string. Bake the loaf with the string still in it, and cut the string and remove it when you are ready to serve the bread. (See photograph in color insert.)

SHAPING A TEDDY BEAR

Once you've made a few of these bears, you'll find each has its own personality! Just remember these whimsical creatures are made of bread—and are definitely meant to be eaten. Don't get precious about them, just dig right in, rip off their little paws, and chow down!

Make one recipe of the dough for Toy's Teddy Bread (page 75). This dough is very malleable and holds its shape better during baking than some of the other doughs we've tried. (Be careful not to make it too wet, though, or your bear will be flat instead of chubby.) Let the dough rise once, then divide it as described below. Keep the pieces covered with plastic wrap so they don't dry out as you work. Weigh out ten pieces of dough as follows:

- One 10-ounce piece, for the head

- One 2-ounce piece, for the nose

- Two $1^1/_4$-ounce pieces, for the ears

- One $13^1/_2$-ounce piece, for the tummy

- Four $1^1/_2$-ounce pieces, for the paws

- One ounce, to make the eyes, nose, and bellybutton

Shape the leftover dough into a boule (see page 26) or a log (see page 22), sprinkle it with a mixture of cracked rye and sesame seeds, and set it on a cornmeal-dusted peel or pan to rise. Bake it with the bear if possible, or retard it in the refrigerator after it has almost doubled and bake it after the bear is done.

To shape the bear:

1. Line a peel or the back of a baking sheet with parchment paper and spray it lightly with cooking spray or brush lightly with vegetable oil. Set it on the work surface next to you with a short end of the sheet facing you. Shape the large piece of dough for the tummy into a compact boule (see page 26) and place it just below the center of the prepared baking sheet. Gently press down the edges at the top and bottom of the dough ball so they slope slightly, emphasizing the curve of the tummy.

2. Shape the piece for the head into a compact boule, then mold it into a rough rounded triangular shape–the apex of the triangle will be the top of the head, the two bottom "points" will be the cheeks. Place this piece on the pan above the tummy so that the flat bottom of the triangle is just touching the ball of dough.

3. Shape the two pieces for the ears into compact little balls, like rolls (see page 27), then roll them gently back and forth on the table to elongate them slightly into chubby ovals. Position one on each side of the bear's head, slightly down from the apex of the triangle and just touching the dough.

4. Shape the four pieces for the paws exactly as you did the ears, into slightly elongated chubby ovals. Put one of the paws on each side of the tummy, about $^3/_4$ inch down from the head, with part of a long side of each oval touching the tummy dough. Put the other two paws at the bottom of the tummy ball, leaving about 2 to 3 inches between them, again with part of a long side of each oval in contact with the tummy dough.

5. Shape the piece of dough for the nose into a compact ball, like a roll, then gently rotate the bottom half of the ball between your palms to form a slight cone shape at the base of the ball. Press a deep indentation into the center of the head, about two thirds of the way down from the ears, and widen it slightly to accommodate the cone part of the ball. Press the nose into the indentation–the cone serves to anchor the ball of dough so it doesn't pop up and separate during baking.

6. Pull off a small piece of the remaining dough and shape it into a ball the size of a large pea, about $^1/_2$ inch in diameter. Form a tiny cone shape on the bottom of it as you did in Step 5. Press your finger firmly into the center of the nose, and place the little ball in the depression, cone first. Press down on it slightly to anchor it. (This gives further definition to the nose.)

continued

7. Make two more little balls slightly smaller than the first one and mold cones on them as well. Make two deep depressions in the head, one on each side of the nose and about halfway between the nose and the top of the head. Put one ball in each depression, cone first, and press down on them slightly to anchor the eyes.

8. Finally, make a little ball of dough just a bit larger than $1/2$ inch in diameter and shape a cone. Make a deep indentation in the tummy, just slightly down from the center, and drop in the ball, cone first. Press gently to anchor the bellybutton.

9. Cover the teddy bear loosely but completely with a large piece of oiled plastic wrap and let it rise at room temperature (75° to 77° F) for 2 to 3 hours, or until it has doubled in size. The bear will flatten out slightly and broaden considerably.

10. While the bread is rising, make a cornstarch wash: Put $1/2$ cup cold water in a small saucepan and whisk in $1^1/_4$ teaspoons of cornstarch. Bring to a boil, stirring frequently until it thickens. Remove from the heat and cover to keep a skin from forming. Set aside to cool.

11. Thirty minutes before baking, preheat the oven to 425° F. Place a baking stone in the oven to preheat and place an empty water pan directly below the stone.

12. When the bear has doubled, carefully slide it, parchment and all, onto the baking stone. Work quickly but carefully: You don't want to deflate the dough or separate the head from the body by being too heavy-handed. Quickly pour 1 cup of very hot water into the water pan and immediately shut the door. After 3 minutes, using a plant sprayer, mist the top and sides of the oven 6 to 8 times, then quickly shut the oven door. Repeat the misting procedure 3 minutes later.

13. Bake for 15 minutes, then reduce the oven temperature to 350° F and bake for 10 minutes longer. Open the oven door and use a pastry brush to paint the bear quickly but thoroughly with some of the prepared cornstarch wash. Then bake for 10 to 15 minutes longer, or until the bread is a uniform glossy dark golden brown. Don't try to pick it up and tap it on the bottom–the head might drop off! The bear is fragile until completely cooled.

14. To get the teddy out of the oven without breaking it, hold an upside-down baking sheet or a peel level with the baking stone and carefully slide the bear onto it by pulling gently but firmly on the parchment paper. If the parchment rips because it's become too brittle, use a pot holder or an oven mitt and carefully slide the bear onto the pan or peel. The idea is to avoid taking the bear out at an angle that might put pressure on the head and cause it to separate from the body. Slide the bread onto a cooling rack, keeping it level with the rack, then carefully pull the parchment out from under the bear and discard it. Immediately brush another coat of the cornstarch wash all over the bear. Let cool completely.

15. To finish the teddy, tie a colorful ribbon around its neck, making a decorative bow in front. It can be stored for a day or two in a plastic bag at room temperature, or you can wrap it in aluminum foil and several layers of plastic wrap and freeze it. Let it thaw at room temperature for 3 to 4 hours.

MAKING DECORATIVE PATTERNS AND SCORING

Shape a piece of dough that weighs at least one pound into a boule and let it rise until it is still slightly underproofed. Place the loaf on a peel or upside-down baking sheet generously sprinkled with cornmeal. Place a **circular cooling rack** on top of the loaf and sift or strain flour over the surface. Remove the cooling rack to expose a circular pattern on the top of the loaf. Score the bread along the straight lines that radiate out from the center. Bake, being careful not to spray the loaf when you mist the oven walls, or you will ruin the flour pattern.

Hold a wide **chef's knife** over the length of a log or a triangular-shaped loaf that is slightly underproofed and sift or strain flour over the top of the bread. Remove the knife and score a series of short cuts across the loaf in the unfloured stripe. Bake the bread immediately.

Using a circular cooling rack to make a floured pattern on a loaf

Using a chef's knife to make a triangular pattern on a loaf

Saucisson cut, tic-tac-toe cut, and crown cut

Allow a round loaf to rise, then score a **tie-tac-toe pattern** on the top. You can vary the angle of the scored grid, forming square- or diamond-shaped openings.

Dust evenly with flour a one-pound boule that has just been formed, then press a **cake cutter** (a ring used to mark portions on a round cake) into the top of the loaf. Press down on the bread firmly enough to make indentations that resemble flower petals. Remove the cake cutter and let the dough rise. Just before baking, dip the rim of a glass in flour and press it down into the middle of the loaf to form the center of the flower.

Saucisson is an attractive cut for log-shaped loaves made with stiffer, denser doughs such as our Dense Rye Bread (page 85). Form the dough into a long firm log. Sprinkle the surface evenly with rye or white flour, then score the loaf: Hold a *lame* or a sharp razor blade perpendicular to the loaf and make a series of slightly diagonal cuts about $3/4$ inch apart. Let rise and bake normally.

Troubleshooting: Answers to Questions About Mixing, Rising, and Baking

♦

How do I determine the proper temperature of ingredients when mixing dough? For our recipes we like the dough to have a temperature of 75° F when it is fully kneaded. To achieve that, we regulate the temperature of the various elements that influence the dough–the flour, the air, and the water.

Here is a formula that will help you reach the optimum dough temperature. The magic number for us is 225° F, that is, 75° F multiplied by the three components. Since the flour temperature and room temperature vary depending on the weather, we adjust the temperature of the water, the one variable we can control.

First check the temperature of the flour you'll be using, then check the temperature of your kitchen. If, for example, the flour temperature is 78° F and the room is 80° F, the sum of the two is 158° F. Subtract that from 225° F and you get 67° F, the desired water temperature. The warmth of your hands and the friction caused by kneading will raise the temperature of the dough by three to five degrees, so you should lower the water temperature slightly, to around 63° F, to compensate. If you are using a mixer, be aware that the dough temperature increases by one degree each minute it is mixed on medium speed. After using this formula, check the temperature of the mixed dough with an instant-read thermometer to find out how close you came to your desired result.

In the recipes in this book, we have given basic water temperatures that work fine for small batches of dough mixed on moderately temperate days. But if you're making bread on a very hot day, or if you're mixing very large batches of dough, be sure to use the formula given here for each batch of dough.

How can I improve the flavor of my bread? Many bread-making techniques can improve the flavor of the bread. Of course you should start with good ingredients. Using the best-quality ingredients will make a big difference in the flavor of your bread. Consistently using whole grains and less-refined products, organic flour, fresh nuts, and seasonal produce from a local farmer means your bread will taste that much better! Here are some of the other factors that make a difference:

Proper dough hydration: Making moist dough will improve the flavor of the finished bread. If the dough is too dry, the flour is unable to absorb enough water to become fully hydrated and reach its full flavor potential. Most of our doughs are mixed to achieve a hydration rate of 65 to 70 percent, but wetter doughs, such as Italian ciabatta, can have hydration rates of 75 to 80 percent. To calculate the hydration rate of a dough, add the weight of all of the liquids, then add the weight of all the flours or meals in the dough, and divide the weight of the liquids by the weight of the flours. If a dough includes a starter, the hydration rate and proportion of starter in the dough should be factored into the formula. In our opinion, the lowest hydration rate that would still result in a workable dough would be 62 percent, but we don't like to work with dough this firm. If you have other bread recipes that you would like to analyze, after determining the hydration rate of the dough, you can adjust the rate by adding or reducing the amount of water to reach the hydration rate you want. Experimentation and experience will tell you the best hydration rate for a specific dough.

Proper mixing: Dough that is made with an autolyse, or rest period, requires less kneading time than dough that is not allowed to rest, so it will be less oxidized by the mixing process. Mixing dough too long, and incorporating too much air into it, destroys the carotenoid pigments in the flour and causes a bleaching effect. This is a common problem in commercial bakeries. The carotenoid pigments in the flour give the dough a fragrant smell, a full flavor, and a crumb with a creamy yellow color. The autolyse also lets the gluten in the dough absorb more water with less kneading. And the autolyse makes the dough easier to handle and to shape and creates more volume in the risen loaf.

Using a ripe starter or sponge: As important as any other factor for developing flavor is the ripeness, or readiness, of the sourdough starter or sponge you mix into the dough. If you're using either a starter or a sponge, be sure it has been allowed to mature fully but is not so old that it doesn't have the strength to leaven the bread properly. A starter that is too mature will be high in acid, and the acidity will break down the gluten in the dough, causing the bread to collapse, tear, or be very sticky inside–almost rubbery–even when cooled. A properly matured sourdough starter or sponge starter should have all of the characteristics of ripeness described in Chapter 2, Making Bread Rise.

If you are making a sponge for a dough that incorporates a sourdough starter, you can determine the sourness of the final dough by the amount of time you age the sponge. For an example of this method, see the recipe for Tangy Twenty-Four-Hour Sourdough, page 129. If you want to make a sponge bread that is not very tangy, you can use the sponge before it has reached its full sourness. If the same sponge is allowed to mature to a more sour, slightly acidic stage, it will make a tangier, more assertive sourdough bread. The optimal stage is when the sponge tastes slightly sweet with a tangy, slightly sharp aftertaste.

Using less yeast and more time for rising: By reducing the amount of yeast used in standard dough recipes, you can lengthen the fermentation time, allowing the flavors of the other ingredients in the bread to develop and to become more pronounced. They will not be masked by a strong taste of yeast. A slower fermentation gives the protein in the flour time to absorb more water, resulting in a loaf with a moister crumb and bread that won't get stale so quickly. Fermentation can also be slowed by retarding, or chilling, the dough. Retarding the dough allows more time for the development of organic acids in the dough, which help produce a fuller flavor, a moister texture, and a crunchier crust.

Proper fermentation: To get the best flavor from bread, the fermentation of the dough should be carefully controlled. Try to keep the rising dough at a relatively cool temperature, between 75° F and 77° F. Bread dough should be covered when it rises so it stays moist. Let the dough rise as slowly as possible to obtain the fullest flavor from your ingredients.

If you're working in a cold kitchen, it may be necessary to place the bowl of kneaded dough in a sink filled with warm water to get the dough moving. As long as you keep the dough in the 75° to 77° F range, it's fine.

Make sure to allow the dough to rise completely (it should nearly double) on the first rise. (With bread dough that is refrigerated overnight, we consider the first rise to be the rising time before and after it is refrigerated, but before it is shaped.) The first rise is most important because most of the flavor development of the dough takes place during that time. Each subsequent rise takes less time and contributes less to the final flavor.

Browning the crust: Baking a loaf until the crust has a deep rich brown color will enhance the flavor of the loaf. A dark-crusted loaf of bread has a much fuller flavor than a pale loaf. The reactions between sugars and amino acids in the dough that result in browning occur only at a temperature above 220° F. As the baking bread reaches this temperature, the crust begins to brown. If the crust is allowed to color fully, the flavor of the caramelized crust will affect the flavor of the whole loaf, because the natural by-products of the sugar–amino acid reaction penetrate inward. Much of the flavor from the crust is transferred to the crumb in the first ten to twenty minutes after the bread is taken from the oven.

> ### Starch to Sugar Conversion
> *Flour is partially made up of starch granules. During fermentation, starch-breaking malt enzymes attack the starch granules, converting them into sugars that the yeast cells use as food.*

What factors other than baking time affect crust coloration? Chilling the bread briefly after it has risen, just before baking, will give you a glossier, deeper brown crust. Two factors are involved: First, condensation occurs in the refrigerator, leaving moisture on the crust. The moisture has the same effect as steam in your oven during baking, resulting in a shinier, crisper crust. Second, the greater difference between the dough temperature and the oven temperature after refrigeration causes the bread to brown better. Presumably this is because the yeast action has been slowed down enough to keep the yeast from consuming all of the starch and/or sugar in the dough, allowing those sugars to caramelize in the oven into a golden brown crust.

Sometimes the crust takes a long time to color and never seems to brown enough. If the oven environment is too dry, because steam was not created in the oven or the steam escaped from the oven, the crust will not become as brown as it should and it may have a white, streaky look. Providing adequate moisture around the bread during the first ten minutes of baking is crucial.

Sourdough breads, leavened only with a natural starter, may take longer to brown or may not brown at all because the dough has become too mature and high in acid. The acid-alkaline balance may be off because the dough or the starter fermented for too long, leaving more acid and less alkaline. (A high-alkaline dough browns better than a dough high in acid.) The yeasts may have consumed all of the starch and sugar in the dough, leaving no sugars to brown or caramelize in the crust.

Salt in the dough may also affect the color of the crust. Dough made without salt will rise relatively quickly because the yeast is not inhibited. Since the fermentation is accelerated, the yeast quickly uses up the supply of starch and sugar in the dough, leaving little natural sugar to color the crust during baking. Dough that is very salty, on the other hand—such as a salt crust used to roast a chicken—won't brown either, because too much salt inhibits caramelization. The perfect proportion of salt will result in a golden-brown crust.

I usually mix my dough using warmer water and more yeast than your recipes. What will happen if I modify other recipes by decreasing the yeast and reducing the dough temperature? As the yeast in a dough feeds on starch and sugar, it multiplies. At a lower temperature, this multiplication occurs more slowly than at a higher one. But even with less yeast than in standard recipes, dough that is allowed a long fermentation time will rise as much as yeastier dough once the yeasts build their strength and power. In contrast, if you use a larger amount of yeast or give the dough a warmer rise, the yeast is more quickly exhausted, giving an acidic raw yeast flavor to the bread. And as the dough temperature gets warmer, from about 82°F up to 95°F, the yeasts multiply more rapidly and produce gas so the dough rises, but they also give off more sour and unpleasant smelling by-products that affect the flavor of the bread. That's why we prefer a long, cool fermentation.

How do I convert standard yeast dough recipes to recipes that use a sponge starter? Begin by reducing the amount of yeast by half—but don't use less than one-half teaspoon per pound of flour. Add one and a half cups (twelve ounces) of sponge per one pound of flour and decrease the water in the recipe by a tablespoon for each one and a half cups of sponge added. You may need to add a little more kosher salt, about one quarter teaspoon per pound of flour, to adjust for the volume of the added sponge.

COMMON PROBLEMS IN BREAD MAKING

The crumb is too dense: The dough was too dry, the dough did not rise enough on the first rise, or the flour used was too strong (i.e., too much high-gluten flour).

The crumb is wet and gummy: The dough was too wet or the dough was too cold when it was placed in the oven or it was retarded too long.

The loaf is flat: The dough deflated because it was overrisen; the dough was made too wet, so it spread when rising; or the loaf was shaped too loosely (the skin and the seal of the loaf were not tight enough).

Common Mistakes

This photograph shows several mistakes. The loaf on the left is underproofed, it cracked open on the left side, the crust is pale and streaked, the crumb is too tight. The middle loaf is perfectly proofed, has good color and an even crumb. The loaf on the right is overproofed and has become flat. The crumb has developed a sponge-like network and is coarser.

The crust didn't brown or has white streaks: The dough–or the starter–was too mature and too acidic or there wasn't enough steam in the oven.

The loaf cracked: The dough was not proofed enough or the scored cuts on the loaf were too short or shallow; if the loaf is a rye bread, the dough became highly acidic during the rise, causing the gluten in the dough to break down and the loaf to crack or split before baking. (Rye flour feeds on yeast more rapidly than wheat flour, creating acids that break down the weaker gluten structure of rye dough.)

The loaf burst open: The loaf was not proofed enough and/or it was scored too lightly–or not at all.

The bottom of the bread is dark and the top is too light: The oven heat was uneven or the loaf was baked too close to the bottom of the oven.

The crust is very thick and tough: The dough was too dry, the dough did not ferment enough on the first rise, there was not enough steam in the oven, or the oven temperature was too low so the bread had to be baked for too long.

The crust is squishy: The loaf was not allowed to brown enough during baking or the bread was not baked long enough after it browned–or the humidity in the air has caused it to soften.

The bread has a big air pocket inside: The dough was not shaped well or the dough was dry and/or too cold when it went into the oven, creating a pocket under the crust during oven spring.

Closing

◆

Eating good bread reminds us all of why we have devoted our lives to baking. Bread is beautiful, earthy, rich, healthful, humble in its primal simplicity, ancient in its ingredients, satisfying to our bodies, and pleasing to all our senses.

We hope our book will help you enjoy the process of making bread as much as you enjoy eating it.

Good luck and good health!

Amy and *Jay*

glossary

Ash content A measure of the amount of minerals in a specific flour. A sample of the flour is burned and the ashes, which are composed of minerals, are weighed. Ash content is not considered as important in determining flour quality in America as it is in Europe.

Autolyse The French word for a rest period given to dough during mixing, which allows the gluten in the dough to relax so that the flour can absorb more water. Since kneading time is shortened, the loaves have better flavor because the dough is less oxidized, and they also have a fuller volume.

Baguette The French word for wand or stick, and the name given to a bread shape about three inches wide and twenty-five inches long. Traditional baguettes are made with yeasted white dough and are light and airy with a thin, crisp, golden crust.

Banneton A special basket, often with a canvas lining, used for letting dough rise. These baskets work well for soft doughs. Flour is rubbed into the cloth, or the grooves of the basket, to keep the dough from sticking. The baked loaf has an attractive flour coating and a thicker crust than a loaf risen free-form.

Bâtard A medium-length loaf that is wider in the center and tapered at the tips, often referred to as a French loaf.

Biga The Italian word for a sponge starter made from flour, water, and a tiny bit of yeast. It may be mixed wet or firm and is used to give breads a light, chewy crumb.

Boule The French name for a round ball-shaped loaf. *Boule* is the root of the word *boulangerie,* "bakery." Before the baguette was introduced in France, most loaves were shaped into large or small boules. The person who shaped the bread was the *boulanger* (boule shaper).

Chef We use the word *chef* to describe a piece of dough saved from one day's batch of dough to be mixed into the next day's dough.

Cool rise A rise (of dough) at a temperature of between 75° F and 77° F, it gives the dough a better texture and flavor than a warmer rise would.

Couche The French word for a heavy baker's canvas that is dusted with flour and used to let dough rise. The couche is particularly useful for long, straight loaves like baguettes, ficelles, and bâtards, which are placed side by side on the cloth. The couche cradles the loaves, keeping them straight and preventing them from sticking together.

Crumb The interior of the loaf, also referred to as the *mie*. The crumb is the soft part of the bread, surrounded by the crust.

Culture The word used to refer to the first fermented mixture of flour, water, and wild yeast that results when a new sourdough starter is made. The mother starter is built from the culture.

Epi A bread shape that looks like the top of a blade of wheat. A long baguette is snipped with scissors and alternating cut sections of dough are pulled in opposite directions to form a decorative pattern.

Extensibility A term used to describe the extent of the gluten development in a kneaded dough, which can be demonstrated by seeing how far a piece of the dough can be stretched without breaking.

Fermentation A bread-making term used to describe the process of dough maturation. Flour and water are mixed with a leavener and allowed to rise and age, resulting in a breakdown of carbohydrates in the dough. The by-products are released in the form of carbon dioxide and alcohol.

Ficelle A slender version of the long thin baguette loaf. The ficelle is traditionally half the weight of its larger cousin.

Focaccia An Italian flatbread with a dimpled surface. Focaccia can be dressed simply with olive oil and herbs or topped with other ingredients, such as onions, olives, and tomatoes. *Focaccia* comes from the Latin word *focus,* which means "hearth."

Fougasse A beautiful flat, lattice-like bread that originated in the south of France. Some fougasse are filled with ingredients from the Mediterranean, such as black olives, anchovies, or orange flower water. The name comes from the same Latin word as *focaccia.*

Free-form loaf Bread that is shaped and allowed to rise on a flat surface, rather than in a loaf pan, basket, or bread mold that would give it a particular shape.

Gluten The stretchy elastic strands of protein that form when wheat flour is mixed with water and kneaded. The gluten forms a web that traps the carbon dioxide given off by the yeast, causing the dough to rise and creating a network of bubbles in the crumb of the finished loaf.

Hearth The floor of an oven, usually one made of stone, brick, or cement. Loaves are placed directly on the preheated hearth to bake. A stone hearth can be simulated in a home oven by using a baking stone.

Hydration rate The ratio of water to flour in a dough. See page 181 for instructions on how to determine the hydration rate. In our recipes, the rate is between 65 and 70 percent.

Knead To work a dough by pushing and stretching it in order to develop the gluten in the flour.

Levain The French word for a natural sourdough starter that is made by fermenting a mixture of flour and water until it is ripe enough to leaven bread. *Levain* usually refers to a firm, stiff starter. (We call the final starter used in our Country Sourdough Boule *levain*; see page 141.)

Mother The word used by some bakers to describe the healthy sourdough starter that is built into the final starter used in various dough recipes. The mother is maintained through regular refreshment with flour and water. When dough is to be made, some of the mother is used to prepare a *levain* starter or rye sour for the recipe. It is the starter from which all other starters come.

Old dough starter A piece of dough saved from one batch of dough to be used as a starter in another batch. Fresh dough can be made specifically to be allowed to ferment until it is ripe enough to act as an old dough starter.

Oven spring The bursting action that occurs when risen dough is placed in a hot oven. When the yeasts get hot, they become very active until they expire at a temperature of 140°F. Their rapid action releases carbon dioxide, which is trapped in the web of gluten in the dough, causing the loaf to "spring up" in the oven and creating a full, well-risen loaf.

Overproof To allow dough to rise too long. Overproofed dough will not rise to its full potential volume in the oven because the yeast supply in the dough has dwindled and the gluten strands have already stretched to their limit, causing the loaf to spread or collapse in the oven's heat.

Pan loaf Bread that is baked in a standard rectangular loaf pan.

Pâte fermentée A French term meaning "fermented dough"; we use the name "old dough" in our recipes. *Pâte fermentée* is used in the same way as a starter to add flavor and texture to a dough.

Peel A wooden paddle used to slide loaves onto the oven hearth or a baking stone in the oven. The peel can also be used to remove baked bread from the oven.

Poolish The French name for a wet starter made of flour, water, and a bit of yeast. The *poolish* is allowed to bubble, rise, and ferment until it nearly triples in volume. When it is ready to use, it will look bubbly and will have tiny folds or creases in the surface where it is just beginning to sink. It should not have completely fallen. *Poolish* is a sponge starter, similar to *biga.*

Proof To bring dough to the proper lightness, or to rise. Dough that is fully proofed should have doubled in volume.

Refresh To feed or replenish a starter with flour and water.

Retard To slow the fermentation process of mixed dough. Dough can be placed in a refrigerator or moist retarding chamber to slow the rise, allowing the flavors in the bread to develop more fully over a longer time.

Rise Used interchangeably with "proof" when referring to dough maturation; the action of the dough as it inflates after it is kneaded or shaped into loaves.

Rye sour The sourdough starter made from a rye mother, used to leaven a batch of dough.

Score To cut or slash the crust of a loaf before baking to create a place for carbon dioxide in the dough to escape. Bread is also scored to give it a more attractive or decorative appearance.

Seam The place where a loaf is sealed after it is shaped. In French it is known as the *clé* (key).

Sourdough bread Any bread made with a natural or wild yeast starter. A sourdough bread can be mild or very tangy depending on the fermentation procedure used. "Pure" sourdough breads are made without the addition of commercial yeast, but tiny quantities of yeast are sometimes used along with a natural starter.

Sourdough starter A mixture of flour, water, and wild yeast that is allowed to ferment and used to leaven bread.

Sponge A mixture of flour, water, and a bit of yeast that is allowed to ferment and is mixed into a dough. In some of our recipes we make a sponge using a portion of the flour, water, and yeast or sourdough starter called for in that specific recipe. This mixture is allowed to ferment for thirty minutes to several hours before it is incorporated into the dough. In other recipes we use a previously made sponge starter that we have maintained.

Sponge starter In this book specifically, a starter made from flour, water, and a little bit of yeast that is allowed to ferment until it nearly triples in volume, then begins to crease, fold, and sink slightly on the surface at its peak of ripeness. *Biga* and *poolish* are both sponge starters.

Starter Generally, a mixture of flour, water, and some type of leavener–either wild or commercial yeast–that is allowed to ferment and develop to maturity. It is then mixed into bread dough to leaven it.

Underproof To keep dough from fully rising or doubling. It is best to bake some breads when they are just slightly underproofed so they get maximum oven spring when they are put into a hot oven.

Mail-Order Sources

Arrowhead Mills
P.O. Box 866
Hereford, TX 79045
(713) 364–0730
A wide variety of stone-ground organic flours (carried by most natural food stores); organic seeds and grains.

The Chef's Catalogue
3215 Commercial Avenue
Northbrook, IL 60062-1900
(800) 338–3232
Baking stones and peels, KitchenAid mixers, baking pans and bread molds in a variety of shapes.

Community Mill and Bean
267 Route 89 South
Savannah, NY 13146
(800) 755–0554
High-quality stone-ground organic flours of all types. Call for a products and price list.

King Arthur Flour Baker's Catalogue
P.O. Box 876
Norwich, VT 05055-0876
(800) 827–6836
Everything for the dedicated baker, including

proofing baskets and cloths and a complete list of excellent flours, both organic and nonorganic; knowledgeable staff, courteous and willing to answer questions about any of their products and services.

Pamela's Products
156 Utah Avenue
South San Francisco, CA 94080
(415) 952–4546
Giusto's flours, some of the best flours available– a large variety of both organic and nonorganic stone-ground flours. Call for a products and price list.

Walnut Acres Organic Farms
Penns Creek, PA 17862
(800) 433–3998
A full range of natural foods, including organic flours, grains, nuts, and seeds; grain mills.

Williams-Sonoma
P.O. Box 7546
San Francisco, CA 94120–7546
(800) 541–2233
High-quality kitchen equipment, including KitchenAid mixers, baking stones, baking pans, circular cooling racks, and other kitchen tools.

Organizations

Bread Bakers Guild of America
P.O. Box 22254
Pittsburgh, PA 15222
(412) 765–3638
Fax: (412) 765–1694
National nonprofit organization for artisan bread bakers,
both professional and nonprofessional (see page xviii).
Annual dues are tax-deductible.

Bibliography

The Bread Bakers Guild of America Newsletter, May 1993. See item number 2 in the Translator's Notes, page 7, by James MacGuire, for information on ash content in flour.

—, July 1993. See Special Feature section, page 6, for Professor Raymond Calvel's views on natural starters.

—, September 1993. See Technical Baking column, page 6, by Danielle Forestier, on wheat and flour classifications.

McGee, Harold. *On Food and Cooking.* New York: Charles Scribner's Sons, 1984. Valuable reference on food science, culinary lore, and food history.

Wood, Ed. *World Sourdoughs from Antiquity.* Berkeley, CA: Ten Speed Press *and Today.* 1989. An interesting and enlightening book by a pathologist with a passion for sourdough. History and lore, plus recipes for using ten sourdough cultures from around the world; includes an order form for the packaged/dehydrated sourdough cultures.

index

Page numbers in **bold** refer to recipes.

prosciutto, olives, mushrooms, and artichoke hearts, quattro stagione with, **108**

prosciutto and grilled chicken sandwich filling for wands of walnut scallion bread, **147**

hand shaping, *see* shaping, of loaves

hard red spring wheat flour, 2, 4

hearth, 186

herbs, fresh vs. dried, 8

high-gluten flour, 3

hominy, as cracked corn substitute, 73

honey, 7, 154

in dough starters, 170

measuring of, 13

hot cross buns, **160–162**

hot peppers, handling of, 74

hydration, 187

see also moisture

I

ingredients:

coarse, kneading of, 17–18

corn, 5

eggs, 7

fat, 7

liquids, 6

oats, 5

rye flour, 4–5

salt, 6

specialty, 7–8

sweeteners, 7

wheat flour, 2–4

instant flour, 2

instant-read thermometers, 12

instant yeast, 39

Italian loaf, Amy's crusty, **62–63**

Italian semolina loaves, golden, **92–93**

J

alapeño pepper, in coarse cracked corn with four peppers, **72–74**

K

Kalamata olives, 8

King Arthur Flour Baker's Catalogue, 189

KitchenAid mixers, 9

kitchen scales, 10

kneading, 15–16, 187

autolyse, 14–15, 180, 185

with coarse ingredients, 17–18

with electric mixers, 17

by hand, 9

of rye dough, 77, 86

testing, 19

of wet dough, 14

knot shapes, 172

kosher salt, 6

L

La Cloche, 10

lactic acid, 168

lactobacilli, 168

lame, 11

for decorative cuts, 29–30

leaveners:

baker's yeast, 36–39

old dough starter, **41–43**, 53, 71

sourdough starter, **43–47**, 76, 188

sponge starter, **39–41**, 188, 189

leavening, 20, 188

chemical activity in, 168–169

tests for, 21, 22

lentil rolls, **144–146**

veggie burger, onion, tomato, and radish filling for, 147

levain starter, **50**, 187

liquids, *see* moisture

loaf pans, 10, 28–29

log shape, 22–24

Lovera, Henri, 61

low-fat milk, in dough, 6

M

mail-order sources, 189

maltose, 168

maple syrup, 7

in dough starters, 170

maple walnut and fig bread, **158–159**

measuring:

equivalents, 38

techniques, 13

utensils, 10

microbes, in sourdough, 168

microwaving, 34

milk, in dough, 6

millet, 7

millet seeds, grainy whole wheat and, with apricots, prunes, and raisins, **68–71**

milling, of flour, *see specific types of flour*

misting, 11, 32, 34

mixers, 17

electric, 9

mixing, 180

mixing bowls, 10

Modern Products, Inc., 5

moist potato-rye wands with dill, **115–117**

moisture:

in dough, 6, 14, 179–180

fermentation and, 46

in yeast, 38

molasses, 7

Toy's Anadama bread, **88–90**

molds, for shaping, 28–29

mothers, 187

rye, 43, **47–48**, 76, 188

white sourdough, 43, **49**, 50

mushrooms:

olives, prosciutto, and artichoke hearts, quattro stagione with, **108**

portobello, and onions with fresh sage and grated imported Parmesan cheese pizza or focaccia, **108**

mustard:

and caraway seeds, Amy's organic rye with, **127–129**

seed, anise, and coriander, aromatic twigs with, **112–114**

N

nonorganic flour, 2

nutritional yeast, 37

nuts, 7–8

autumn pumpkin bread with pecans, **163–165**

coarse-grained whole wheat with toasted walnuts, **66–68**

maple walnut and fig bread, **158–159**

organic whole wheat sandwich bread with oats and pecans, **80–82**

pecan sticky buns, **155–157**

toasting of, 68

wands of walnut scallion bread, **124–126**

O

oatmeal buttermilk scones, Suze's, **153–154**

oats, 5

organic whole wheat sandwich bread with pecans and, **80–82**

oil, 7

oil, basil, **107**

rich focaccia with, **105–107**

oil, measuring of, 13

old dough bread:

Amy's organic rye with caraway and mustard seeds, **127–129**

cinnamon raisin, **57–58**

golden whole wheat, **55–56**

old dough bread, overnight:

grainy whole wheat and seeds with apricots, prunes, and raisins, **68–71**

lentil rolls, **144–146**

old dough starter, **41–43**, 53, 71, 187

olive oil, 7

fresh rosemary bread with, **120–121**

olive(s), 8

black, rustic rounds of sweet red pepper and, **122–124**

prosciutto, mushrooms, and artichoke hearts, quattro stagione with, **108**